April 1996

To Ron & June

For the sake of times gone by
and with my very best wishes,

Don

A SHARE OF TIME

Donald Low MC

NEWTON

First Published in Great Britain by
J & KH Publishing (1996)
P O Box 13, Hailsham,
East Sussex BN27 3XQ

Copyright $^{©}$ Donald Low (1996)

British Library Catalogueing-in-Publication Data. A catalogue record for this book is
available from the British Library

ISBN   1 900511 02 9

Printed by:

        Da Costa Print & Finishing Company
        Queensland Road
        London N7 7AH

CONTENTS

LIST OF ILLUSTRATIONS

INTRODUCTION

Years ago, it seems so long now, my three children used to ask me to tell them stories of the war when we were driving fairly long distances as a family. The stories used to make the journeys pass quickly and often there were requests for some stories to be repeated on subsequent journeys. These tales were invariably funny ones designed for entertainment with the nasty bits omitted.

From these beginnings there came the idea of a fuller account to be embarked upon. Particular interest was centred on the novelty that I, in the middle of a war and in Africa, had acquired a piano. The early part of this story had already been started and so, in response to the general feeling, it seemed a natural thing to try to finish the story of Tunisia and perhaps, at a later date, to consider some of the happenings in Italy.

This story of Tunisia is concerned with a small unit of gunners who found themselves launched onto the continent of Africa as part of the design to eliminate German and Italian forces in the southern Mediterranean. It is not an unbiased account of the campaign as an historian would record it. Rather it is a self-centred, insular and prejudiced viewpoint for which I make no apology. Of necessity it is restricted in content since it is autobiographical and if it has any merit, it must be in the fact that it is true and unembroidered. I have avoided exaggerations and dramatisations in an attempt to portray feelings and events as faithfully as I am able. In retrospect, I might have included more expression of everyday things: of the interminable night marches; of scorpions and a few snakes; of sunsets and frosts at night; of being wet and getting wetter; of the cries of the wounded men; of fellowship and fun.

When I began to write about those months concerning the first half of 1943, events were still quite vivid in my mind, but during the later years when I completed the story, the facts became hazy, yet the incidents recorded here are those which remain still bright in my memory. A memory that cannot be so far from accuracy because I have just returned from my first visit to Italy since the war and there I was able to find, and verify, the exact spot where my battery crossed over Oxford Bridge on the River Rapido at Cassino in 1944. This was in October 1990.

The landings in Algiers took place in November 1942 and almost at once the Allied forces were thrown onto the defensive. An invading force has, by definition, the image of an offensive force - otherwise why invade? However, as I have explained elsewhere in this story, the Germans and Italians were able to assemble troops and tanks far more quickly than were the British and Americans. For this reason they were able to wrest the offensive from us and instead we had a desperate job to hold on to the ground we had occupied in the first weeks.

The anti-tank gun is a defensive weapon in its recognised form; it can do nothing until the enemy attacks with armour. In such circumstances it becomes the essential ingredient in the defence. In the conditions of North Africa, where the enemy had greater numbers of tanks with better armour and much more powerful guns, the humble anti-tank gun was the only answer and ensured that our presence was welcomed by all. This continued into April '43 when the First Army took to the offensive and we became less important in the order of things.

At the end of the North African campaign my battery was re-equipped with self-propelled guns of a more powerful nature. They were called 'M10s' and were high velocity 3" guns mounted on the hulls of Sherman tanks. They had the further advantage of being used as conventional artillery by firing high explosive shells in addition to armour piercing. This meant that our role in Italy was very different from that assigned to us in Tunisia.

Looking back at North Africa, I am more than a little surprised at my own good fortune. Beginning at Tebourba where we were left behind; continuing to Ouseltia where my troop left just in time; the fiasco at Robaa where the war should have ended for us one way or another; on to Sedjenane and no-one knows how we got out unscathed; to Djebel Kournine and our survival without casualties compared with our successors who were badly mauled. Due to promotion I never commanded a troop again but 6 Troop lost three successive troop commanders in Italy and I cannot but feel that their luck must have deserted them. I felt then that I should have stayed with the troop and somehow it would have been different, which was nonsense of course, but so was everything in those days.

If you are looking for a war story as exemplified in the films then don't bother to read any further. If perhaps, you have any curiosity about the everyday life of a troop of gunners in action over a period of months, then I hope your interest may be maintained through the following chapters.

Donald Low

FOREWORD

'A Share of Time' is a compelling story by a war time soldier about what fighting at the front is really like. The author describes lightly the movements and tasks of his anti-tank troop in 72nd Anti-tank Regiment, the discomforts that had to be faced and overcome and the hopes and fears of the soldiers he led. He also gives us a revealing glimpse of his personal thoughts about warfare in general and his own motivation and concerns. Professional soldiers will realise that his account is very modest, clearly he was a brave, resourceful and most effective officer who maintained the best traditions of the Royal Regiment throughout his time in the army.

Many millions of words have been written about what keeps men fighting in adversity when their lives are severely at risk from happenings totally out of their control. Donald Low's book adds another important chapter to that debate. He cites comradeship as one of the major factors and I entirely agree with that. 6th Armoured Division was a true team in every respect through all the ranks. One very senior visitor asked why it was that all the officers in the division had doubled barrelled names; the reason was that they always referred to each other by both christian and surname. Throughout the rest of his life my father was proud to have been privileged to command such a crack formation. The breakup of a close-knit team is inevitably a sad affair. The final paragraph of this book neatly sums up the tremendous blow it always is to be told one's unit is to be disbanded or amalgamated with another.

It has been an honour to write a foreword to 'A Share of Time' and a humbling experience to read about the deeds of those who gave so much that we, the next generation, might live in peace and freedom. This book gives a fascinating insight into what life is really like in action and will be of great interest to all professional soldiers, but most particularly to young men at the start of their military careers. Donald Low is to be congratulated on writing this readable and inspiring account of his time in 72nd Antitank Regiment.

1 October 1993

MAJOR GENERAL R C KEIGHTLEY CB

ACKNOWLEDGMENTS

My grateful thanks go to Mrs Joan East for providing the diagrams in the book. Maj General Keightley for his Foreword and certain helpful corrections. Derrick (D L) Smith and Ian Robinson for arranging typescripts. Frank Lacey for allowing me to quote his poem "November 11th", Phil Drake for his drawing in Chapter XIV. The Bovington Tank Museum for the photograph of The MK VI Tiger Tank taken at Robaa, Tunisia.

Lastly to my wife, Daphne, who started it all on a very old portable typewriter whilst incubating our first child, and who persuaded me to continue to the end.

ABOUT THE AUTHOR

The Author, born January 1920 was educated at Dulwich College. On leaving school he joined a firm of Quantity Surveyors in London as a trainee.

Upon outbreak of Second World War volunteered for RAF but was told that they had too many pilots, so volunteered for the Royal Artillery. Joined 5th Field Training Regiment RA at Dover in February 1940 and was commissioned as a Field Gunner in 1941.

Joined 72nd Anti-Tank Regiment RA in Summer of 1941. The Regiment was sent overseas to North Africa with 6th Armoured Division in November 1942 at the beginning of 'Torch'. Fought throughout Tunisian campaign and awarded the MC in March 1943.

After the North African war the Division was sent to Italy in Spring of 1944 and took part in final battle for Cassino in May. Continued fighting in Europe until 1945. Promoted Major and Battery Commander in 1945; discharged from Army in July 1946.

In 1948 started farming in Devon with fellow Officer, Lieutenant Ted Newman, who later became his brother-in-law. Married June 1951 to Daphne Whitehead, they have three children.

Left farming in 1954 to train for the Probation Service. Served in Berkshire, Devon and finally as Chief Probation Officer of the Dorset service. Retired in 1982. Joined Came Down Golf Club in 1968, elected Captain in 1972 and again in 1989, has been President of the Club since end of 1989.

Captain Donald Low MC, the author

CHAPTER I

NOVEMBER 1942

"Sailing down the Clyde,
Sailing down the Clyde,
Back to Bonny Scotland
And your own fireside. "

The strains of this tune, sung with a certain forced cheerfulness, must have been audible along the busy banks of that same river. If any man among those thousands in that convoy wished to cherish a memory of Britain during the years to follow, he could not have wished for a lovelier panorama than the November sun on those Scottish hills as the convoy seemed to drift out through the Firth of Clyde.

I thought of the friends I had made in Scotland, I thought of my relatives in Glasgow - I'd meant to visit them again last weekend but it had not been possible. Well, there would be a good many wet months in Glasgow before I saw them again and they were welcome to them. For my part I hoped that, wherever we were going, the weather might be just a little more cheerful. Six months under canvas at Ayr race-course had tested our tempers to the full, to say nothing of our boots. And the sound of falling rain on the outside of one's tent had become as natural and as constant as the clock ticking in Grandmother's sitting room. Goodbye to all that we thought.

At home they would receive my last hurriedly written letter from Ayr telling them not to worry if they didn't hear from me for a week or two - which meant, of course, that they would worry all the more. My mother would interpret all kind of hidden meanings into every news bulletin and if there was nothing of any consequence she would certainly exercise her inventive faculties. We in our turn were speculating upon the interval of time before we once again saw the coast of England - England or Scotland, it was all one to us. I supposed that many of us would not return and looked round at the men I knew so well, better than my own friends at home it seemed. I couldn't honestly believe that they wouldn't come back. It was too usual, too mechanical, too well 'laid on' to be the real thing. There were rumours that it was just another scheme. The men had openly forecast for the last eighteen months that the 6th Armoured Division was obviously ear-marked for the second front across the Channel. "And you don't go launching a frontal attack in a bleedin' great luxury liner," maintained one of the young 'old soldiers'. "It's probably another bloody 'Dryshod'."

'Dryshod' was the last outing the higher command had invited us to, during which everybody had been soaked for four dismal days. For two years our division had been training hard. In our regiment - the 72nd Anti-Tank Regiment RA - we had trained energetically as anti-tank gunners. Drills, ranges, schemes, inspections, making drivers into gunners and gunners into drivers, making NCOs and breaking NCOs, map reading, gun siting, route marches, forced marches, night deployments, painting and repainting vehicles. The whole rigmarole had continued and repeated itself until, after a series of inspections by higher and higher 'ups', the whole thing culminated in the disappearance of 'A' Battery who motored off furtively one dull day after a lot of hushed whisperings.

We in 'B' Battery received our orders to march down to Ayr station four days after the departure of 'A' Battery. We had assembled on the station at 4 am on November 10th and, after the usual delays to which we had long since become accustomed, clambered and cluttered into the train which puffed and clanked us through the murky smoke-stacked factory district of Clydeside and on to the little dock-side station at Greenock. Thence we were ferried, together with an RAF regiment, in a tiny pleasure-type steamer across to the waiting large transport ships. Soon after my troop boarded this little ferry boat there was a rifle report followed by a scuffle somewhere near the funnel. One of the RAF regiment, who had decided it was now or never, had shot himself in the foot and blown off a toe.

We waited at anchor in the Clyde for four days whilst the convoy gradually took in its cargo of youth. Besides our battery and several units of our division, we had in our ship - the Windsor Castle - a large detachment of American troops. These American soldiers provided a constant source of interest for the British rank and file throughout the days to come. It wasn't long before a few Tommies were able to give a creditable showing of American arms drill, marching up and down the decks with their rifles held the wrong way and yelling "About face" at one another. And very soon it was not unknown for gunner Bloggins to jump smartly to his feet and deliver the slickest of salutes - palm downwards. These originalities to the British army were subsequently discouraged by the sergeant major organising a short but brisk refresher course in marching and rifle drill. Soon the letters to home had been written (to be retained by the rear party for several days before posting). Then on November 14th, with no bands playing and no fluttering handkerchieves, we moved off. Slowly the great ships felt their way down the river, each one wrapped in a cummerbund of faces. "Sailing down the Clyde."

* * * * * * * *

The last I remember of the Scottish coast line was a large dark lizard which was as near as I could get to identifying the Isle of Something. Then the dinner gong sounded. Dinner for the officers, late tea for the men, was an encouraging sample of food to come. I cannot remember the menu but I know it would have rivalled the best hotels in London. Throughout the 10 days at sea the cuisine department of the Windsor Castle maintained a standard to which few of us had been accustomed and none of us had anticipated. This applied equally to what the ship's crew termed 'the lower deck'.

The next morning found us with an escort of six destroyers and a Sunderland flying boat. We were alleged to be off the coast of Ireland though nobody knew off which coast and certainly nobody knew which coast was preparing to welcome us. Nobody, that's to say, except perhaps the captain. We had been introduced to the new drill of manning the lifeboats. This drill was heralded by a crescendo of ringing bells which were, as far as I could see, the signal for the outbreak of complete chaos.

For my part, I had been elected to the status of "Guns". This position carried with it the privilege of ignoring the cacophony of bells in order to devote my attention whole-heartedly towards the mixed bag of men nominated to man the twenty-two different sorts and sizes of guns carried by the ship. These weapons ranged from a large 6-inch gun which stuck out like a tail from the boat's stern, to twin machine-guns mounted at various points of vantage. And in particular I was personally responsible for the well-being of a brace of 12-pounders which were positioned just outside the window of the captain's cabin. I was permitted to man these two with men from my own troop (No 6 Troop) though it was pointed out that on no condition were we to fire them - not even in the case of attack. They were strictly naval guns and consequently were coveted by the ship's company.

The voyage continued and was, as far as I was concerned, one of the pleasantest periods I spent in 6½ years in the army. In between the daily parades I liked to slip away to my troop's guns which were higher up in the ship and from where I could obtain a better view of the dolphin fish. These dolphins could be seen most days during the fine weather and seemed the most playful of creatures. They would follow the boat for miles, leaping out of the water and apparently bowling themselves along just for the fun of it. We were sorely tempted to throw them food but there were very strict orders prohibiting the jettisoning of anything. A paper bag or cigarette packet might float for days and offer unnecessary clues to enemy aircraft.

Fortunately I must have inherited from my father a seaman's stomach, because we were soon to enter, or traverse, the Bay of Biscay, where we encountered a fairly heavy sea. Soon there were obvious signs of distress among the ship's many passengers. In November 1942 I was twenty-two years old and young enough to be unaffected by the suffering of others so long as I enjoyed the sea as I did. I fell foul of Major Hamilton, my battery commander, seriously for the first time. He made no claim to being a good sailor and although he wasn't showing it at the time, was feeling the first effects of the ship's rolling and pitching. I expressed my hope that we'd have it good and rough for a bit - just to make it exciting. He called me a selfish young bugger who deserved to have his seat kicked. I think that was our only tiff in the eighteen months he was my battery commander. When presently I visited the men below in their sleeping quarters, I could see his point of view.

The rough sea passed and the weather became warmer. Battle dress blouses were discarded and shirt sleeves were the order of the day. Still the speculation as to our destination continued - India, or the Middle East were favourites. Then, after a week at sea, there came the call for unit commanders and the news was out. We were to follow a force which had just landed or was just landing at Algiers and were to press on towards Tunisia and Tunis with all possible speed.

Little books on the country were issued giving conditions of roads and descriptions of the terrain and climate. Thousands of maps were handed out to be sorted. Some of us were issued with comic little compasses disguised as collar studs and other agreeable little toys such as might be found inside a Christmas cracker. These were not amusements for the troops but were supposed to stand us in good stead if, as prisoners of war, we ever wished to make good our escape.

As the convoy approached the Gibraltar Straits our escort, now of some 15 destroyers and one cruiser, took on a new lease of life and began to hurry and scurry to and fro at speed. Then - CRUMP - our ship shuddered and bounced very slightly. Someone suggested we'd hit the Rock of Gibraltar - then we saw that one destroyer far out to port was dropping depth charges. A second crump and a third were felt rather than heard and everybody looked towards the water to see if any torpedoes were coming our way.

It was dark by the time we came abreast of Gibraltar Rock and it seemed strange to see the lights twinkling along the Spanish coast - the first lights we had seen outside since leaving Scotland. Major Hamilton gazed at the dark, yet somehow comforting, shape of Gibraltar Rock. He had been stationed there for some time just before the war; as he leant on the ship's rail and stared through the darkness towards Gibraltar he spoke nostalgically of the gay times they'd had there. His voice was even quieter than usual and as I stood beside him I knew we were thinking similar thoughts: it couldn't be long now and what would it be like?

My own war experiences so far consisted of books I'd read of the first war and stories I'd heard from elderly relatives and friends of the family. Some of them had been lurid enough; of course there had been a few air-raids at Dover in 1940 and some better ones at home, but that wasn't the same. Somehow this pleasant and thoroughly enjoyable trip could hardly be a prelude to another Somme or Dunkirk. Perhaps it would be a walk-over; there were vague reports of the 8th Army chasing the Germans along the north African coast - we might only be needed for 'mopping up' operations. We were soon to learn that it was neither a Dunkirk nor a walk-over.

Looking at the convoy ships around us, as I had done night after night, I tried to think of an apt description but nothing seemed to fit so exactly as the ordinary adjective "ghostly". They were a bunch of ghost ships that thrust silently through the waves clinging together for reassurance. Well, if I were going to get bumped off I hoped it would be on land - even Africa was better than the sea.

During the voyage my 12-pounders had been manned day and night by my troop: A section (2-gun detachments) by day and the other section by night. I had visited them from time to time throughout each 24 hours and found the night visits preferable to my stuffy cabin below, shared with three other officers. The memory of those ethereal nights has been preserved in my mind. The wind and spray in my face, the moon exaggerating the movement of the waves and enhancing the shadows of the ship and, above all, the tumbling and sportive juggling of phosphorus lights that capered round the ship's bow as she drove on through the waves. It was a picture that might only be described in music.

Presently Ken Hamilton pointed out the lights of Tangier. He had visited the place a couple of times and said that, at the time, he'd been quite taken with it. As I looked I could just make out the high cliffs of Africa even though the moon was scarcely up. Africa for me, until that moment, had limited itself to a large head of a poodle in a school atlas, a poodle with its nose to the ground. A continent populated by black men and wild animals and colonised by practically everybody who ever had a leaning towards colonising. The world's poor relative from whom people borrowed but never recompensed. Now, suddenly, here it was and I felt rather like a new boy arriving at the first day of term, or as a chick ought to feel when it has just hatched from its egg; I wished I could run to some place of security and just think things over for a while.

As we pursued our course up the Mediterranean I became fascinated by the brilliance of a star dead ahead. This star changed colour so frequently and so vividly that it must be the heavenly traffic lights. Algy Collins claimed it to be Sirius. Lieutenant Collins was a bright and enthusiastic officer who took his job seriously. He commanded 7 Troop and was a comparative newcomer to our battery and he and I enjoyed some earnest but friendly rivalry between our troops. Since he was educated at Harrow I bowed before his astronomical erudition. He continued to name several more of the constellations and whilst I listened with half an ear, I thought of the years 1914-1918 and how many hopeless faces must have gazed up at the same Great Bear from their frigid parapets. And, as Algy pointed out that we were in much the same position as the Malta convoys that had run the gauntlet along these same waterways, I could readily understand the rancour felt by the wiring parties towards this risen moon of twenty-five years ago.

However, our convoy arrived and anchored out in Algiers harbour shortly before dawn on November 22nd. The navy had seen us safely there as we had confidently expected it would. The navy equally confidently prophesied that it would have to take us off again when we ran back to Algiers in the near future. News came to us that French resistance had ceased almost as soon as the initial assault had gone in. We had understood that the idea of our coming here was to fight the Germans not the French - still, apparently that had been sorted out and we need not worry ourselves further on that account.

Most of us anticipated dawn in our eagerness to glimpse Algiers and soon we were rewarded by a splendid sight. Now that we were in a confined space the harbour seemed full of shipping. The navy was much in evidence and the whole scene reminded one of a recruiting poster. Join the Navy and See the World. With this romantic and sparkling white port as a background and the battle-grey ships snugly settled in the bluest of seas, the hills studded with palm trees - all these produced an air of cordiality which could not fail to bring response. A nearby soldier remarked that it was a good thing his missus wasn't here as she'd want to come every year for her holidays.

* * * * * * * *

Now followed a day of intense activity attended by all its orders and counter orders. Baggage parties were organised, loading and unloading parties were detailed. The battery sergeant major's boots lost some of their lustre but he was compensated by the gain in venom of his tongue. The orderly sergeant condemned all ship's constructional engineers to perdition. The voice of the ship's adjutant blared over the loud speakers every eight minutes and Major Hamilton became decidedly prickly. I believe it was at this time that Ken Hamilton first described the officer's conversation as, "A statement of fact followed by a flat contradiction, followed by a stream of abuse."

To Lieutenant Newman was consigned the task of baggage officer. Lieutenant Newman was one of the battery HQ subalterns and was known as 'Honest Ted'. He was about the only one among us who could possibly be expected to extricate the battery's paraphernalia from that of several other units of the division who were our fellow passengers. He could also be relied upon to curb, or at least retard, some of the partisan activities of various unit NCO's.

That evening the convoy began discharging its various cargoes. Our turn was not to come for many hours yet so, as darkness approached, we began to make temporary arrangements for a few hours' sleep. During the day some chap, with a particularly able pair of eyes and a diligently cultivated flare for aircraft recognition, pronounced a black speck which appeared in the sky and as quickly vanished, to be a Heinkel something or other. The truth of this statement will never be known but if indeed it were a hostile reconnaissance aeroplane its pilot's report must have born fruit.

Soon after dark there came the unmistakeable throb of aeroplane engines. Abruptly the searchlights were flicked on and hundreds of eyes followed them as they probed the skies this way and that. Then it started. Our nearest neighbour, some one hundred yards away to starboard, was a cruiser with its backside shot off; literally the last ten to fifteen feet aft were missing and it ended in a few jagged-edged compartments. This cruiser may have felt embarrassed but she threw off her shyness with startling effect. Suddenly she let off five hair-raising wallops in quick succession that drove my teeth together like a mouse trap. Having relieved herself of this invective in the shape of five 3.5 or 4 inch shells, she obviously felt better and forthwith set to work with two or three sets of multiple Pom-Poms.

The effect of all this upon the assembled shipping was practically simultaneous. As if the cruiser had been the starter's gun, they all let rip with such alacrity and enthusiasm that a casual onlooker might have mistaken it for the principal set-piece of a combined service gala that had been rehearsed for weeks. I don't know how many ships were in the harbour that night, certainly at least twenty troop carriers; in addition, there were a couple of cruisers and about ten destroyers. Of the twenty-two assorted guns on the Windsor Castle, nineteen of them opened fire to my certain knowledge. The three exceptions being the 6-inch tail gun whose ammunition was locked away in some inaccessible place (under the circumstances perhaps it was just as well) and my two 12-pounders. But even allowing for the absence of these three defaulters, the resultant din was pretty stimulating. Apart from the navy's big stuff, all the other guns were firing tracer ammunition. Bofors ack-ack guns, multiple Pom-Poms, heavy machine-guns, lighter twin machine-guns, all of them sending streams of coloured lights skywards. And, above it all, like the big bass drum in a brass band, the next-door cruiser keeping time as it crashed out five beats to the bar.

The reason for the 12-pounders' silence was that, at the sound of the alarm, six members of the ship's crew had taken over the two guns whilst two more commenced bringing shells and charges up a vertical ladder. When I asked what the idea was, they merely stated that those were their orders. It also appeared that they couldn't fire the guns unless given the order by their own officer. Meanwhile 6 Troop were getting impatient and so was I, so, telling the seamen that I would accept full responsibility, I replaced them with my own gun crews and told them to act as ammunition numbers.

At this stage it is necessary to mention the position of those two guns more exactly. From the main decks where the troops paraded and were allowed to roam in their free time, there arose three or four tiers joined together above and below by those infernal vertical step-ladders. Somewhere near the top of these tiers rested the bridge and underneath the bridge was the captain's cabin. Immediately outside the captain's cabin, on a miniature deck of their own, were my troop's adopted guns, one to port and one to starboard. If you stood between the two guns and looked straight ahead you were faced by the foremast and its attendant rigging. This of necessity limited the scope of each gun to a 90 degree traverse and throughout the following hour I made it my business to answer for the ship's safety by ensuring that the guns kept within those limits. It wasn't so difficult for the gunners to overlook the mast in the dark and gunners Chalky White and Bert Walters were as capable of landing one in the middle of the crow's nest, or whatever it was the mast carried, as the next.

The vociferous cruiser was thumping off her salvos methodically and presumably guided by information unavailable to us. So, reckoning they'd do less harm if they added weight to the cruiser's barrage than if left to their own devices, and more as a reward for my troop than with any idea of hitting anything, I directed them to fire accordingly. The starboard gun entrusted to sergeant Williams' detachment was the only one able to engage the cruiser's bursting shells. Presently, the fuses having been set at maximum range, the shell was rammed into the breech and the charge inserted. Sergeant Williams yelled "Fire" and there followed the grandfather of bangs together with blast to match. Standing a little to one side of the gun I was propelled against the captain's cabin. In a confined space and with very little gun shield for protection we hadn't bargained for such concussion.

It transpired that we had not endeared ourselves to others. There came a torrent of oaths and profanity from just above us by the bridge. There were a couple of heavy machine-guns mounted there, one either side of the bridge. These had naturally felt the effect of our 12-pounder being discharged and their response was crude to say the least. Gunner Gardener (known as Spit and Blink) began to join issue but I intervened and ordered the gun to resume firing.

Gunner Gardener earned the title 'Spit and Blink' because of his nervous habit of shaking his head sideways whilst blinking in an obvious and oft repeated manner; at the same time he made a spitting noise without actually spitting. The more anxious or worried he was, the more pronounced this affliction became. He was small of stature, partially bald even though still a young man, very sparsely endowed with intelligence, illiterate, ugly and cunning as a fox. He was born and reared somewhere in the east end of London and I had the impression that he had served his apprenticeship as a burglar. He asked nothing of life beyond the usual social necessities and it was obvious that his social blessings had always been threadbare. Even so, he was a source of laughter and held a philosophy of "Do unto others before they do you". Life had dealt him the poorest of hands but it was the only one he had and it was precious to him.

7

Meanwhile, after two more deftly placed rounds the target apparently moved across the arc of fire of No 1 detachment. Sergeant Varney's orders to engage and fire came in one breath and he had scarcely time to get them out before the gun went off and promptly blew out the window of the captain's cabin.

With the departure of the captain's window and its 'blackout' there came a shaft of light which seemed as though it must be lighting up half the harbour. Sergeant Varney was a big bruiser of a man with a masterly voice; he acted with commendable speed and initiative in addressing gunner White, "Chalky, stick your arse in that window an' be quick about it." His orders were carried out to the letter. Acting as the occasion demanded, gunner White, assisted by two others, mounted onto gunner Gardener's shoulders and assuming a sitting position was thrust trouser-seat first into the vacant porthole. There he remained for some half-an-hour effectively screening the window. And, as Bombardier Bullen afterwards remarked, "It was the first and last time he was ever likely to have his 'picture' framed."

The barrage continued and every now and then was punctuated by the shock of a bomb bursting. How it was that the boats were missed I never understood. But only one ship was hit and that by a plane which flew in at water level and launched a torpedo. The ship did not sink and the chief loss was the convoy's mail which was in its hold. Nor did I see any enemy plane hit and that seemed even more remarkable. Though it was rumoured next day that seven aircraft had crashed in the district.
Eventually the planes made off and the gun-fire ceased. The ensuing silence seemed to accentuate the ringing in our heads. But we thought we'd done pretty well to see them off with practically no casualties to ourselves. After cleaning up the mess of empty cartridge cases and general debris there was very little time left for sleep that night.

The next day was spent in maintenance of the guns and further preparations for the coming disembarkation. It also provided me with the opportunity to seize five of the Windsor Castle's best toilet-rolls together with some tablets of soap and put them into my large pack. An action upon which I subsequently congratulated myself a hundred times. It was all a rush and scramble, lots of shouting and people getting lost. Suddenly we were on the cobbled quayside feeling and looking like pack horses. Major Hamilton went off to seek instructions from somebody as to our route and assembly point with the rest of the regiment. During his absence another relay of German planes arrived as our battery was forming itself up, and the colossal bombardment started over again. This time it wasn't such fun, shell splinters were falling all around us making vicious metallic clanks as they hit the ground. One or two bombs fell too close for comfort and we all felt thankful when Major Hamilton returned and gave orders for the battery to prepare to move off.

It did not take much preparation and in a few moments we moved off on a march none of us would ever forget. Let me explain that Lieutenant Jimmy James, the other battery HQ subaltern, had left Scotland in a separate convoy with the vehicles and guns. No-one knew exactly where he was nor whether our guns and transport had yet arrived in Africa. The first thing was to meet up with the regimental HQ who no doubt would tell us where to find Lieutenant James. So, leaving Lieutenant Newman with his baggage party to unload the biggest part of the battery's stores, the remainder of us set off at about 0200 hours to find the regimental assembly area.

We carried with us 'only the essentials' consisting of the following: Large pack, spare pair of boots, 2 blankets, 1 towel, 2 pairs of socks, 1 great coat; side haversacks - emergency rations, shaving kit, first aid dressing, rations for next 24 hours, any personal belongings (in my case some chocolate and a couple of books), gas mask, gas cape, ground sheet, tin hat, filled water bottle and a rifle or tommy gun together with 50 rounds of ammunition. Each gun detachment also owned a bren gun which was carried in turn by the men together with boxes of ammunition. I've never worked out how many pounds weight each man carried but it wouldn't have been much less than half a hundredweight.

So it was that the battery began a march of approximately 28 miles, 18 miles to a wrong map reference given to Ken Hamilton and 10 miles back again. Our backs were bent under the weight when we started from the docks but at least we were in three ranks and bore some resemblance to marching soldiery. 18-20 hours later we looked a grotesque contrast.

* * * * * * * *

Now for the first time I had an opportunity to look around me and realise that this was Africa and these, although deserted, were the streets of Algiers. The place I had associated with romance and intrigue had looked from the ship every bit as I imagined it should. The white buildings had sparkled so in the sunshine the day before, the high- domed mosques offered a hint of the 'Arabian Nights'. It had all looked so glittering and clean as it lay there - a perfect compliment to that blue sea. Now it was quite another story. My impression of Algiers both by night and day can be summed up in two words - filth and disgust. As we passed through the streets we encountered every vile smell imaginable. Those dazzling white houses assumed a dirty grey, the air was hot and contaminated by the stale smells that filtered through the windows of those houses. The roads were littered with dirt and decaying vegetation, the excreta from a host of different animals, and occasionally human beings, was lying about everywhere. The whole place savoured of unwholesomeness and corruption, of gambling places and brothels, and one instinctively wished for a week's rain to wash it clean. This wish was to be granted much sooner than we'd anticipated.

I don't think I have ever felt so lonely and far from home as I did then. As I looked around at this desolate reeking place, I wanted to run from it all - it was a horrible sensation. The light, supplied by searchlights and the multitudes of tracer bullets, instilled a grimness, made all the more forbidding by the hollow clanking of our hob-nailed boots on the cobbles. I had a kind of premonition that if I were shoved into battle from Algiers, launched as it were from sordidness, there could be only one result. I began that march with a hopelessness that persisted until five days later we sailed again from Algiers.

I have already said that is was with bent backs that 'B' Battery left the dockside with the air-raid becoming more and more unpleasant. Due to our overloaded condition we were compelled to make frequent stops and as time went on it became increasingly difficult to get to our feet after a halt. Lying on our backs in a ditch, or at the side of the road, we were like upturned turtles and equally unable to right ourselves. We passed a dog lying in the middle of the road; it had been dead perhaps a couple of days. This was a busy road approaching the Algerian capital but apparently none of the passers-by nor adjacent shop-keepers had seen fit to remove it.

Eventually Algiers was left behind and, with the coming of dawn, its firework display ended. Soon after dawn Ken Hamilton decided upon an hour's rest, partly to give us time to brew some tea and partly to allow the stragglers to catch up. By this time our shoulders and backs were feeling a little raw and our feet beginning to protest. Soon the whistle blew again and we helped one another on with our packs and all the rest of the Christmas tree. On we staggered again, every minute was an hour and at every halt it seemed impossible that we could go another hundred yards. At the commencement of the march the battery extended over something less than 100 yards, by mid-morning it was spread over nearly a mile. Our feet were sticky from the blood of broken blisters and our shoulders felt as if we'd been flogged. We looked to the world like an exhausted batch of walking wounded; men were trying to help one another along, officers armed with revolvers instead of rifles were taking turns with rifles, tommy guns, bren guns and ammunition boxes. And whereas in the earlier stages the men had cursed and blasphemed their way along, they were now silent, a sure sign that they'd reached the end of their tether.

It was mid-day when we reached the map reference which was our destination. Just over 10 hours it had taken to cover 18 miles. There we expected to find RHQ and there, to quote a censored version of one of the men, we found 'A womanless expanse of nothing at all'. However, none of us worried on that account except perhaps Hamilton and soon the men were busying themselves with the brew cans. The four troop commanders, Lieutenant Fulton - 5 Troop, myself - 6 Troop, Lieutenant Collins - 7 Troop and Lieutenant Maclean - 8 Troop, held a foot inspection which did more harm than good. It merely confirmed what we already knew, that every man in the battery had blistered feet: and, having removed their boots with some difficulty, many of them couldn't get them on again so swollen were their feet.

A cup of char, a snack from our haversack rations, a wash and shave and spirits soon began to recover. Then, as the men began to spread themselves in assorted attitudes of rest, the CO's car turned the corner and pulled up in a cloud of dust on the road alongside.

Colonel Davidson was an imposing man. Tall, athletic and good looking, his patch over one eye adding distinction, dressed always in riding boots and breeches and equipped at all times with a shooting stick and often with a bag of boiled sweets. As a figurehead he was excellent but he spared no man in the execution of his duty. Two qualities he certainly had: the first was knowing just what he wanted and getting it, and the second was bravery. The first we knew all about, the second had yet to be demonstrated.

He sprang out of his car and strode towards Major Hamilton who was hobbling to meet him. A hurried consultation, an acknowledged salute, and he was gone. "That bugger's up to no good," prophesied one of the gunners.

Ham, as he was known to the officers, approached us wearing one of his forced smiles which usually meant that things were not altogether what they might be. He was not given to sudden outbursts of rage nor did he show his pleasure very forcefully. Some people might describe him as undemonstrative yet this was not strictly true. Those of us who knew him well - and they were not many - quickly learned to recognise his various humours at a glance. We learned too that, for all his youth, he was not a man with whom one took liberties. For the most part he was mild and pretty easy-going and his pleasantly boyish face took on in repose a thoughtful expression. He had a naturally good-humoured disposition and enjoyed pulling our legs - particularly mine. To him I was known as 'The little man' or 'Little Donald'. (The emphasis on the word 'little' had more to do with my age than my size). And to me he was as much a friend as a battery commander. Some of the regimental officers thought him rather slow and ineffectual and I believe Captain Whitting, our battery captain, shared that opinion. Slow he may have been, ineffectual he certainly was not.

There was nothing good-humoured in the tone of his voice as he explained the purpose of the colonel's brief visit. "The divisional artillery are now assembling in a place called Polygon d'artillerie about half way back the way we've come," he said tersely. "The colonel has just ordered me to take the battery there as quickly as possible." Then, as an afterthought, "I wish to Christ people would make up their minds."

We seconded his vote of censure as bluntly as we knew how and then called to our troop sergeants (a kind of troop sergeant major) to prepare to move again. The order "Prepare to move" was soon to become the most disliked and most often heard of all orders given and received in North Africa, at least as far as we anti-tank gunners were concerned. Orders were shouted and fires were hurriedly extinguished, mess tins were scraped clean and, to the accompaniment of oaths and curses, the troops began to collect and buckle on their equipment. As I have said, many of them could only struggle into their boots with extreme difficulty.

"Cigarettes out and form up in three ranks," yelled Sergeant Oakley (my troop sergeant). "What shall I do with this bren gun, sarge? 'Taint my turn to carry it," demanded Gunner Roberts. A strong recommendation volunteered by his nearest neighbour left him no better off. More reiterations from Sergeant Oakley to, "Get a bloody move on," the scuffle of boots, the rattle of rifle butts on the ground. Finally I limped up to Ham, saluted, and reported, "Six Troop ready to move, Sir."

Before long 'B' Battery was on the move again. At first there were outbreaks of singing but gradually, as the spirits of the men succumbed to the pain of their blistered shoulders and feet, the singing died away and the battery reverted to its former shambling condition. Once again the halts became more frequent and of longer duration; then mercifully a 3-ton lorry came along the road towards us, a swirling cloud of dust in its wake. The colonel had sent one of RHQ's 3-tonners to take on our baggage or as much as it could. A cheer went up as Hamilton halted the battery and ordered every body to divest himself of his large pack and bedding roll. Bren guns and ammunition boxes were loaded together with as

11

much stuff as could be pushed into the lorry.

I was sent on with the lorry, taking with me half a dozen of the most seriously crippled men, to get things organised at the assembly area. Six other men were left on the roadside to guard the remaining packs to be picked up on the second trip. During the last half hour there had been a cool breeze and a few clouds had passed teasingly overhead. Now, suddenly, it became very overcast and as we drove away the rain began with welcome spatters on the windscreen.

Driving back towards Algiers the refreshing drops of rain changed into a deluge that made a "Scotch mist" appear a mere April shower in comparison. (The incessant rains we had endured in Scotland during the six months prior to leaving were always classified as "Scotch mists".) In a short while we reached the much sought after Polygon d'artillerie and there we encountered a fitting end to this first day's introduction to overseas service.

The Polygon d'artillerie was the name given to a sandy wooded enclosure, rather circular in shape and perhaps 200-300 yards in diameter. In amongst the trees the ground was covered like a mushroom bed with small two-man bivouacs. These had been erected by an optimistic body of men to provide shelter and sleeping accommodation for the divisional artillery. The divisional artillery consisted of four regiments and its own HQ staff, of which something less than half had so far landed. These frail little tents stood only two foot six inches high and one could just crawl into them and lie full length inside them. As our lorry entered this refuge, none of the several hundred soldiers were making any pretence of lying in them. Looking around at this sorry sight I could see that about 80 percent of the tents had several inches of water running through them and as the rain continued, things were not improving.

I was conducted to a vacant colony of bivouacs which had been assigned to my battery. I thought of the others still grimly staggering along the last remaining miles and obviously by now they must all be drenched. I imagined their reactions to the prospect of taking their first rest lying in three inches of water. In the trees not far away I noticed two large huts of corrugated iron; on closer inspection they were found to be locked. Knowing that it was only a matter of time before HQRA staff ensconced themselves in the dry, I considered my battery could lose nothing by getting there first, even if we were kicked out later. So walking back to the lorry I told two of my six sufferers that I'd be back in a few minutes and hoped to find both doors of the huts open when I returned. They needed no further encouragement.

With difficulty we coaxed the 3-tonner through the trees over the sodden slippery ground so that is was nearer for unloading. There were two grinning gunners sitting on the floor of one of the huts - the doors of both were wide open. I didn't ask any silly questions so I didn't get any silly answers. These were the first smiling faces I'd seen for nearly 24 hours.

Having unloaded the 3-tonner and sent it off for the remainder of the kit, we improvised a cook-house and started some fires to brew some tea and generally made the place ready to receive the rest of the battery. We hadn't long to wait before Ham arrived with the vanguard as it were. Within half an hour the whole battery was accounted for including the 3-tonner with the last of the casualties.

A pretty sorry sight we all looked. The only comforting thought was that we were at least under cover and had a promise of some sleep, whereas hundreds of other chaps of various units were still enduring this soaking rain. Ham was certainly pleased to see those two huts and we managed to cram everybody inside without any persuasion.

The next two or three days were employed in doctoring our sores, drying our clothes, providing guards and performing sundry fatigues. We learnt that neither our guns nor our vehicles were within 100 miles of Algiers and it was not decided yet where we were to meet up with them. 'A' Battery had motored off from Algiers heading east over the Atlas mountains as part of a fighting group called 'Blade Force'. This force was to push on as fast as possible and make contact with any German troops advancing westwards from Tunis. In this objective they certainly succeeded. 'B' Battery's equipment was still at sea and, depending upon where and how hard Blade Force bumped the enemy, a decision would be made as to where our fighting tools should be discharged. In fact everything was in the air and depended on something or somebody else. Tactical RHQ, with colonel Davidson at its head, had departed from Polygon d'artillerie and was heading for Tunisia and, in particular, a town called Beja.

'B' Battery was then ordered to march back to Algiers, about 8 miles, and be prepared to embark on another ship at very short notice. We were not sorry to see the back of Polygon d'artillerie with its rain, mud and confusion, and spirits were considerably higher when we arrived at a football stadium and noticed with approval that it boasted a large sheltered grandstand. However, the rain had now stopped and Algiers smelt a little fresher than it had been five days ago. Nevertheless, my feelings for the place were unaltered and after a further 24 hours at the stadium I was almost overjoyed to hear that the battery was to leave Algiers by boat that evening. Apparently the handful of 78th Infantry Division and a rather battered Blade Force were yelling for anti-tank guns, so we were to rush up to the port of Bone - some 200 miles from Algiers - collect our guns there and travel post-haste for the "sharp end". Just where the sharp end was we didn't know but we'd no doubt meet somebody who did.

On the evening of November 29th 'B' Battery embarked again in a Dutch motor-ship 'Princess Beatrice' which had been converted into an assault landing-craft. There was a similar motor-ship, whose name I have forgotten, which made up a party of two. No escort, and precious few guns carried. These two boats were nevertheless capable of a handsome turn of speed, a point greatly to their advantage as far as we were concerned.

The sun was waning as the two comparatively small boats slipped out of Algiers harbour. Of all the men who stood leaning on the ship's rails not one expressed a single word of regret at leaving this so-called city of gaiety. For myself, I felt like someone suddenly released from toothache; as the fresh breeze whipped my face it seemed to cleanse the dirt from my nostrils and the depression from my mind.

After leaving the harbour, Princess Beatrice and her companion quickly turned eastwards and, hugging the coastline, they sped us away up the Mediterranean into the gathering darkness. The ship's engines changed from a subdued hum to a wrathful clatter, one had to shout to make oneself heard and the vibration was most alarming. We all thought the rivets must fall out of the ship's plates as the Beatrice shuddered and seemed to twist herself as she thrust through the fairly choppy sea at a cracking good pace.

Soon most of us were in bed. We were tired and didn't know what was before us and I remember wondering how long it would be before I once again slept in a comfortable bed between sheets. It was nearly four months later when I next took off my clothes and donned a pair of pyjamas and nearly three years before I experienced the luxury of clean sheets!

MAP OF TUNISIA

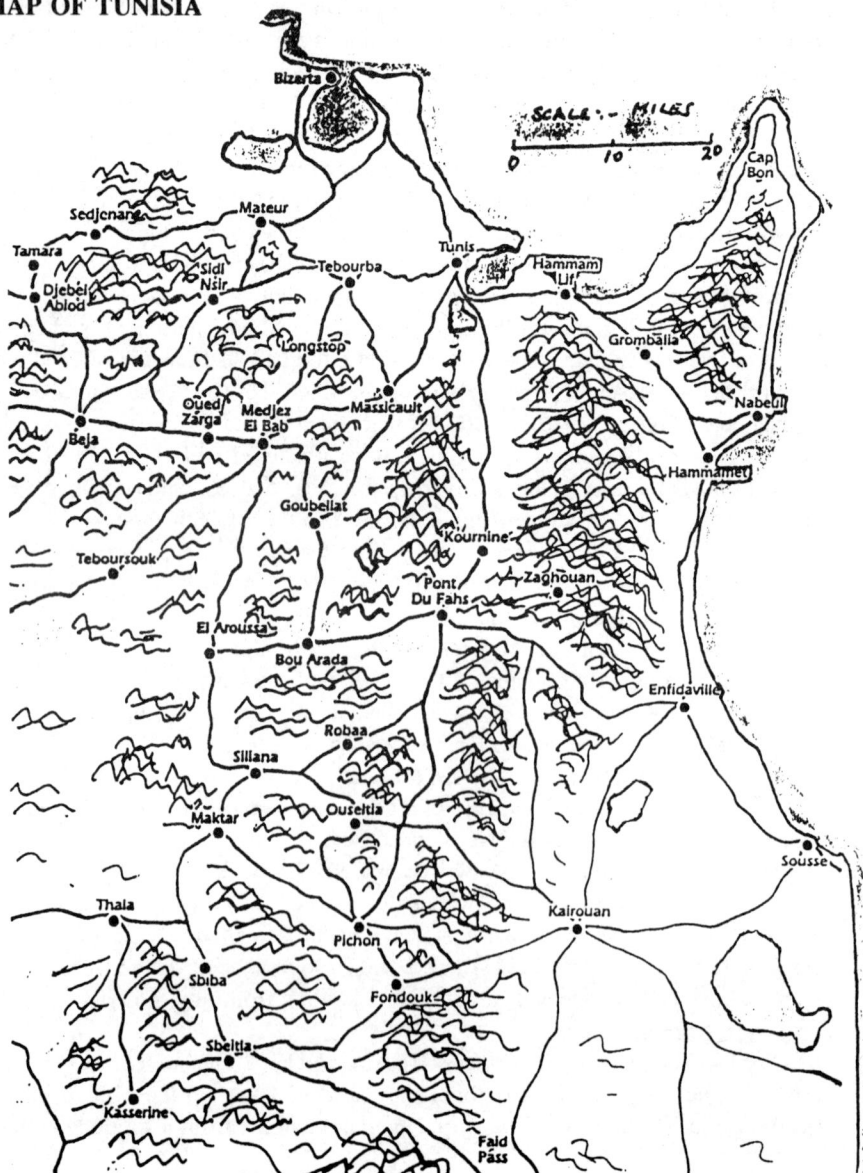

14

CHAPTER II

DECEMBER 1942

'B' Battery disembarked at Bone at eleven o'clock on the morning of November 30th. Spirits were high as we left the docks and marched a short distance to a tobacco warehouse. This warehouse consisted of several vast chambers very high and unfurnished; alongside were long loading platforms three or four feet high. The impression was of an empty covered-in railway station. On the platforms were a number of large square-sided heaps or stacks of tobacco. They looked like stacks of silage with a similar penetrating smell. There was an obvious reaction to this which was to stow as much of this natural blend about one's person as could conveniently be carried. Sadly it was soon realised that the immature leaf was practically unsmokeable.

Outside the warehouse our guns and vehicles were waiting in the proud custody of Lieutenant Jimmy James. Having delivered them into our hands he expressed the hope that he could now be permitted to return to England in peace. Drivers were reunited with their respective troops and, over a hurried lunch, stories about the journey from the UK and happenings after landing in Africa were swapped. Then the whole battery set about making ready for things to come: Battery HQ to its stores and paperwork, the four troops to their guns and gun-towers. Before leaving Ayr the guns had been entirely coated with thick grease; this was a necessary precaution taken against inclement weather during the voyage.

For the benefit of those who are unfamiliar with guns and their bits and pieces, I will mention briefly the sections that go to make up the whole. In front there is the barrel, known in artillery circles as the Piece. Between the two wheels is the Gun Carriage which embraces the breech and breech block, firing mechanism, gun sights, traversing and elevating gear, and the whole is protected by the gun shield. Sticking out behind the gun carriage is the long Trail; in the case of our anti-tank guns the trail was split into two trail legs each with a spade at the end which digs into the ground when the gun fires. On the end of one of these legs is a trail eye, a thick metal ring that slips onto a towing hook on the gun-tower.

All of the above mentioned parts had to be thoroughly cleaned of all dirt and grease before the guns could go into action. Apart from the cleaning there were many stores to be checked over: picks and shovels, camouflage nets, water and food containers, ration boxes, fuel containers, boxes of Mills bombs, Bren guns and magazines of ammunition, Tommy guns and ammunition, rifles, maps and a dozen other miscellaneous articles apart from the men's personal kits. By the evening of November 30th we were ready at last and Ham had the battery paraded in order to brief us. After explaining that we had a long and arduous march in front of us, he gave us all words of encouragement and wished us well.

It was 2100 hours when Major Hamilton led the gun group off towards the east and Tunisia. Captain Whitting, the battery captain, had now joined us but was left to bring on his 'A' echelon, with all the battery stores and water cart plus the 3-tonners from each of the troops, in his own time. The gun group totalled 23 vehicles and 6 dispatch riders in addition to Lieutenants Newman and

James also on motor cycles.

Darkness fell very soon so there was little opportunity to form any opinion of this new part of Africa. I remember nothing other than the fact that the road was good and that we passed an ordinary looking stretch of railway siding with its usual shabby warehouses and heaps of scrap metal and bricks. In a few minutes Bone was left behind and we were permitted to switch on our side-lights only. During the hours of darkness the convoy closed up to about 15-20 yards between vehicles and at each road junction or cross roads a DR (dispatch rider) would act as policeman until the whole column had passed by; he would then return to the head of the column again.

The road became narrower and more winding as we began a long ascent and, as the night wore on, the drivers found it increasingly difficult to keep awake. We halted for 10 minutes every 2 hours, more to awaken ourselves than to stretch our legs. It was not the easiest task to maintain 18 miles in the hour over strange and hilly roads with only a fraction of our side-lights to see by. (All vehicle lights had been 'blacked out' except for a tiny hole in the centre of each lamp). During the early hours of the morning, when the column had halted, Sergeant Barlow of 5 Troop had walked ahead to speak to his neighbours in front. In doing so he crossed over a bridge the sides of which were only wooden railings. Suddenly there was a yell and a splash. Two men ran to the bridge and discovered it to be under repair; at the left side against the rails there was a gaping hole about 6 feet long and 2 feet 6 inches wide. It was easy to see what had happened to Sergeant Barlow. He had fallen 20 feet into the water below. Fortunately he fell into a deep pool and apart from being soaked to the skin and a little shocked, was unhurt. Had he chosen almost any other spot to fall from the bridge he would certainly have hit some ugly rocks.

Soon after dawn next morning we stopped for breakfast; for this we were allowed an hour which was to include washing and shaving and generally tidying ourselves up. We had hardly dismounted from our vehicles when from a large swampy area on our right there came a succession of awful screams. After a few minutes the screams became moans and were approaching us through the tall reeds of the swamp. I ran towards this noise wondering just what I should encounter when, with much smashing of bushes and trampling of rushes, there appeared an elderly Arab. In one hand he grasped a large thick stick and in the other a young boy; as he hurried and pushed the boy before him he continually glanced over his shoulder. My first thought was that he had been belabouring this boy for the last five minutes with the cruel-looking cudgel. My temper rose fittingly as I strode towards them not knowing quite what I was going to do.

Then, as I neared them, I noticed the boy clutched a badly wounded arm. His right upper arm was mutilated to the extent of the bone being laid bare from elbow almost to shoulder. There was a hole deep and large enough to house a banana. The old man was almost as distressed as the boy and, making devil's horns with his fingers from his head, gave me to understand that the lad had been savaged by a bull. I ran back to my truck and found a 'field' dressing and, having bound this over the wound, they both seemed much comforted. Then with a peculiar gesture of thanks, in the form of salutation, the old man placed his arm around the boy's shoulders and steered him off down the road.

Returning to my troop and feeling like a boy scout, I smiled to Ham and prepared to explain the distressing incident. He cut me short by blasting my eyes and demanding to know why my bren-gunners were not posted. I retaliated with the smartest salute and the dirtiest look I could muster and mumbled something about seeing to it at once.

Our small convoy wound its way slowly onwards throughout the day. The hills seemed interminable, up and down, round and round, past noisily splashing waterfalls and through sheer-sided rock gorges. Miles of cork forests extended over these mountains, tall trees with an exterior rugged like an oak but slightly spongy to the touch. Had we known we should have gazed more intently on these trees for during the next six months we saw practically none.

Every once in a while the precipitous countryside would give way to small terraced fields or olive groves; at this time of year they were often under the plough. I was amazed to see such steeply inclined ground under cultivation - no tractor of the 'advanced countries' could have remained upright on such slopes. The ploughing was accomplished with teams of oxen whose horns would have won prizes at any Highland cattle show. These terraced fields usually proclaimed the existence of a village near by, villages that appeared devoid of women but always there were small groups of lean, bare-footed men. Their feet and swarthy expressionless faces were the only indication of life beneath the hoods and cloaks which were their garments.

One had the impression that time had rested here, nothing had altered since the days of the Romans. The sparsely cultivated countryside, the primitive villages (apart from the scattered French villas), the oxen, the unhurried attitude of the Arabs, the hollow-backed donkeys plodding the dusty roads, receiving a prod from behind every few yards of the way more, I suspected, with the purpose of keeping both beast and master awake than of increasing speed. All of this conspired to erase a thousand years of history.

We followed the coast road which twisted and turned and weaved its way up to and away from the coast for mile upon mile. Looking far below at the end of the seaward tack one frequently glimpsed the sea as if from an aeroplane, the waves appearing mere ripples on a pond. Then, turning abruptly inland, the road would ascend into low cloud with thick mists and fairly heavy rain. It was a picturesque route that continued until, at Tabarka, we turned southwards away from the sea and on into the second night.

During the second night the column motored slowly on to Souk el Arba. It was a treacherous journey to make at night even in good conditions, for most of the way it meant a hideous drop for any vehicle leaving the road. And we were not only driving by shielded sidelights but had been without sleep for nearly two days and two nights. The gun teams snatched a few hours as we went along of course, but for the drivers it was a supreme test. Tired eyes trying to pierce the darkness, tortuous roads, steep hills, mists and those almost sheer drops into space if the drivers made a mistake. This was the sort of stuff our drivers were to contend with for the next six months and all possible praise is due to them for the magnificent way they carried out their task.

From Souk el Arba we turned east and dawn on December 2nd found us somewhere near Souk el Khemis on the road to Beja and Medjez el Bab. We breakfasted, washed and refuelled and were off again under the hour. Beja was reached and now we felt suddenly alert and anxious. Beja had just recently received the closest attentions of the German Stukas. These dive-bombers had made a proper job of the place; although we'd been warned of the ferocity and persistence of the Luftwaffe, we ourselves had not been bothered by it nor had we seen any evidence to alarm us. So the sight of Beja, torn, twisted and charred, jerked us into an alertness that needed no further inducement.

Regimental HQ was alleged to be at Oued Zarga, the next village after Beja. It was still the early hours of the morning when we left Beja behind us and now the countryside had changed to low rolling hills covered with scrub and large clumps of cactus here and there. Considering we were approaching a regimental HQ and therefore presumably in a fairly forward area, we hadn't yet seen any signs of a British or an American army. Where was everybody? The whole country was apparently deserted; perhaps the war had moved on since we last had news; they might even be nearing Tunis, in Algiers they'd prophesied the fall of Tunis within ten days.

* * * * * * * *

It was just after six o'clock on the morning of December 2nd when we found RHQ tucked away in some trees just outside the village of Oued Zarga. The Quartermaster greeted us with a solemn glance upwards towards his Maker and remarked that unless we wanted the living daylights knocked out of us, we'd better get our stuff under cover. We accepted his advice and scattered the column under what remaining cover there was. That done, we sought out the various office staffs, hungry for news of the battle.

The sundry groups of men who went to make up RHQ had one thing in common - they were all reluctant to move farther than 10 yards from the nearest slit trench. And whilst they knew little or nothing about the battle situation, they were more than ready to recount the narrowness of their escapes from Messerschmitts and dive-bombers. In our view this was just RHQ talk and to be treated with suspicion. Nevertheless, we were debating whether or not to dig a few holes for ourselves, just in case, when Ham returned from the CO to say that we should be moving shortly.

The battery was to be placed under command of the 64th Anti-Tank Regiment RA who belonged, we thought, to the 78th Division. Ham was to contact their CO somewhere in Tebourba at 1700 hours but meantime the whole battery including 'A' echelon would concentrate nearer Tebourba in readiness for deployment. Studying our maps, we troop commanders marked the map reference where the battery was to rendezvous - a place about two-thirds of the way between Medjez el Bab and Tebourba, a short distance beyond a hill on the left of the road where a small rivulet crossed underneath the road. Ham was going ahead and would meet the vehicles at this point to give them further orders. We were to move one vehicle at a time at 5-minute intervals. This was a precaution against air attack.

Just then Lieutenant Laycock of 'A' Battery drove into our secluded oasis in his 15 cwt truck. He looked haggard, tired and dirty. He was yellow with dust and as I hailed him I noticed how bloodshot his eyes were. Lacy, as we called him, was one of the brighter officers, always highly polished, beautifully dressed,

and with a taste for expensive boots; I had last seen him before he left Ayr with
'A' Battery. He looked round at me now and half smiled, "Hello, Donald." His
mouth tightened and he ran his hand nervously through his hair, "Oh,
everything's fine, I've just lost my bloody troop; at least, if there's any left I
can't find them, nor my battery either for that matter." He walked off to find the
CO in the hope of learning where, if anywhere, he could find his battery again.
Shortly afterwards he returned, climbed into the driver's seat of his truck, nodded
to me and drove off wearing the same unfamiliar gaunt expression.
Ham's talk with Colonel Davidson revealed that 'A' Battery had been badly
knocked about. In company with Blade Force they had been caught by a strong
force of German tanks in the fairly open ground to the north west of Tebourba
and had virtually lost numbers 3 and 4 Troops. The 17/21st Lancers (with
Valentine and Crusader tanks) and a Field Battery of the 12th Royal Horse
Artillery, both of our division and of Blade Force, had also been badly done by
and the whole of Blade Force was now concentrating in the olive groves around
Tebourba. Our battery was going there to join a brigade of the 78th Division and
a troop of medium guns to allow Blade Force to withdraw.
    None of this news was at all indicative of our marching into Tunis within the
next week or so. In fact, judging from the snatches of news, Lacy's face, and the
general gloominess of Oued Zarga, it seemed far more probable that we should
all be heading at a brisk canter for the sanctuary of those mountains that we'd
cursed so heartily last night. To put it plainly, we were all suffering from a slight
attack of the jitters. It's one thing to imagine yourself bashing an enemy when
reading the reports from the front in a newspaper at the breakfast table, it's quite
another prospect when the opportunity becomes a reality, particularly if the
evidence points to the enemy being more advantageously placed to bash you.
    At about 1330 hours Ham, after having cautioned 5 Troop to be ready to
move, drove out of our refuge and down the road to Medjez el Bab. There was
a glum silence as we all watched his truck bumping away out of sight, as if we
fully expected a Messerschmitt to swoop out of the sky and pounce on him like
a hawk. Precisely five minutes later Lieutenant Fulton followed in Ham's tracks,
his head stuck out through the unbuttoned canvas hood of his 15 cwt, and turned
from side to side as he scanned the skies. Captain Whitting, who had left Bone
with his 'A' echelon some hours after us, had reached Oued Zarga during the
morning. He stood beside me in his field boots and breeches and, unlike myself,
looked forward eagerly to "our first meeting with the Boche" as he put it. My
feelings were very similar to those I experienced whenever I was in a dentist's
waiting room.
    One by one 5 Troop's guns left their hiding places and then, with a few words
of advice to my sergeants, I got in my truck beside my driver who had the engine
already running. At 1400 hours I told Lance Bombardier Foster to drive on. The
canvas hood of the driver's cabin was folded back so that I could stand with my
head and shoulders out above the top. My batman, Savage, reckoned two pairs
of eyes were better than one and accordingly posted himself on the tail board.
Our journey was of some twenty miles and for the first two of these Savage gave
me his private but unsolicited opinion of German aircraft, their pilots, Africa,

Arabs and so forth. It must be explained that in no way could Savage be described as a willing participant in the affairs of an army on active service. In fact his constant prayer throughout his three and a half years' of overseas service was to change places with one of the 'War Workers'. It is equally fair to add that he was an excellent soldier and a blessing at all times when he wasn't grumbling.

Medjez el Bab was just short of half way to our rendezvous; it lay on a bend in the river Medjerda and what it lacked in size it made up for in importance. 'B' Battery came to know it pretty well during the month of December. But I was not concerned with Medjez just now and, as we turned the last corner of the drunken road from Oued Zarga, I remember only the dazzling whiteness of its buildings in the strong African afternoon sun.

The road slopes down from the hills into the town but we had to turn off beforehand to join the main Medjez-Tebourba road. As we came upon this road I noticed a number of shallow, blackened holes dotted all around and about. Medjez el Bab was the first town I'd been near that had been really contested and scars were everywhere to be seen amid its outskirts. Leaving Medjez on our right we passed the station, and that too bore evidence of recent combat, and headed towards Tebourba.

Now we passed a few farm houses and buildings. The Medjerda valley was an extremely fertile one and the number of farms dotted about bore witness to that fact. It may have been a populous neighbourhood in normal times but at the moment it was deserted and soulless as a dead land. Suddenly we came upon a burnt out vehicle, then another and a third; charred hulks that sprawled by the wayside, their blackened contents spread all around them. Another black object lay beside a barn; as we drew closer the vilest stench I'd ever encountered made me hold my breath. It was a dead mule; a million flies buzzed around it and about the dark patch where its head and neck lay. It had swollen to twice or three times its normal size so that it looked as if it must burst at any moment. Two of the stiffened legs pointed vertically upwards, the other two propped the carcase on its back. The thick lips were drawn back revealing large, hideously grinning teeth. We passed several more along the road, each looking equally frightful and each having a sickening effect upon me.

My 15 cwt continued northwards at a perceptibly faster speed. The road was rather more open than before and one felt akin to a fox that has broken cover and bolted across open country; it seemed that the eyes of the pack must pick us up. Our eyes and ears were never more attentive and we cursed the cloak of dust that followed in our wake. I pulled up my map case at intervals to check our position then quickly thrust it away lest the glinting mica covering should betray us.

On our left, some 3000 yards from and running parallel to the road, there was a vast rocky structure; it looked immensely high and almost sheer. A much lower hill grew out at right angles from the main mass like a short stubby limb and extended almost to the road. This smaller tributary was nevertheless majestic enough, itself rising to 900 feet from almost sea level but as we passed it by we guessed nothing of the tragic importance it was to assume under its subsequent name of 'Longstop Hill'.

On the right, the river Medjerda snaked its way down to Tebourba and on to the sea and beyond the river the flat Medjez plain had merged into gently-rolling hills. So that now we were entering a narrow valley with the river and rolling hills on one side and a miniature mountain-range on the other. This range discharged a number of streams from its heights which flowed under the road and into the Medjerda. And it was by a bridge over one of these that Fulton and Ham were standing ready to usher us off the road.

Leaving Fulton to intercept the first of my guns, Ham took me off to show me my troop area. We were not deploying for any state of emergency, simply spreading ourselves well out to avoid presenting the Luftwaffe with a concentrated target. I had just time for a quick glance around before a growing swirl of dust announced the rapid approach of Sergeant Varney's gun. The maximum speed permitted for the guns was twenty miles per hour but, judging from the way the gun was bouncing behind its tower, number 1 detachment were doing between 30 and 40mph. Bombardier Foster, my driver, remarked that, "If any of them Messyschmitts wants to do Sergeant Varney they'll 'ave to get 'im 'ead on 'cause they'll never catch 'im from be'ind."

This attitude of urgency seemed to prevail throughout the whole battery; one by one the guns arrived at the finishing post as though there were a monetary reward for the detachment achieving the shortest time. By four o'clock in the afternoon most of the battery had reached the rendezvous and Ham left for Tebourba to find the commanding officer of the 64th.

Whilst he was away, the remainder of the battery commenced brewing tea. The method of boiling the water was a simple one. A medium sized tin was filled with earth; the earth was soaked with petrol and a match applied. This stove would burn for a very long time. True, the resultant product, after heating a tin of water and adding the mixture of powdered milk, sugar and tea, was very much an acquired taste. Often, if the tea tasted too strongly of petrol fumes and smoke, a number of wooden slivers were placed in the water while it was being heated; these were supposed to absorb the offending fumes - with what success I shouldn't care to say.

* * * * * * * *

Ham returned at about seven o'clock in the evening with the news that all was not well at Tebourba. Second Brigade of the 78th Division were trying desperately to hold a conical hill just outside the town; this hill completely overlooked Tebourba and its loss would enforce a withdrawal. A large German tank force was in the neighbourhood and had been attacking constantly, and in particular it had been trying to work round the left flank to the west and south-west and so cut off Second Brigade. About five miles up the road the range of hills on the left, and the river Medjerda on the right, converged to make a narrow pass; at this point there was a large cactus grove astride the main road. We were to leave one troop at this cactus grove to safeguard the rear, while the remainder of the battery continued another mile or so into the southern outskirts of Tebourba. There they were to form an anti-tank hedgehog and, together with Second Brigade, were to hold the town until reinforcements could be brought up. There was a battery of medium artillery in the olive groves to the south of the town, so we should be in good company.

The troop to be dropped off at the cactus grove would not be on its own but would join Lieutenant Heslop of 'A' Battery who had moved up there last night; there would be no infantry support so a watchful eye must be kept for night patrols. The HQ of an American armoured combat-group was also rumoured to be there but no one quite knew. The battery would move under cover of darkness and no lights of any kind were to be used.

We left Ham to have some food and returned to our troops wishing we had more cheerful news to tell them. It would be a few hours before we could start so, in order to alleviate the tension of waiting, we busied ourselves writing letters or darning a sock; some of the men spread themselves on the ground and dozed, their heads lolling back in their tin hats. We troop officers were obliged to censor our men's letters and with one accord they were expressing their dissatisfaction at not having received any mail since before leaving Scotland. Mail meant more to us than anything else; the war we could throw off when the danger past, discomfort and sleeplessness could be suffered and laughed at, but a prolonged absence of mail engulfed us all in a mood of fretful discontent.

I wandered across to Algy Collins and began chatting with him; all sorts of fears and doubts were in my mind as to my own performance in action and I wanted to quell them. Fears of my own courage and doubts of my ability to lead my men through whatever was coming. I remembered Laycock's face - he had lost his troop, was it his fault, I wondered, or was it damned bad luck? My mind envisaged all kinds of catastrophes and I wished to hell we could get started.

Algy was as cheery and confident as ever. "We'll soon see whose troop can shoot the straightest," and he grinned at the prospect. We indulged in a bit of harmless backchat when, startlingly, there came four loud bangs of field guns from just over the hill to our right, or so it sounded. A pause and then a repeat dose. We realised that these were the first shots we'd heard fired in anger since leaving Algiers. The explosions of the bursting shells could be heard easily and Algy pointed out that they were probably the mediums and therefore sounded much nearer than they really were.

Ham, who had been talking with Captain Whitting, called the sergeant major and all officers over to him. He gave us further orders concerning the next move. "Donald, I've decided to leave you in the cactus grove. It may not be for long and you'll probably join us in Tebourba in a day or two. The order of march for the battery will be myself, followed by the wireless truck, Mr Newman on his motor cycle, 5 Troop, 7 Troop, 8 Troop, 'A' echelon ending with the fitters and the sergeant major. 6 Troop will bring up the rear and drop off at their position. Mr James is to report to the Colonel as liaison officer and will not accompany us. The route will be along the main road as far as 6 Troop cactus grove, then via a track which runs through olive groves and follows the river to Tebourba. No lights will be used so vehicles travel nose to tail. Any questions?"

I felt a slight resentment at being selected for this secondary task but long afterwards Ham told me the decision came about because Little Donald was the youngest. And, as it turned out, it was just as well for me and for 6 Troop that I was.

CHAPTER III

TEBOURBA

The night of December 2nd began by being dark as a coal-mine but improved to bright moonlight during the early hours of the morning. The battery crawled out of the harbour area and along the main road and, as always when we had been without sleep for a long time, we felt stale-mouthed and shivery. The last time we had slept was on the boat to Bone; this was betrayed by vehicles constantly straying across the road. But apart from a gun and quad of 8 Troop's, and the sergeant major's motor cycle, both of which broke down, they all completed the journey without mishap. (A quad was the official name for a gun-tower).

There was no mistaking my cactus grove even in the practically impenetrable blackness. For the last couple of miles I had been alternately staring at my map with the aid of a screened torch and leaning out of the truck probing the darkness for any feature that would corroborate our position lest I should overshoot the place. But a solid wall of cactus ten feet high both sides of the road gave me all the confirmation I needed. So, leaving the troop parked on the verge of the road, I walked forward with Sergeant Oakley to the front edge of this cactus in the hope of stumbling across Peter Heslop or one of his guns.

Walking along the road from rear to front of this cactus measured about 150 yards; in the darkness it seemed three times that distance. As we drew near to the front we became aware of a reddish light in the sky; at least it enabled us to see a little better but it was an eerie sensation. In a moment or two we stood at the front or northern edge of the cactus and understood the source of this weird light. Ahead of us the ground was open and flat as far as we could tell, anyway for some distance, then it rose up not very high to where two or three mammoth bonfires were burning. Every few minutes one of them sent a shower of sparks cascading upwards like a miniature eruption. Even in our greenness we could identify burning tanks when we saw them.

We turned left along an uneven track and crunched our way towards a looming mass of rock reflected in the peculiar light. As we approached this craggy bulk a voice called out, "Who's that?" I replied, "An anti-tank troop commander and I'd like a word with you if you don't mind." The owner of the voice left the shadows and came to meet us. "You're a bit late aren't you? Should've been here yesterday." Major Blank introduced himself but I have forgotten his name. I only remember he was from 78th Division. "We had thirty enemy tanks trying to frighten us here yesterday. They did too but the little 'pack' gunners gave them a bloody nose, though at some cost to themselves."

The little pack gunners were a troop of Light Mountain Artillery equipped with four 3.7 inch howitzers. They had held their fire until the German tanks - firing their 75mm guns as they came - were only 300 yards off, then all four of them opened up at point blank range. After a short but savage encounter the tanks withdrew leaving six of their number on fire or disabled. A number of the light artillery were casualties but they had more than proved themselves in that brave action against stern odds. They had repulsed a considerable number of tanks with their four tiny guns. As it happened, one of their officers came to my aid three months later in a remote spot called Sedjenane.

I asked the major if he could tell me exactly where the Germans where. Pointing with the stem of his pipe towards the burning tank he said, "They've been there all day today and, of course, at Tebourba", indicating the right hand side of the plain, "But God knows where they'll be tomorrow". I asked about night patrols, pointing out the isolated position of gun detachments without infantry cover. He replied that they'd been all right so far because the enemy had been too busy round Tebourba but supposed that we couldn't count on that indefinitely. This major apparently accepted things as he found them and reckoned that if the outlook was a bit obscure for us, there was no need to suppose that it was any clearer for the other side. It took me some time to understand the truth of that.

As Sergeant Oakley and I retraced our steps to the road, the moon, still hidden from us by the crest of the hills, promised to make things less tedious for the remainder of the night. This was a considerable relief to me since I had to deploy my troop before dawn. The essentials were that tank approaches should be recognised, that guns should be sited so as to cover the likely tank approaches, that the guns should have a reasonably uninterrupted field of fire and that the guns, if possible, should be able to shoot at a tank at a killing range without other following tanks being able to see or, at any rate, shoot in reply. This meant tucking the guns behind some feature or building or group of trees etc. In the darkness it would have been an even chance that the guns would have been sited in totally inappropriate places; with the moon for assistance things might not be so difficult.

We reached the road again and walked back between the high cactus towards our waiting guns. On the way we found Peter Heslop behind a gap in the hedge asleep in his camp bed. The moon, now fast rising, afforded sufficient light to disclose the cactus to be a large outer fortification protecting an orchard of olive trees within. The trees were in straight military lines similar to the average fruit orchard in Kent or Worcestershire. However, in contrast to the silence of an English orchard, these were the rowdiest collection of trees it's possible to imagine. Each and every twig and stem was a platform designed to amplify the half croak, half cheep, emitted by thousands of crickets, if they were crickets. They strove to shout each other down until the noise was absolutely penetrating.

I wondered how Peter could possibly sleep with such a din about his ears. He, on the other hand, lying in gaudy, poplin pyjamas, transmitted an air of convincing indifference to his surroundings. Having gained a little idea of the size and shape of this cactus grove, and the whereabouts of Peter's guns, I returned with Sergeant Oakley to my waiting troop. It was now about one o'clock in the morning and bitterly cold so, telling Sergeant Oakley to collect the four gun sergeants, I turned to my truck to pull out my greatcoat.

The six of us then set out to explore the interior as well as exterior of this cactus grove. We walked its length, its breadth, its perimeter and its centre. Its shape resembled two open-ended squares, one on either side of the road. The western side, on our left, was closed by the steep ridge of hills mentioned earlier. The eastern side sloped down to the river Medjerda. Inside these rectangles the closely planted olive trees would afford a certain amount of cover though they were not large enough to conceal a vehicle adequately.

By 4 am the gun positions were selected and the troop deployed. The quads were camouflaged fairly near to their guns and were thus automatically dispersed against an air attack. Now all that remained was to dig the gun-pits and dig slit trenches for ourselves. As the soil was three parts sand, this sometimes lengthy task was accomplished in little more than half an hour. I established my troop HQ towards the rear of the western side not far from the foothills of the ridge. At dawn on December 3rd we unrolled our blankets and fell asleep for the first time since November 29th.

* * * * * * * *

Like the circulation returning after numbness, my senses gradually realised that something was up. I started up in my camp bed trying to throw off my stupor, forced open my eyes and winced as they met a bright sun. "Bastards," said a voice. Its owner, Savage, was able to put more intonation into that particular noun, whether it be singular or plural, than anyone else I ever encountered. With the accent on the first syllable, he invested the word with extra expression and meaning. Sometimes it was preceded by a suitable adjective but it was the word itself that really carried the weight. Having been delivered, no other contribution was necessary; one might say that any further comment would have been pointless.

On this occasion it heralded the noise of approaching aeroplanes. Looking over my shoulder, I saw two fighter aircraft coming towards us and flying very low. With an adroit twist I catapulted out of bed and made for the slit trench. Even so I came a bad fourth to Savage, Rowe and Bombardier Foster; Sergeant Oakley was slightly handicapped by corns on his feet. As the planes flashed over our heads, the black and white crosses could be plainly seen. Savage informed us that they were Messerschmitts and that they had flown over us twice. We watched them wheel left-handed over the river and away northwards towards Tebourba. The time was six-thirty - we had been asleep for two hours and it had seemed like two minutes.

Soon my small canvas basin was fixed on its stand and used in turn by the other members of my troop HQ. Having washed and shaved, I left Savage and Foster to prepare breakfast, Sergeant Oakley to improve the camouflage and Gunner Rowe, my DR, to deepen and lengthen the slit-trench whilst I set off for a brief tour of the four guns. Only one of them had to be moved and that only a matter of fifteen yards. All the men were washing and every gun had beside it a can of tea brewing.

Before eight o'clock I was back for breakfast. Our 'compo' rations, as they were called, came in large wooden boxes and contained one day's rations for fourteen men or two days for seven men and so on - as far as one's mathematics would stretch. Inside was a square tin of hard biscuits, dozens of them and very hard, which normally acted as coinage for the purchase of eggs or 'oeufs' from Arabs; they were only eaten by us as a last resort or to keep awake during long night marches. A much smaller tin contained a mixture of powdered milk, tea and sugar. There was a collection of tinned meats and vegetables; these varied according to the label on the box. 'A' might include Irish stew, box 'B' possibly Bully beef, 'C' might be Steak and Kidney and so on. The puddings also varied with the box letterings: treacle puddings, date, mixed fruit, rice were the ones I particularly remember. Breakfast dishes were mainly baked beans or some awful sausages which, after a month or two, I could no longer face. There would also be a tin of jam and another of margarine. Lastly, there were two tins of fifty cigarettes and a ration of boiled sweets, and some toilet paper.

We were munching slabs of bread and jam (the bread had been purchased from an Arab bakery at Oued Zarga on the drive to RHQ) and sipping mugs of hot soupy tea when, from Tebourba, there came the banging of 25-pounder guns. Their range was short because the crashes of exploding shells came almost immediately after the bangs. It became apparent that it was no casual target they were engaging; the guns continued to thud and thump until the whole valley thundered with noise.

Presently the harsh crackle of machine-guns contributed their share towards the din, then the squeaky grind of moving tanks could be heard. One by one the various instruments of war joined this orchestration of destruction. Smoke and dust drifted across the open plain in front of us. Sergeant Oakley ventured that it sounded like a big attack. I agreed that it did and felt decidedly less confident of our ability to withstand a tank attack than I had during my last visit to the gun teams. Suddenly I thought how silly it would be to get wiped out defending eight or ten acres of North African olive trees; they weren't even part of a line.

The noise around Tebourba eased for a while then swelled again to further heights. I knew the gun detachments must be feeling anxious at all this clamour so I set off with Sergeant Oakley to make sure that all was well. As was to be expected, they were all busy deepening slit-trenches and digging weapon-pits for bren guns. (Bren guns were the ordinary machine guns used widely throughout the army). Without exception they were expressing concern for the others of 'B' Battery at Tebourba. It was not possible for us to imagine what was going on there but it sounded quite ghastly.

For two hours or more the pandemonium alternately raged and lulled until at midday it reached its climax with the arrival of several waves of Stuka dive-bombers. By now I had found myself an observation post a little way up in the rocky foothills behind my troop HQ. From here I had a good view of Tebourba and the steep hill that overlooked it. I was climbing to my vantage point as the first instalment of Stukas began circling their target. They spaced themselves out until they formed a complete ring whilst around and about them small dark puffs of smoke indicated the bursting shells of the ack-ack guns.

Having located the target, the leader dipped his wing and slipped sideways and downwards out of the circle. His dive became steeper and was accompanied by a wailing noise that rose to a screech as the speed of the diving plane increased. It dropped almost vertically until at the last moment it released its bomb, flattened out and began to climb away again. There followed a violent, tearing explosion and, within a few seconds, another and another as one by one the bombers had peeled off and followed the same pattern as the leader. I felt a succession of shocks as waves reached me from the bomb bursts. Then, as the last of the Stukas made off towards Tunis, a huge pall of black smoke and dust rose and covered the entire area.

My first reaction was one of pity for those who'd suffered that battering. The outward appearance of those Stukas was simply devastating; the sheer noise must have been stunning. Pity gave way to anger when I thought of the air cover we'd been promised on the ship when we'd been told of our destination. Our air force was going to see to it that the Luftwaffe would not fly, at least during the hours of daylight. There was going to be close co-operation with the ground forces and so on. I didn't stop to think that Tunis boasted a fine, large aerodrome with concrete runways unaffected by rain; whereas, before our fighters could operate over the battle areas, forward aerodromes had to be constructed and that would take some time.

Then, as I scrambled down the rocks, and as if in answer to the German knockout blows, I heard the deep throated roars of the medium guns and saw their shells blasting away chunks of the hill that the Germans had occupied. I took comfort in the knowledge of their survival but wondered at the fate of my battery. If the truth were told, I thought also of myself. If what I had witnessed was an average sample of what was to come in this particular war, then it might be better not to contemplate the future.

The afternoon brought no respite for the poor devils trying to hold that little town. As I periodically looked through my field glasses, I could clearly see the vicious spurts of earth and smoke of the bursting shells and mortar-bombs. I wondered what the verdict of it all would be. Had Frank Whitting's first meeting with 'the Boche' exceeded his expectations? Had Algy Collins' troop shot straight and bagged a few? They were having their baptism of fire, mine was yet to come; I just hoped that mine would be a considerably gentler experience.

* * * * * * * *

It must have been about five o'clock in the evening before the battle showed signs of burning itself out. Gradually the gunfire grew more hesitant and the bursts of machine-guns more spasmodic. At last it all seemed to come to a spluttering standstill. I had seen Peter several times during the day and we'd exchanged opinions on the situation, mostly with an optimistic flavour. But I think neither of us was deceived by the other's outward calm. I asked him, in a casual sort of way, whether this was a typical day in our particular war? He replied that in his ten days' experience he had been mortared a bit and been subjected to sundry air attacks but that was about all. At that time I would have given a lot to have had his ten days' experience behind me.

Now that the din had stopped we all felt a resurgence of confidence and faith in ourselves. After all, so far as we could tell, there had been no breakthrough and apparently Tebourba was still in our hands. Dusk graduated to darkness and I stood talking to Peter and his troop sergeant near my HQ. We had just completed the evening tour of our guns. The night guards had been organised and the crickets had begun their shrill chorus.

We were smoking a cigarette and I was thinking what an anti-climax the darkness had brought after the pounding of the day. The tension of not knowing what had happened over there and the watchful anticipation of a possible attack, together with the lack of sleep, had left me feeling overwrought and oddly limp. I was hoping for some message from my battery so, as we talked about Scotland and leave and any other comfortable subjects, my ears were alert to any sound that might be a motor cycle or a truck.

With a sudden stiffening the three of us stopped talking and listened. The sound we heard was that of moving tanks coming, so it seemed, from the rolling ground on our right and behind us. "Christ!" said Peter, "If they attack in this darkness it'll be a proper bloody cock-up." We hurried towards the rear gun positions and his troop sergeant paused saying that it sounded as though they were coming along the road from Medjez towards us.

As we considered this possibility the side lights of a vehicle could be seen coming slowly along the road. As it approached, a voice was clearly heard to say, "Say easy there, driver, I guess we're here." Peter began to laugh, "It's those Yanks again. They've been here once and apparently they've come back to have another bash." To our great relief a jeep slid to a standstill near Peter's HQ. The colonel of the combat-group stepped out and prepared to intercept his tanks as they trundled on behind him.

I learned from Peter's sergeant that two days earlier this same combat-group had launched seventeen of their Grant tanks at the German tank force which had been throwing taunts at them from across the plain in front of us. The American tanks had burst out of the cactus and charged across the plain at the enemy armour in true cavalry style. The Germans had turned about and rolled back over the crest of the sloping ground at the far side of the small plain. Gaining in confidence, the Grants chased over the ridge in pursuit and, in doing so, they ran right onto the waiting 88mm guns. There had been a short and unhappy exchange wherein the Americans lost rather more than half their number.

Now they had returned reinforced and ready to exact a bit of revenge if given the chance. In fact, they were called upon to do nothing other than churn around with their tanks inside our cactus grove for two more days. Still it was comforting to have them there and during their brief sojourn we found them always ready to help and co-operate in any way they could. They were friendly, generous and unceremonious. I had only to remark to an American sergeant that I could do with a saw to cut down a particular tree - which was hindering the field of fire of one of the guns - and he turned to his driver, without reference to higher authority, saying, "Take out that tank and roll down that tree for the lootenant here." They also invited us to help ourselves to fuel and water from their supply trucks.

We had more to do with the Americans later in the campaign and always found them generous and anxious to please. They liked to be liked and were apt, during any conversation, to dive into their pockets and thrust snapshots of their wives, children, sweethearts etc into your hand and invite your scrutiny. They were proud of themselves and of their country and they had reason to be. Yet their zeal and determination to show that Uncle Sam meant business, led them into too many imprudences.

Our second night's sleep in action was about as short-lived as the first. At about 2 am on December 4th, I was awakened by a vigorous shaking and an impatient voice shouting, "Donald, Donald, wake up!"

My eyelids seemed weighted down with rocks but as I forced them open I looked into the begrimed and concerned face of Major Hamilton. "Hello Ham," I said rather stupidly, "glad to see you again." "Blast it, Donald, where's the battery?" Hamilton thundered his question in such a way that I realised something was expected of me. Sitting up I answered, "Battery? I thought you had it." "It left Tebourba over two hours ago, should have been here." His voice snapped with alarm and he stared into the moonlit olive trees as if unable to believe that the rest of the battery were not huddled there somewhere. I suggested, as I shiveringly pulled on my greatcoat, that we went to Sergeant Williams' gun which was nearest to the track leading to Tebourba and he would know if anybody had passed that way.

Gunner Barber was on guard when we reached Williams' gun position; he had been on from one to three am and had seen a few medium guns pass through, also Major Hamilton with Lieutenant Newman on motor bikes, but that was all. There had been nothing else, nor had he heard anything. "Good God," said Ham and he briefly told me what had happened.

It appeared that the battery had arrived in Tebourba at about six o'clock the previous morning. 8 Troop had been deployed to the north of the town, the remainder had harboured in olive groves to the south. The Germans attacked during the morning and eventually took the hill overlooking the town. At 3.15 pm the East Surreys had counter attacked unsuccessfully. Enemy tanks had closed in on the town and some bloody battles had taken place. The tanks and enemy infantry had been halted by our infantry charging with rifle and bayonet but it had all been in vain. After much confusion the whole force was ordered to withdraw in the evening.

Captain Whitting had been told to take the battery back to my cactus under cover of darkness. Ham and Ted Newman had remained behind to see the battery safely away. The battery had followed behind the infantry but Ted and he had somehow got themselves mixed up with the medium guns so that they had followed some twenty minutes or so afterwards. Although they both travelled on motor cycles, the track was too narrow to allow them to overtake the mediums. So they were obliged to follow slowly along through the olive trees in the darkness. From time to time the German tanks machine-gunned around the place and altogether the retreating columns had a difficult and hazardous time.

Eventually, after many doubts and scares, they were clear of immediate danger and simply rode along until they reached my position. Ham was near to breaking; he kept on asking what had Frank Whitting done with them? I felt desperately sorry for him; he looked all in and he was at his wits end to know what to do. He had not slept for days and had been under great strain, not to mention danger, for the last 24 hours. On top of everything, he was faced with the fact that he had lost his battery, not part of it but all of it, except for my troop. Eleven guns he had taken into Tebourba, plus a fair amount of transport, and not one of them had returned apparently. I knew he was thinking that Colonel Davidson would not be impressed by a battery commander returning unscathed from a battle without his battery.

Ham sent me back along the track towards Tebourba in a faint hope that I might hear something whilst he himself went back to RHQ to report to the colonel. It was a useless quest as far as I was concerned and after bouncing about on my motorcycle through the olive trees for about half an hour, not knowing where I was going in the dark, I returned not unwillingly to my troop HQ to await the return of Hamilton.

Not long afterwards he returned with Ted Newman who had ridden on to RHQ ahead of him. We were a glum party for the next half hour. It seemed that

Lieutenant James, whilst on a mission for the colonel, had fallen off his motorcycle and cracked his knee cap. He had been evacuated and, in fact, we never saw him with the regiment again.

After holding several inquests on the withdrawal of the battery, I finally persuaded Ham that since we could do nothing now, it might be as well if we all snatched a few hours' sleep. Ted habitually carried much of his kit on his motorcycle so he was less bereft of personal belongings than was Ham. Captain Whitting had taken my troop 3-ton truck with his 'A' echelon so all my troop stores and spare bedding had been lost with the battery. However, we each contributed a blanket and, as it happened, I had bought a new camp bed before leaving Scotland and my old one was in my 15 cwt truck. This was gratefully accepted by Major Hamilton.

Next morning we woke at 6 am and after the usual ablutions, Savage got to work with the brew can and tin opener. Rowe began extending the slit-trenches to provide for two more and his toils were soon rewarded.

Halfway through the first mug of tea our two Messerschmitt visitors came whizzing towards us. They roared over our heads, circled the cactus grove twice and rushed off as quickly as they had come. Savage raised his tin-hat in salutation and with equal solemnity pronounced his usual judgement, "Black bastards" and went back to his breakfast. Bombardier Foster merely forked his fingers in the direction of the departed Me109's. At 7.30 am, just half an hour later, Ham's prophecy of a following Stuka attack proved correct.

Staring into the sun we could see nothing but the drone of approaching engines was unmistakeable. Soon they were overhead, seven of them, and, as I'd seen them the previous day, so they began the same ritual. They broke formation to form a large circle above us then, after three circuits, the leader plunged down into his dive.

Instinctively we all pressed tighter into our slit-trenches and I confess that my heart was pounding fit to burst. The sirens fixed to the plane screeched with frenzied volume until the aircraft pulled out of its dive, then there was a loud swishing as the bomb fell. The very air, the ground, the trees all seemed to split and erupt with the explosion that followed. The noise of the screaming Stuka and the bomb exploding nearby was incredible. There was scarcely time to realise that we at any rate had been missed before the second plane was tearing down at us.

So they came, one close upon the other and after each explosion we could feel a sudden suction like a vacuum collapsing. Earth, stones, branches of trees and great lumps of cactus flew over our trench. Then suddenly there was quiet, except for the receding throb of the Stukas. Ham and I set off hastily to visit the gun positions. The nearest to my troop HQ had suffered the most anxious time but there were no casualties in any of the detachments. I thought of yesterday and realised that, although very frightening, these Stuka attacks were not as devastating as they looked. Unknown to us at the time, this attack was of much greater help to us than to the Germans.

About an hour later we heard a faint cheering and shortly afterwards the grinning figure of gunner Smith came round the corner of the cactus hedge. He was running cap in hand, since he tended to wear it on the back of his head and it was apt to become unseated if he ran. He came to a halt and saluted, still with his cap in his hand, thereby breaching one of the army rules about Good Order and Military Discipline. Just now we were more concerned with his purpose than with his appearance. Gunner Smith conveyed Sergeant Williams' compliments and the fact that they had got seven of them there having a cup of char. "Got back just now, Sir" gunner Smith completed his evidence with obvious delight. He confirmed that these were seven of the missing battery so, sending Rowe back to RHQ with a message for Major Hamilton who had gone there earlier, I accompanied Smith back to his gun to hear the news from the seven stragglers.

Their story was not an encouraging one. It seemed that Captain Whitting had led the battery column in darkness behind mixed troops of infantry and ack-ack gunners. They were following a narrow track which wound along the high bank of the river Medjerda. Before long one of the infantry carriers was hit and set on fire, completely blocking the road. They tried to push it over the cliff into the river but the heat and flames prevented them from getting close enough for more than a few seconds. Having the impression that the enemy was not far away, the order was given to abandon all vehicles and make their own way back.

At this point the river took a wide sweep westward and then northward before swinging south and passing my position. To follow the river would be to risk walking into the enemy and their tanks which were still sweeping and searching all around that area. It was decided to swim the river, if necessary twice, in order to get back to my position. The river was deep with quite a current and with very thick muddy verges. They thought many of their number had not reached the other side. The Germans were machine-gunning up and down the river and, although they couldn't see their targets in the darkness, it had made things most unpleasant. Captain Whitting had led them into the river, he was swimming and carrying his greatcoat etc above his head. No-one had seen him come out on the other bank.

In the darkness confusion prevailed and the whole force had become split up. They had tried to cross the river from many different points and many of them had been swept down stream in the attempt. Some of the battery, on gaining the other bank, had decided to lie up in the shelter of the river bank until morning. This particular party had decided to push on into the thick olive groves before dawn arrived. Daylight found them completely lost and without maps they couldn't even identify any features. Fortunately for them they saw the Stukas fly over en route for my position. Naturally they saw the subsequent attack and straight away turned their steps towards it. They assumed that the area attacked would contain friends of some sort and they were greatly assisted by the great cloud of black dust and smoke that rose from the bursting bombs.

Major Hamilton returned and the story was repeated for his benefit. His worried face brightened at last at the prospect that the battery might not after all have fallen into enemy hands and that they might yet find their way back. He said that Peter Heslop's troop had been placed under his command temporarily, as also had Steve Lindsay's troop from 'C' Battery. He had sent Steve to occupy the hill called Djebel el Ahmera, about seven miles or so back on the road to Medjez. He was to act as a sort of longstop, explained Ham, and he later claimed that at that moment he had christened the infamous Longstop Hill.

Throughout the day small groups of missing battery members filtered into our position but their numbers did not amount to many. They all had a similar tale to tell and most of them had been guided by our early morning dive-bombing attack.

During the afternoon, after I had been round the perimeter of the cactus with Peter, we were walking back through the middle of the olive trees when Peter went to earth shouting, "Down, Donald!" I flung myself down without knowing why but as I did so there came a hollow bang. I felt more surprise than alarm. "What the devil was that?" I enquired of Peter. "A mortar," he answered; the bomb had burst some forty odd yards from us and the fragments had made a curious singing noise as they flew over us. We walked on rather faster than before; suddenly he stopped, "There, did you hear the plop? There's another on the way." I looked for a hole or ditch to dive into but Peter assured me that this one was OK - you could tell by the sound the missile made through the air. Trusting his judgement, I remained standing by his side and sure enough the second bomb fell a good 100 yards to our left.

Much impressed by this demonstration of front line expertise, I asked for a few tips. Peter said there was no magic formula, it was just a matter of having a few lobbed at you and around you until you learn to pick the wrong ones from the passers-by. Several more mortars were lobbed over before I gained the sanctuary of my troop HQ with its comforting slit-trench. Ham asked if any of them were near me, to which I replied nonchalantly, and thinking of his recent experiences at Tebourba, "Nothing nearer than about 30 yards."

* * * * * * * *

The next day, December 5th, was spent in trying to sort out the stragglers and fit them up with bedding and all the other essentials. At precisely the same hour as the previous day we had been treated to another attack by the Stukas. This time it had painful though not disastrous effect upon two of my troop.

We had suffered the first attack in silence, due to an order forbidding any action against aircraft and absolute stillness when they were overhead. The enemy were not supposed to know of our presence in this particular olive grove! Even so, I had given orders that any future Stuka attacks should be regarded as fair game for the bren gunners, particularly since the Americans were cheerfully and belligerently advertising their presence to all enemy planes that approached anywhere near.

The nearest gun to my troop HQ was sited right in the thick cactus hedge. A hole had been cut through the hedge to accommodate the gun and two slit-trenches had been dug just inside the hedge behind the gun. Bombardier Harper, one of the best and most reliable members of 6 Troop, and Gunner Tisor, one of the more difficult and least predictable, had one thing in common - neither believed in turning the other cheek. They had been hammering away at the Stukas as they dived down at us, Harper with the bren and Tisor feeding him with magazines; but after the fourth bomb there was an abrupt cessation of firing from them.

The Stukas flew off and I jumped out of my trench and ran towards Sergeant

Agambar's gun which was screened by the usual thick blanket of dust. I knew that two of the bombs must have been very close. As I came to the gun I could hear yells and foul language in about equal proportions. The yells came from the centre of a large uprooted cactus, a vast bush which Sergeant Agambar was dismantling with a machete. Between swipes he explained that the two men were pinned in the slit-trench beneath. When the others of the gun detachment and I had joined the rescue with an axe and three spades, the two unfortunates were released in a very few minutes.

Their lack of gratitude was understandable in view of the spate of mirth and derision they suffered when they eventually emerged. While the many spikes were being plucked from their persons, Bombardier Harper gave a graphic account of how they had been spraying tracer bullets at each diving plane in turn until they both realised that the fourth bomb was coming straight at them. In a second they were both down in the slit-trench behind the hedge where they were the unhappy recipients of a couple of hundredweights of cactus. The bomb had severed and lifted this huge hedge, full of 2-inch spikes, and dropped it on them. These spikes were not just prickles, they were more like hypodermic needles and injected a painful substance that brought up a lump. However, both Harper and Tisor were able to enjoy the misfortune of another before many hours had passed.

During the afternoon the German mortars began another session; beginning with our right flank or river side, they systematically worked over the whole olive grove. It transpired that Sergeant Williams was taken short a few minutes before all this started. So it was that the first bomb sailed over and found him with his trousers down about 25-30 yards away from its point of impact. The bursting mortar caught him bending, as it were, and inflicted a flesh wound where he offered the most flesh. Unable to take cover where he was and unwilling to remain a sitting target, he made back towards his gun with as much haste as circumstances would allow. From all accounts he made an interesting spectacle as he covered the ground in leaps and bounds with his trousers round his knees, giving a fair imitation of a village sack race.

First aid was administered and it was found that he had suffered most injury to his dignity. The Americans had one man wounded as a result of the mortaring, otherwise all was well. Ham wasn't at all happy about things; he mistrusted the negative attitude of the enemy, especially as they must know of our vulnerable situation and depleted forces since Tebourba. He had expected them to exploit their local success and press on to Medjez el Bab. We all knew that we couldn't hold a sustained attack, for one thing we had no infantry whatsoever. If he lost the remainder of his command in similar circumstances as before, poor Ham would have been finished.

Those responsible for the disposition of our small force must have shared these views for, the following day, Ham was ordered to withdraw his two troops. The Yanks had pulled out during the night leaving us the olive trees, the cactus, the stars and the crickets. I remember lying in my blankets that night, looking up at the Great Bear and thinking what an age it seemed since Algy and I had been discussing the stars as the Windsor Castle rocked us on towards Africa and an uncertain future. Now, a week or two later, out of the eight officers who had been together in Scotland, only three of us were here now.

Next day in the late morning a DR came towards us at high speed. To our amazement he shot past us and through the cactus grove into the open plain beyond. In disbelief we followed his progress to the German forward localities in farm buildings that straddled the road some 1500 yards in front. The DR rode right into the farm and then, seconds later, came hurtling back along the road towards us again. The rider was lying flat along his petrol tank and we heard shots coming from the Germans. Nevertheless, in inspired fashion, he reached our cactus and the waving arms of the gunners. His bike slid to a stop on its side as he landed sprawling at the feet of the gun team. The DR was white-faced as he sat on the ground receiving an enthusiastic welcome. The gunners were not used to seeing a member of RHQ so ready to engage the enemy. He, in turn, could only repeat, "Holy Jesus!" His mission was to summon Ham to the HQ of 138 Field Regiment RA.

Ham returned later with the news that we were falling back to Medjez. My troop was to be dropped at Steve Lindsay's Longstop Hill for the night while Peter Heslop and Battery HQ were going on to Medjez. The move would take place this evening and my troop was to cover the river crossings to protect the withdrawal. I was to set out at once to make a reconnaissance of the river and any tank crossings in order to occupy and secure the crossings before the remainder moved off.

I looked at my map and pointed out to Ham that I was being asked to defend five or six miles of river with four guns. Did he seriously think it possible? Ham smiled and said he didn't but that there may be only a few places in that distance where tanks could cross. If I could take care of the most likely places it would keep the force commander happy. The force commander was Colonel Dick Hull, CO of the 17th/21st Lancers, and I had met him earlier with Ham before he had decided to pull back to Medjez. The next time I met him was many years later in 1966. I was having a short holiday with my family and was fishing on the River Torridge in Devon. One rainy morning I encountered a fellow fisherman and we talked together for a few minutes. I still was able to recognise the man who stood beside me, though he had earlier become Field Marshal Sir Richard Hull, Chief of the Imperial General Staff.

As I bumped along the deserted road with a folded map in my pocket and my revolver at my side, I thought to myself how ridiculous it all was. Here was I alone on a motor bike with the whole of north Africa laid out before me: the extremely lovely mountain ridge full of colours was now on my right, the river Medjerda winding slowly along on my left and beyond that the handsome Medjez plain. There was no sign of life, not even a cow or a donkey; the sun was warm and I thought if only it could stay like this. Away from the others it all felt like a game, war was unreal, it was the denial of man's evolution and his sensitivity. The thought of German tanks rolling down this plain with the intention of blowing to pieces anything they saw moving in front of them, seemed absurd and unbelievable.

Leaving the road I reached the river by a track and then followed its course as best I could across country. I marked on my map any places where tanks might cross, giving them a scaled priority of markings. At the end of an hour and a half I was riding along the road and pondering a mathematical problem. I'd covered scarcely half the distance and I'd found at least a dozen easy crossings so far; if I doubled that, then 24 crossings would be a fair estimate to be covered with 4 guns. At that moment my problems were interrupted by other agencies. Six Focke Wolfe fighter-bombers were coming fast upon my tail.

On the right of the road was a deep ditch which of necessity had to pass under any tracks that joined the road. Just ahead was a farmhouse and a few trees and opposite was a track running up towards the hills. I skidded to a sort of halt under the trees, that is to say, I left the bike when it was nearly there and was across the road and down into the ditch before the engine had stopped. In a few more seconds I had wriggled feet first into an 18 inch culvert beneath the track.

Lying dry-mouthed in my drainpipe, I watched the low flying, black-crossed aeroplanes roar over and on towards Medjez el Bab. A day or two later I remembered that it was in that drainpipe that I must have lost my rather good pair of leather gloves. And that episode terminated my reconnaissance of river crossings. Instead I returned to Ham and reported that the river couldn't be covered with twice my number of guns. The best I could do would be to select four crossings at random and hope for the best. He agreed it was a waste of time and told me to forget it.

The plans having been rearranged to include my troop in the move, Peter and I were buzzing around arranging to extricate our guns without telegraphing to the enemy the news that we were pulling out. We had no wish to invite their mortar fire at such a time. My troop was to form up above and below the road and, naturally, facing the road. As soon as Ham had seen Peter's troop safely off on the road to Medjez, he was to accompany me to Longstop Hill, lend a hand in deploying the guns and then he would motor on to Medjez el Bab.

6 Troop were ready and waiting behind the hedge and the time for Peter to leave had come and gone without any of his guns having left. Presently Ham appeared red-faced and agitated. He told me I'd better push off on my own as one of Peter's quads had turned over and God knew when they'd get it upright again. He complained bitterly that this would happen to him but at least he wanted to get one troop out complete. He told me to find positions on Longstop covering the road but hoped to get me back to Medjez next day.

With a wave of his hand Ham returned to Peter's overturned quad and I gave the signal for 6 Troop to start up. Once again, we set off down the Medjez-Tebourba road but in the opposite direction. Still we were a complete troop. Complete, that is, except for dear old Henry Carter, our 3-tonner driver. He was one of the simplest, jolliest, brainless and most popular men and was one of those missing at Tebourba.

Four days had elapsed since we had travelled up this road and those four days had cost 'B' Battery eleven guns and quads, the whole of 'A' echelon, four officers missing and one evacuated, and fifty-three other ranks missing.

CHAPTER IV

MEDJEZ EL BAB

Early on the morning of December 7th a dispatch rider came bounding along the road from Medjez and turned off along the track leading to my position on Longstop. As expected, he brought orders for me to retire to Medjez where I should be met by Ham. Our stay had been a mere bed and breakfast, so it took little time to assemble the troop and make a brisk dash along the six miles or so. How soon it was before the German armoured cars probed up the track by which we left I do not know, but two or three weeks later the first battle for Longstop took place. The Guards Brigade and later, units of 78th Division, had terrible reason to reflect upon that frowning mass. The toll of lives it took on both sides was excessive by any standards.

Medjez el Bab was a small, rather straggling market town. It boasted a number of fairly prosperous-looking villas and what must have been a very old and fine-looking bridge over the river Medjerda. The closely surrounding land was fertile and rich in corn though at this time of year the corn was a promise rather than a fact. To the north and south of the town there were high, steep and rocky ranges of hills. To the east the valley gradually opened and continued virtually the thirty miles to Tunis. There were some lesser, rolling hills in parts of this valley and a few more formidable ones south of Tebourba.

The relative absence of natural defences and obstacles between Medjez and Tunis and its proximity to the capital, plus the fact that it was amply served by good roads, all combined to identify this little town as the most likely launching platform for an attack on Tunis. This realisation was confirmed by the tenacity with which the allied forces hung on to Medjez and constant effort the enemy exerted to take it or to neutralise it.

Our entrance and introduction to Medjez that morning reminded me vaguely of the promenade at a coastal resort. On reaching the town the road went perfectly straight for nearly a quarter of a mile. On our right were shops and houses, on the left the river Medjerda, with the plain extending for miles beyond it. There were no buildings on the river side of the road but there was a fine straight line of eucalyptus trees. Looking through them one felt that the plain ought to be a sea with the noise of lapping waves where the river ran slowly past.

The buildings which had gleamed dazzling white as we had skirted the place five days ago now assumed the usual drabness and the inevitable variety of indelicate smells pervaded the air. Most of the buildings had already sustained damage varying in severity, and outside one of these semi-battered places 'B' Battery's sign indicated Ham's latest HQ. I drew 6 Troop up under the trees and met Ham as he came out of his carpenter's shop. He was his brighter self again and was obviously pleased to see my troop back in one piece and not partly incapacitated in some rocky crag on Longstop.

Until now, the second in command of the regiment, Major 'Pinkey' Burne, had been responsible for the defence of Medjez. He had been provided with neither troops nor guns for this task but he saw no reason to hold back on that account. As second in command it was rare that he was offered the opportunity to act freely on his own. So, pocketing his brandy flask, one could imagine him wandering off, only he knew where, in pursuance of some off-beat scheme that often turned out to be more effective than others had prophesied. His moustache, a reddish-gingery colour, matched his hair and bloomed luxuriantly upon his face giving the impression of the flower of the plant. The plant itself had been allowed to grow unpruned and, in consequence, had developed a comfortable shape but totally unsuited to army transport on African roads.

The outcome of Pinkey Burne's exertions over the past week was praiseworthy, all things considered. Having collected some willing sappers, he had allowed his imagination some freedom of expression in the distribution of mines all round the countryside. With impish delight he had sprinkled an arc of invisible defences in front of the town and around and across the Tunis road. This action enhanced his position overall since he alone possessed the key to their whereabouts.

My job was the defence of the Tunis road and to break up any tank attack from that direction and, having received my orders from Ham, I set off to deploy my troop. I had been shown on the map where at least some of the mines were supposed to be but I was advised against wandering far from the beaten track.

Leaving Battery HQ to their own domestic devices, I continued to the end of the promenade where there was a T-junction. The road to the right forked almost at once, straight on for Teboursouk and doubling back to the right for Oued Zarga and Beja. But my way was left and over the Bailey bridge (the name given to the steel sectional bridges erected by the engineers) and so on to the Tunis road. As we rattled over the bridge there was plenty of evidence of recent contest. Virtually all the buildings were badly knocked about and the river banks and surrounds were a rash of shell-holes. There were bomb craters here and there with debris lying about everywhere.

We picked our way through the rubble and followed the road as it swept round to the right. About a quarter of a mile from the bridge a secondary road from the Goubellat plain joined in from the right. Then, just beyond, where the left of the road was bordered by iron railings, we stopped in front of some queer pattern of small excavations across the road. I got out of my truck and looked more closely at these broken surfaces; at the same time some excited French soldiers materialised. They appeared to come from a dwelling beside a mosque that was inside the railings. There were three of them and I imagine they were supposed to be on duty attending to traffic wanting to cross over this section of road. I was given to understand that they didn't stay by the mines all the time because this area of the road and down to the bridge was subject to shellfire all too often.

After our friends had made it safe for us to pass through, we were in the area allocated to me. I privately hoped that this spot would be better attended during the hours of darkness or I visualised my rations going up in smoke. We were now out in the open. There were a few scattered farmhouses on our right where the land rose gradually towards a large long ridge which were the hills south of Medjez. This ridge was soon to be named 'Banana-Ridge'. On our left there was a field that sloped upwards, as did the road as it left Medjez. Beyond this field was the Medjez plain which, as we proceeded, fell farther below us. Spacing the guns out to right and left of the road, Sergeant Oakley and I set off on motor-bikes to make a recce up the road and along the few tributary tracks. Our infantry support consisted of a few isolated French detachments badly armed and manned for the most part by Moroccan troops of sometimes indifferent loyalty. The officers and NCO's were French and, in contrast, were in high spirits and willing to have a go at the 'Boche' with whatever was available.

The road rose gradually uphill for about 400 yards then dipped quite steeply down the other side and ran straight and level for 1000 yards or so. There it rounded a significant ledge of rock that stuck out like a finger from Banana-Ridge. The road was completely concealed behind the ledge as it meandered on towards Tunis. As Sergeant Oakley and I rode up the road to the top of the incline we took note of any features to our right and left, any places that might provide concealment for a gun and where there might be a decent arc of fire over the ground where attacking tanks would choose to approach.

At the top of the incline there was a large white farmhouse standing almost on the skyline some 150 yards up a track to the right. It transpired that this housed the most forward troops of the French together with the gunners serving a couple of French 75's. The two 75's were pointing forwards down the Tunis road and, being on the skyline, I wondered just how long they would last if indeed there was an attack. On the other side of the road to our left there were farm buildings, a haystack or two, some old machinery and bits and pieces.

It was obvious that here were positions for a section of two guns: one behind the white house, the other in the buildings. They should both be able to shoot to right or to left. We returned more slowly down the road examining different possibilities. The other two guns would be needed to support the front two and at the same time provide additional defence in depth for this sector of Medjez. We found what was needed: one well-placed and shooting out over the plain, the other tucked into a fold in the ground and shooting out towards Banana Ridge. It was with relief that I saw the last of the four guns being shuffled into its appointed place. It was early evening now, I'd located the French company HQ in a large barn nearer to Medjez and half-way across a ploughed field towards Banana Ridge. I decided on the same site for my troop HQ. Throughout the afternoon I'd been fighting off a fever that would not be denied.; by now I didn't much care what was happening, I simply wanted to climb into my blankets and be left alone.

Thinking the barn was fully occupied, I selected an adjoining haystack and told Savage to unroll my bedding beside it. Leaving the details of administration in the capable hands of Sergeant Oakley, I cast off my boots and wriggled sweating yet shivering into bed. Very soon it became suddenly cooler and then heavy spots of rain followed. The French company commander, a captain, invited me into his barn, an invitation that was readily accepted. There was ample room for the five of us to spread our blankets on the floor along one end wall, so, excusing myself in schoolboy French, I once again crawled into bed.

The first night spent in these new positions was memorable in that sleep was so frequently interrupted. I woke a number of times in order to inflict further casualties on the scores of fleas that pranced about my person. From what I could hear from those around me it seemed that the invasion was an epidemic, yet the French were sleeping soundly. They must have been immune or insulated. We were not sorry to get out of our blankets at dawn to rid all our clothes of unwanted tenants.

We washed and breakfasted and tried a very faltering conversation with our French comrades but somehow we were never able to establish any worthwhile contact with them. We took a fresh look round our new surroundings and felt pleased that we were such a comfortable distance from the enemy positions. It meant that we could move about without being seen by them and we were out of range of their mortars. Had we known it at that time, we would have been surprised by the distance that actually separated us from the enemy. After Tebourba both sides had to sit back and reflect for a while.

Our meagre forces comprised little more than a brigade of 78th Division, a small American combat group and Blade Force, which was a small part of 6th Armoured Division. The whole lot wouldn't amount to anything like a division. These troops had been sorely battered and depleted in these early battles; by the end of Tebourba they were almost spent and hence the withdrawal to Medjez el Bab. The Germans had acted quickly at the invasion of North Africa. They had diverted troops that had been intended for Rommel's Afrika Corps to Tunis, plus others which were soon mustered in southern Italy. All of these had been thrown in against our forces in order to stem our advance upon Tunis. Their position had been critical at times and they too had lost heavily. Thus they were unable to follow up what we thought was their success at Tebourba. They, like us, had to sit tight and wait for reinforcements. We, who were mere soldiers, knew nothing about such details and less about logistics. We knew we were very thin on the ground and that our defensive strength at Medjez had more pretence than reality. Now the distance between the opposing forces offered a tinge of reassurance. Anyhow, we felt a little easier than we had a few days ago. Having said which we were quickly reminded that, although out of sight, we were not out of mind. The first shell whistled overhead and stopped all conversation until it banged inconsequentially into the buildings somewhere near the Bailey bridge. Several more followed and all thumped with reverberant explosions into the same area. Obviously the bridge was their favourite target and was no place to loiter in the future.

These were the first shells, as opposed to mortars, that we in 6 Troop had heard coming our way and it was interesting to note the difference in sound of approach the shells gave out. There was also a distinct distant banging of the guns when they fired. We were aware that the French had disappeared and noticed a large hole in the corner of the barn. The hole had steps leading down and under the stone wall of the barn and became a trench that continued out into the ploughed field.

We were contemplating this when, with a swish and a roar, the first shell exploded some 40 yards away and sent us scurrying into our slit-trenches. The shell fragments zipped like angry wasps and some of them clanked against the stone walls of the barn. A further half dozen or more shells crumped and crashed in quick succession all around us, then all was quiet once more. This was our first "stonking" by shellfire and, although brief, was frightening enough. However, we had no casualties and this first experience served to demonstrate that a great deal of noise, smoke, earth and flying bits did not necessarily mean death and destruction.

I was astonished to see how small the shell holes were relative to the commotion they had made. They might have given shelter to a dog but certainly not to a man. I had somehow thought of shell holes in terms of Old Bill of the First World War, roomy enough to house a couple of men. The hardness of the ground and the very sensitive fuses used in modern ammunition probably accounted for this. I noticed though that none of us ventured far from our slit-trenches for the next half hour.

My sickness of the day before seemed to leave me almost as quickly as it came. No doubt the liberal helping of wine pressed upon me by the French company commander had played its part. Not long after the stonking, I rode off on Rowe's bike to visit the guns and to explain more fully their tasks and fireplan. After that I rode back the half mile or more into Medjez to report to Ham. There I learnt that the battery was to come under command of the 1st Guards Brigade of our division with effect from this day. They, the Guards, were due to take over the Medjez sector this morning.

This was the first I'd heard that there were any Guards in North Africa and I made no secret of the fact that I was delighted to hear it. I had been told that Medjez must be held at all cost, the kind of phrase and order that the army is over fond of. It is a meaningless order anyway and one that holds no credibility outside the films. It was difficult to find any infantry in my area and, if and when found, they had only a few ancient rifles with which to keep body and soul together. Now the Guards, a brigade of them, this was more than one had dared to hope for. Apparently I was to be in the custody of a battalion of the Grenadiers and I was to expect a recce party of their officers later in the morning followed by the battalion itself.

I returned to 6 Troop feeling as though the war was practically won. The whole troop was greatly encouraged by this news except Spit and Blink who determinedly kept to his oft repeated belief that "Jerry's got more than us." This belief had evidently been refuelled by the sound of the shells we'd received an hour previously.

* * * * * * * *

At approximately 10.30 am the sound of marching could be heard coming from Medjez el Bab. Soon we were watching a company of the Grenadiers moving up the road. They halted by the track leading to my No 1 gun, the one tucked snugly into a cutting in the rocks and shooting out over the Medjez plain. Then something happened that we hadn't expected. A succession of shells exploded along the ridge of the incline, where my two forward guns were deployed. This time there was no warning whine, only a short vicious hiss before the bang. Then to confirm the thought that had crossed my mind, there came the unmistakable burr-burr of the German machine-guns. It was a slightly higher and much faster crackle than our own bren guns.

Telling Sergeant Oakley I was going to see what was going on, I went bumping off across the field. Reaching the Tunis road I turned right up the incline towards my forward guns. The Guards were all waiting philosophically on the left, having dispersed off the road and a subaltern called out to me to watch my step up the road. "What's it all about?" I asked, though I was pretty sure already. "Tanks," he answered.

As I was about to push on, the air just above my head, or so it seemed, was split by a hail of machine-gun bullets. I ducked involuntarily, left my bike at the side of the road and ran to join the company of guardsmen who were lying down behind the lee of the slope.

For the next ten or fifteen minutes I could do nothing but lie as close to the ground as possible. The bursts of fire cracked spitefully over our heads and at intervals a shell would fizz past to explode behind with a gust of smoke and dust. I looked around at the Guardsmen as if for inspiration; they were all doing much the same as I was. I thought this was stupid yet to stand up was likely to be suicidal. The machine-gun bullets made the most surprising noise as they passed overhead, like a cluster of little whipcracks.

I thought I ought to be with my guns so, choosing my moment, I bolted back to my motorcycle and reached it as Colonel Davidson's car came up the road from Medjez. The CO stepped out of his car beckoning to me; as usual he was beautifully turned out and completely composed. "I hear reports of some Boche tanks here, Donald. How many and where are they?" "I was just about to find out myself, Sir," I said, pointing out that for the last quarter of an hour they'd been throwing a lot of stuff at us and I couldn't get up the road to have a look. The CO said it looked all right to him and I knew he would have said the same had he arrived 10 minutes earlier. Of course I felt sheepish and inadequate.

Colonel Davidson saw it as his business to demonstrate that Germans and Italians were ineffective and unworthy opponents and that their efforts at warfare were contemptible. He told me that six new guns were on their way up and he wanted me to find positions for them straight away. First he wanted to see my guns and accordingly followed me up the road.

Stopping just below the crest, we walked up the track to the right to No 4 gun and Sergeant Smith's detachment. They had been a bit worried but nevertheless managed a few broad grins in answer to some of the CO's questions. They had been shelled and machine-gunned quite a lot but had felt moderately secure in their trench behind the stone walls of the white farmhouse. There were three German tanks which had pulled off the Tunis road and sat there facing us with their backs almost propped against the rocky ridge (mentioned earlier) about 1000 yards away. They had systematically swept the area with their guns.

The Colonel asked about the whereabouts of my four positions and then expressed his concern about the security of the right flank, the open area between the white house and Banana Ridge. I knew this was the weakness but there was supposed to be some sort of minefield in that area. Colonel Davidson decided to have a look to see whether or not a gun was needed out there.

He strode from behind the white house up to a haystack and on to the skyline. I followed beside him nursing a stomach-full of misgivings. According to my appreciation this was violating most of the rules of survival in war. Furthermore, if we pursued this kind of challenging behaviour, we both stood an excellent chance of getting our names on the roll of honour.

Once on top of the ridge we had a perfect view of the enemy tanks. What was more in my mind at the time was that the reverse was equally true. Davidson was in arrogant mood. He was discussing the defences and possible eventualities as though we were on an exercise in Scotland. We stood there with him waving his shooting-stick to right and left as though it were the best he could think of to attract the attention of the tanks. I remember asking myself how it was that an apparently intelligent man could behave so stupidly. If his intention were to demonstrate to me and the nearby gun team that German tanks were a trifling nuisance, then he failed. I could only think that it might have been amusing had he attempted to stroll along that ridge some 15 or 20 minutes ago. Meanwhile, I felt like a rabbit with its ears cocked waiting for the gun to go off.

Only once after that occasion was I obliged to offer myself on a sacrificial plate so openly and that was some fifteen months later at Cassino. It was a time when my battery commander, in his first experience of commanding troops at the front, took it upon himself to drive me in his jeep straight up to Cassino itself and along in front of Monastery Hill in broad daylight. We must have been within stone-throwing distance of the Germans and why we lived to tell the tale I shall never know.

After a few more timeless minutes with Colonel Davidson, he decided to let things remain as they were and turned his thoughts to the new guns which were about to arrive. We strolled back to the farmhouse just in time. On reaching the haystack close to the house, there was a combination of sounds. The bang of a gun, the last second hiss of a shell and the wompf of its explosion all came as a package. A couple more followed, all of them hitting the brow of the slope along which we'd just walked.

As we walked back to the Colonel's car, he remarked that the tanks needed smartening up. He told me to remain there in case of trouble and that he would send Peter Heslop up with one of his guns to try to shift them. Meantime I should find a spot where he could get a shot at the tanks.

There was no need for me to hunt for a suitable position for Peter's gun; I already knew the area and all its possibilities so I waited by the roadside for Peter to appear. I was most unhappy about these proposals. To place a gun where it could shoot at the tanks meant running it onto the crest of the slope where there would be no cover. It meant engaging them outside our maximum effective range and, just to ensure failure, the tanks were sitting facing us and therefore they presented the thickest part of their armour to us. In fact everything we had been taught not to do was about to be attempted.

Instead of stopping to pick me up, Peter and his gun crew drove past my waving hand and on towards the farm on the crest. I thought I'd better warn the two guns not in that vicinity what was happening and to alert them in case the tanks were moved and sought to make their way round either flank. Also, I hadn't been to see them since all this business started and obviously they needed to know what was the cause of the trouble.

Returning from Sergeant Varney's gun, I passed through the Grenadiers still waiting for deployment orders. I met Sergeant Oakley who questioned me about the situation and shared my misgivings about the 'A' Battery gun and its mission. Our conversation was interrupted by the report of the first shot of Peter's gun. During the next few minutes there were a number of rounds fired by that gun and also one of the French 75's decided that they too would have a bang at the Germans. It sounded as if they were getting away with it because there was no sound of retaliation and I listened for the sound of tank engines that might betray their intentions. Then three shells exploded on the crest at about 10 second intervals, after that all was silent.

Oakley and I went up the road to discover the outcome. In a few moments we stopped as Peter's quad came down the road at full gallop. He was at the wheel and his face and arms were distinctly bloody, his face was pale and half an hour seemed to have aged him by several years. It transpired that the gun had fired about 10 rounds at the tanks and the French had fired about 3 in addition. No apparent damage had been inflicted and, in reply, the Germans had destroyed the French 75 with their first shell and had a direct hit on Peter's gun with the other two. Of the detachment, two or three were badly wounded and the rest were dead.

I was more than a little angry at this calamitous episode. The enemy had retired eventually unharmed having learnt what he came to learn, namely whereabouts down the Tunis road we had decided to make our defensive line. We had shown our whereabouts, thrown away some men's lives unnecessarily, and lost two guns of which we already had too few. If we had kept quiet, the enemy would have been forced to depart knowing little or nothing; or they would have had to come forward to my farmhouse and so on to my guns at very short range indeed. The result then would have been very different. I wondered what the hell was the purpose of spending so much time training troops to develop necessary skills if we were going to throw them away at the slightest pretext.

* * * * * * * *

The next day, December 9th, concerned itself mainly with the arrival of reinforcements and a reshuffle between batteries in order to bring 'B' Battery more nearly to its former strength. Lieutenant Ian McLennan arrived from RHQ with three new guns; these he took to join some of the Grenadiers on a feature of Banana Ridge, to be known as Grenadier Hill. His was the newly formed 5 Troop. Lieutenant Harry Penman arrived from Scotland and took another three guns which he posted around Medjez itself, to become the new 7 Troop. Lastly, lieutenant Bobby Burrowes was transferred from 'C' Battery with his four guns and his full complement of men; they were deployed around Medjez station, north of the town, and became the new 8 Troop.

Bobby Burrowes was one of those tall, languid, elegant, amiable "Bertie Woosters." His main asset was a reliable good-humour which was also his defence. His main talents were good dress sense, tap-dancing and a capacity for deep sleep under most circumstances. He laid no claim to efficiency and would have been slightly affronted had it been considered one of his attributes, rather as if such a quality were in bad taste. Altogether his six feet odd of affability was better equipped for the task of Master of Ceremonies than to grapple with the management of a troop of anti-tank guns.

Nevertheless it fell upon his troop the following day, December 10th, to open fire on enemy tanks which had come down the Tebourba road and explored a little way into the plain in front of Medjez. Bobby claimed that three of the enemy armour had been hit but, to his dismay, they were retrieved by the Germans during the night. Others of us claimed this to be a fisherman's story. Bobby had admitted that the series of unpleasantly close bangs from his own guns had taken him completely by surprise.

For the next ten days the German armour left us in peace, but communications were maintained through their airforce and artillery. Every morning we were roused by fighter-bombers or dive-bombers which arrived soon after dawn. Mostly they concentrated on the Bailey bridge at Medjez but on occasions they would devote their attentions towards the town itself, or the station area or even my farm barn. Their guns were more sinister because they had our range and there was no similar warning of approaching aeroplanes. They plastered us at least twice a day and although this stonking was extremely unpleasant, we soon learnt to 'pick the wrong 'uns from the passers-by' - a lesson that had to be learnt if we were going to survive for long.

During this period the rain began again intermittently. Although nothing compared with what was to come, it continued to make us dirtier, muddier and bad tempered. Morale was made worse as the days passed by and no mail arrived. Mail was the main concern of us all, its absence made us feel far-off and forgotten. The men began to quarrel over the rations and we all cursed the ever present Luftwaffe and ever absent RAF. The only friendly aeroplanes were a few American Lightnings which occasionally ventured over at great height and speed. After executing a couple of dashing circles they would buzz off home again, no doubt to fried bacon and eggs, as we thought.

We had a few field guns somewhere behind Medjez but our enormously stretched supply lines and difficult roads forbade any reckless use of ammunition. So for every shell sent we usually received half a dozen in return. Ham was obliged to leave his carpenter's shop after a direct hit and many near misses; he moved his HQ to a less lively spot near Guards Brigade HQ.

On December 21st orders were received for our relief by a battery of 64th Anti-Tank Regiment. We had been at the sharp end for eighteen days and felt that we were entitled to a rest. Although our particular war had been smouldering whilst both sides were busy trying to build up strength, it had been quite lively enough for our taste. In effect, we were quite happy to leave the defence of Medjez el Bab in the hands of others.

During the night of the 19th, the Guards had sent out a patrol unknown to us. Sergeant Agambar's detachment, the forward gun in the farm buildings, had their suspicions aroused by movement below them. They called out the familiar, "Halt! Who goes there?" and were answered by complete silence. This, in their opinion being an admission of guilt, caused the detachment to open up with bren gun and rifles. Tracer bullets sang around the place in a light-hearted manner and it was as well that the patrol was close to cover. Eventually peace was restored by the patrol NCO yelling out, "Lay off you stupid bastards." This was immediately accepted as a friendly response.

Having liaised with the incoming troop commander, the relief at dusk had just commenced when we were shelled in spritely fashion. After ten minutes one of the shells burst pretty closely and knocked a hole through the radiator of my 15 cwt truck. This provoked a healthy flow of language from my troop HQ. The 15 cwt packed and ready with all our kits could not now be driven. Not, that is, until Sergeant Oakley's resourcefulness was brought to bear; he plugged the hole with a bar of my toilet-soap, Windsor Castle vintage.

As darkness came, 6 Troop motored out of Medjez el Bab, back through the fertile valley following the river to Testour. We were quite pleased with ourselves. After all, we'd survived Tebourba, experienced shot and shell, encountered a few German tanks and had more than our share of the Luftwaffe. In fact, we began to look upon ourselves as practically veterans.

DIAGRAM of TEBOURBA

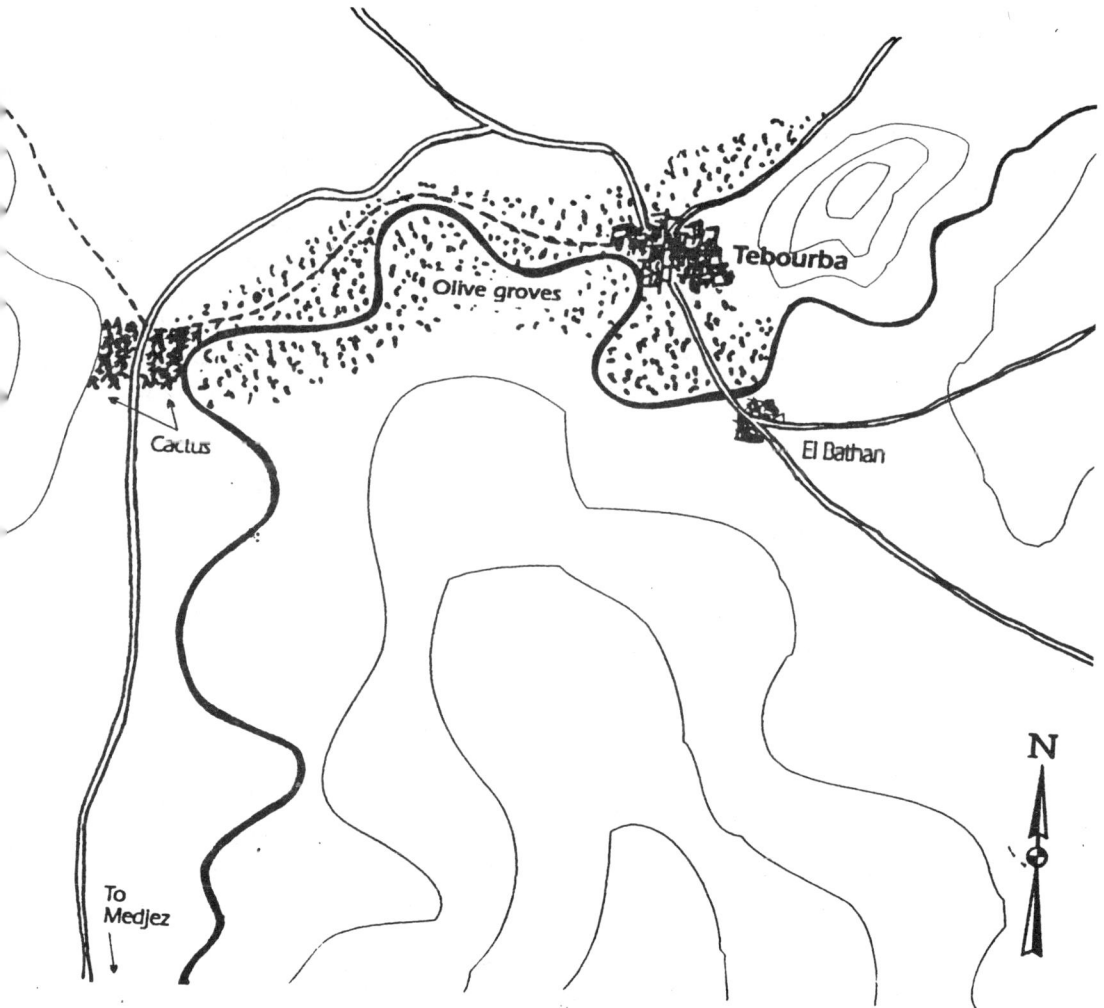

CHAPTER V

OUSELTIA AND BOU ARADA

Teboursouk lies at the foot of some steep hills. It is so disguised by the practically never ending sea of olive groves that the approaching traveller comes upon it unexpectedly. On our arrival there it rather resembled a fishing port when the trawlers were unloading. RHQ were there, so was 'C' Battery and elements of 'A' Battery. We found them all slipping and squelching about in acres of mud. It is surprising what changes to cultivated soil can be brought about by a regiment of men plus their transport and it had rained quite heavily during the last couple of days.

'B' Battery attempted to wriggle its way into its allocated area and in so doing added to the number of already bogged-in vehicles. We were not pleased at the prospect of resting in those conditions but we somehow managed to squeeze our cold and wet selves under the variously improvised forms of shelter.

We now came under command of 26th Armoured Brigade of our division, comprising 17th/21st Lancers, 16th/5th Lancers and the Lothian and Border Horse regiments. This information was received with surprise and reserve. To marry 'B' Battery to the Armoured Brigade could only mean trouble as we saw it, especially so since the other two tank regiments had not been used in anger yet, only the 17th/21st which had been part of Blade Force. Rumours spread and prospered and were mainly concerned with the fact that our Guards Brigade had taken over the Medjez area and now, if our Armoured Brigade had been assembled in the same area, it looked suspiciously like something was contemplated for the 6th Armoured Division.

Soon the plan, such as it was, was unfolded to us. As far as I can remember, the Guards were to advance up the Tebourba road from Medjez and we were to accompany 26th Armoured Brigade who were to attack up the Tunis road on the right of the plain. Their first objective was Massicault and then they were to continue on to Tunis. 78th Division and the American troops were to stage concurrent attacks in order to put maximum pressure on the enemy defences and particularly on their tank forces. All of this depended upon the weather holding fair; the ground was already softening and further rain would prevent our tanks from operating.

As we surveyed ourselves among the olive trees, we wondered at the sanity of the higher command or whether perhaps they were still in the UK. We could scarcely propel ourselves from one truck to another. The mud was thick, heavy and clinging and it was still raining. The slit-trenches were everywhere slowly filling with water and it was as well that the weather appeared to be keeping the Luftwaffe away. We of 'B' Battery were confident that, battle or no, it would take a month to get us out onto a road.

In fact we were out of this particular harbour within three days, three miserable, drenching, soggy days. Everything we possessed was soaking wet. Our clothes, our boots, great-coats, blankets, all were really unfit for human habitation. The nights were worse than the days; sleep was either very difficult or impossible. My troop HQ slept in the back of my Bedford 15 cwt and we packed in like sardines in an effort to gain some warmth. Added to our miseries was the fact that it had turned cold and, being wet, the cold penetrated through and into us so that it became an ache from which we couldn't escape. We swore, we cursed everyone and everything, profanity was on everyone's tongue. And each dawn brought a fresh crop of squelching troubles.

It was nearly Christmas. Surely the army could produce some mail for us in time for Christmas. So far we'd been promised two things - some bottles of beer by somebody and a glorious battle by somebody else. Then on Christmas Eve we had orders to move. Two troops were to come under command of the Lothian and Border Horse, the remainder of the battery, including my troop, were to move with the 10th Rifle Brigade to a place called Sidi Ayed. The 10th Rifle Brigade was the motor battalion of the Armoured Brigade; it was completely mechanised with an unusually high fire power compared with other infantry units. 10th Rifle Brigade were our near neighbours in this present harbour and apparently we were all required to move to this Sidi Ayed via a long, precarious track and in darkness. December 24th 1942 is memorable as being the supreme example of how not to spend Christmas Eve.

It was still raining, of course, and since not one of the Rifle Brigade's admirable vehicles could move, we were invited to assist them in getting onto the track. Our quads boasted a long steel cable winch at the back and four-wheel drive in addition. For half the night of Christmas Eve we toiled and manoeuvred, squelched and winched, sprawled and spattered to and fro until all the Rifle Brigade were safely planted onto the slithery track. The remainder of the night was spent in undertaking a remarkable journey. It could be said to be comparable with Hannibal and his elephants in its absurdity and its difficulty. The track had a kind of clay surface which rain and transport soon converted into a slimy, slippery sludge. Ham said that since the journey was obviously going to be difficult, we officers would ride motor cycles the better to shepherd the troops along the track.

It's true to say that I did eventually arrive at the other end of the track with my motorcycle but I doubt if I travelled more than a hundred yards at a time in the saddle. I lost count of the number of times I fell off, twenty, thirty, I couldn't even guess. I was not alone; all the officers became indistinguishable in their disguise of a thick coating of wet mud. As to conducting my troop, most of the time I couldn't keep up with them, except for those who, from time to time, slid off the track and bogged themselves down.

It took four hours of misery to cover those seven or eight miles before reaching the road at the far end but we finally reached our new harbour area long after dawn on Christmas Day. Later in the morning we learned that the operation against Tunis was off. Considering the night we'd just spent we were not surprised. So, after a short but sincere little Christmas Day service by the side of a tiny railway station, we once more began to clean ourselves up as best we could.

The cleaning up continued for a couple of days and, as luck would have it, those two days culminated in an unexpected inspection by Tiger, the Brigadier. As soon as he had left we were given "Prepare to move" and made our way back to the regiment again, this time by a longer but surer route.

Our harbour was in olive groves again but on a fairly steep hill and firmer ground. Now, we thought, so long as the weather remains bloody awful, the war will be kept at bay.

It was then December 29th. On December 31st, as I watched captivated by the glory of a sunset reflected off the escarpment of a long high ridge about two miles away, I was summoned to Ham's HQ. He was to take my troop plus Bobby Burrowes' troop down south to assist a French force at a place called Ouseltia. We were moving this night.

* * * * * * * * *

Of the move down to the French I remember very little. The distance was over a hundred miles so we couldn't complete it in one night. Major Hamilton went on ahead with a small party of Battery HQ leaving the two troops to follow.

It was a difficult journey, made as usual without lights, over mountains with bad roads forever twisting and turning. Sometimes the road became a mere track between huge rocks in the hillside; often I had to halt to double check our position on the map. An insignificant bullock track would frequently be marked as a road and occasionally a road junction just didn't exist. Gunner Rowe and Sergeant Oakley, on motor-cycles, policed up and down the small column checking the presence of the guns and assisting at any difficult or uncertain places. Always I remember the beastly stale mouth and grimy hands that accompanied those night journeys. The eyes pricked with tiredness, we smoked too many cigarettes and munched the granite-like tasteless compo biscuits to keep ourselves awake.

Thus we progressed through the night, slowly, with much prodding and not infrequent halts for one reason or another. With relief we would notice a gradual paling of the darkness, one more night drive would soon be over and we'd light another cigarette in anticipation of the dawn. As soon as it was light enough we sought out the first reasonable cover or, failing that, a suitable wadi to tuck ourselves into and stopped for a refresher and some breakfast. A wash, a bite of food and a brew and we felt warmed and less irritable.

Our destination was a map reference in the Kessera Forest from where rumour had it that Hannibal's elephants were recruited. We continued in daylight with our vehicles spaced out at about eighty yards, the usual air attack precautions. It wasn't long after our breakfast stop before we came upon the Kessera Forest. As forests go, it was disappointing. A large area of scrub with stunted pines dotted all over. The forest occupied a large plateau about 1000 feet up but here at least we were away from the rain and mud. The sun was shining with real warmth and the absence of Arab villages made it all the more acceptable.

The road through the forest, although dusty, was quite well surfaced. We progressed without hindrance until we encountered the sergeant major waving us to a halt. He guided my troop off the road into our allocated area and I think most of us were glad to be there. Due to the rain and cold, we'd had very little rest or peace since leaving Medjez; to be warm and dry was well worth a long drive.

It was January 1st, New Year's Day, and we celebrated by hanging our wet and clammy clothing over the bushes to dry. Fortunately the German planes were not bothering to patrol down here, it seemed, so we could really relax for a few hours. Ham arrived and said that he had already contacted the French and considering the urgency with which we'd been dispatched they appeared surprisingly unconcerned about any imminent danger. We troop commanders were to go with Ham to the French HQ at Ouseltia the next day when we would decide where we should go.

Leaving the comparative comfort and seclusion of our scrub on January 2nd we passed between two pointed rocky features and at once the road plunged abruptly downwards. The descent was steep and before us a wide open plain extending twenty miles or so. Down on the plain the country was wide open and flat, the road was good and straight and we were able to travel at some speed for a change. There was virtually no cover and, anxious to reach our destination before the Luftwaffe might discover us, we sped along at a brisk 40-50mph. The sky was blue and dazzling as we scanned it for tell-tale black specks and we were relieved to see the village of Ouseltia in the near distance.

The French HQ was established very comfortably in a large, cool villa. We were greeted with much saluting, bowing and hand shaking. An elaborate luncheon was prepared for us on a large table where several bottles of wine stood at one end. They were delighted to see us for social reasons, one felt, as well as military ones.

With difficulty we finally persuaded the French commander to talk about troop dispositions and enemy tanks and other disagreeable aspects of the war. We learnt that the French were even thinner on the ground than they were at Medjez when we first arrived there. They had a handful of troops at one or two strategic points on a very wide front. As before, their arms were few and antiquated: a machine-gun or two and a very few French 75mm field guns. They had nothing that could halt a German tank, in fact their presence was in the nature of sparsely scattered outposts. Their CO said that they had recently been attacked by some Italian units, as a result of which they had acquired some additional arms and ammunition. He showed us a box of Italian hand-grenades. Laughing scornfully he threw one of the bombs at a tree where I was standing. There was a loud bang and that was all, for which I was duly thankful.

It was decided that Bobby Burrowes was to take his troop to a village called Pichon, some twenty miles south of Ouseltia. (Pichon achieved further prominence later in April at the battle of Foudouk). I was directed to occupy a road junction about fifteen miles to the north. Ham, therefore, was responsible for two troops which were deployed nearly forty miles apart and since we had no wireless sets it meant that there were virtually no communications. Either troop could be overrun and nobody would know.

Soon I motored off with my guide, a French officer, in his civilian car. We bounded along the road at an incredible speed so that I had some difficulty in following our progress on the map. We reached my junction and met the lieutenant who commanded the platoon of coloured troops, most of whom appeared to be mounted on horses. After I'd looked over the area, and the two French officers had completed their business, we returned to company HQ as briskly as possible. Saying our au revoirs, Ham, Bobby and I made our way back to the half battery at Kessera Forest. There, wonder of wonders, we were greeted by Ted Newman with not only the rations but mail! It was only then that I realised it was my birthday.

* * * * * * * *

6 Troop arrived at the road junction, map reference 7261, intact and unmolested. Mercifully we were favourably supplied with cover in this position, so we parked the guns and the four gun sergeants together with Sergeant Oakley and myself made an extensive even leisurely recce. My position was at the head of a wide valley, a valley that was at its maximum width at the enemy end and narrowed at my end. Behind me two roads ran from my right and left to converge in front of my position becoming a single road that ran down the valley towards the enemy, like an inverted Y. My guns were deployed between the two arms of the Y where the ground was higher, rockier and covered with scrub.

It was ideal for anti-tank defence and we were quite ready to take on any tank attack from this spot. Our only anxiety focused on the question of these infantry chaps on their horses. We had doubts about their readiness to stay here in the event of things happening. However, it had its compensations as a front line position. For a start, the enemy line was probably three miles away and, so far, nothing had been seen or heard of them. The weather was good and we were able to laze about and write letters to all those at home from whom we had only just received our first mail. There were massive mountain ranges on either side of this valley and the whole scene was really rather beautiful.

Days passed and all was quiet, not a hostile gesture from the enemy. We walked about freely during the day and bathed ourselves in the sun. From Battery HQ at Ouseltia we received boxes of dates and tangerines both gratefully accepted, from the French. All this was fine but it was too good to be true. One had the feeling that something was wrong somewhere and why had we been called down here? We were trying to get to know our infantry friends who were known as Spahis, or some such name. One young brave delved inside his jacket and produced for our inspection a string on which were threaded a whole cluster of human ears. We learnt that they didn't go much for conventional warfare, they preferred to ride off in the darkness, park their horses at a suitable distance and strike at the enemy when least expected. One of their habits was to cut off one or more ears of those they had personally killed. I didn't discover whether these were merely gruesome trophies or whether they were evidence for bonus payments.

About a week after our arrival, the afternoon was interrupted by the drone of aeroplanes. Soon they were overhead, five Italian planes of pre-war vintage. We were all curious about these machines and were standing about looking up at them. To our astonishment they turned and began to circle us. After a couple of circuits one of them began flapping his wings and started a sort of flat dive. Half way down we suddenly spotted a bomb leave his underneath and watched as it came wobbling down in roughly our direction.

For some reason nobody made any attempt to take cover. After the frightening experiences of the German Stuka attacks, this was somehow a comic interlude. When the first bomb missed us by a clear hundred yards, a ripple of derisive cheering broke out from 6 Troop. The remaining four dropped their loads round about us, none of them particularly close, and then made for home. During the latter part of this attack, the men were actually waving their hats at the Italian pilots.

The following night we were awakened soon after midnight by rifle and machine-gun fire. The French had made up their minds that an enemy patrol was out beyond the road on our left. Soon two of my gun teams were banging away with bren guns, firing streams of tracer bullets into the darkness. Running over to the nearest, I asked sergeant Smith what he was firing at? I pointed out that there was no answering fire and his present course of action would only advertise his position. The other gun team were "Practically certain they had heard a move out there" but they didn't know quite where. And that was the end of our engagement with the enemy patrol, or more likely a stray goat.

Two days later Major Hamilton arrived in the early evening with the news that a troop from another regiment was coming down from Bou Arada to take over my position. The take-over would be at dusk this evening. This was sad news for us. We had found ourselves a nice comfortable patch in the war and were told to exchange it with someone already at Bou Arada, about 100 miles north, in order to chase up there for an expected German attack.

The incoming troop commander and his guns arrived as darkness was falling. I showed him the gun placements and the way to get to each of them. That being accomplished, together with a few explanatory details, we wished each other luck; he saying he didn't envy us our journey that night, and me saying he should have damned well stayed where he was and left me in peace.

Once more we set off along the lonely roads, over the hills and far away. This time we were supposed to reach a village called El Akhouat overnight, a distance of some 90 miles. Ted Newman had been dispatched earlier to find a harbour area and we were to travel in company with Battery HQ and 8 Troop. I think only two guns went off the road that night, which was good going. Nevertheless, it was an hour or two after dawn before we drove into the long grass and scrub that Ted had appointed as our harbour.

This was Messerschmitt country and hourly the angry throb of low flying fighters could be heard and usually seen, shooting up anything on the roads and off. Burnt-out supply vehicles were numerous and most road junctions and points of merit had their bodyguard of anti-aircraft guns. The brew cans had hardly got under way when the lookout shouted, "Put those fires out!" Two Me109s came winging over the hills, swished past us, turned down another valley, then came the roar of their cannons and machine- guns. It was always a chilling experience. Quickly the fires were relit in the hope of snatching a cup before the next lot of marauders came screaming out of the sky.

In the afternoon, Ham, Bobby and I set off for Bou Arada, about twenty-five miles away, to liaise with the out-going battery whose positions we were to occupy. The date remains clear because I remember Savage counselling caution saying, "Remember, Sir, it's the bloody thirteenth."

51

Bou Arada was occupied on January 14th after a great deal of fuss and confusion. The positions were not good because the ground where we were deployed behind the village was flat and the only cover available was in the obvious cactus groves. After getting ourselves nicely dug in, we were naturally ordered to move again the next day - this time to immediately behind the village. My orders were to cover the rear of Bou Arada and particularly the road that ran due west from the village. It didn't take long to post a section of two guns in a cactus grove about 250 yards north of the road and the other section plus my troop HQ in another cactus plantation some 300 yards south of the road. In view of the predictability of our gun placements, I made sure that the two sections could support each other. In reality I hoped that the two troops from 'B' Battery and others of 'A' Battery, which were all in front of Bou Arada, would be more than enough to see off any tank attack. The news was that there had been considerable attacking and counter-attacking going on east of the village during the last few days.

Bou Arada was some fifteen miles or more due west of Pont du Fahs. It straddled an important road junction and, so long as it remained in our hands, it posed a threat to Pont du Fahs. The latter was a vital communications centre for the Germans and one of the few gateways to Tunis. We had struggled to make ground towards Pont du Fahs without success; equally the Germans had made strenuous efforts with infantry to capture Bou Arada. Some one and a half miles north of the village a long, low ridge ran eastwards towards Pont du Fahs. It began with a flattish-domed hill christened "Grandstand" which dipped into a saddle and then rose again to a second feature named "Two Tree" after the two stunted trees that stood uncertainly on its top.

Grandstand was in our hands and the enemy held Two Tree. The Inniskillings a regiment of the Irish Brigade, had recently had a bad time attempting to take Two Tree. After several hours of being pinned down by heavy machine-gun and mortar fire, they had eventually made their escape back to Grandstand. It was now expected that the enemy would advance from the security of Two Tree in an endeavour to cut the Bou Arada-Medjez el Bab road. Had they done so they would have threatened the rear of the small 1st army which, for the most part, was stemming the line to the north. The importance of holding Bou Arada was accordingly impressed upon us.

All around and about our area our divisional artillery had been deployed and a battery of French 75's was dug in just in front of us near the road running south from the village. For a day or two we sat quietly waiting for something to happen. The days were warm but the nights surprisingly cold. Dispatch riders kept arriving with messages to do something and then subsequently to do something else. Shells whined over from the east and mostly they were destined for the cross roads but now and again they were sprayed about the area in the hope of catching somebody unawares. German air patrols were active and constantly causing us to dive into our trenches.

During the night of 18th/19th January, a company of the 10th Rifle Brigade with 5 Troop of our battery, very stealthily wriggled onto a forward hill south of the Bou Arada - Pont du Fahs road called Argoub. They had been there only a short time and were still digging in when, soon after dawn, thirty or more German tanks presented themselves chugging down the road from Pont du Fahs. One of Lieutenant Mclennan's guns galloped down the hillside into range, was unhitched from its quad, brought into action and hit three tanks before being knocked out.

This extraordinary piece of bravado was executed with total casualties of one sergeant and one gunner wounded. Fortune must certainly have smiled upon them. After this interruption the tank force proceeded on its course. Had they known how many eyes were watching and how many guns were standing by, I doubt if they would have continued with such artless disregard. Yet, by and large, the Germans were better at defence than they were at attack. They tended to rely upon their armoured forces to bludgeon and frighten the opposition into submission. This attitude may have grown from earlier experiences in the war when their panzer divisions had enjoyed almost unlimited success because of inadequately armed opposition. Now this cavalier advance was heading for trouble.

Since the whole of the divisional artillery was at Bou Arada, it was only natural that our CRA (Commander Royal Artillery) should be taking an active interest in what was going on. Brigadier Lyon-Smith was a positive legend within his divisional artillery. A man of great drive, determination, pride and apoplexy. He was held in awe and esteem by gunners and colonels alike; he was unreasonable in his demands yet fostered a rare loyalty even though he would suffer neither failure nor excuses. He was known to all as Tiger.

Tiger's idea of military fulfilment was to assemble crowds of field guns and be provided with a suitable and adequate target, then to be left alone for an unspecified time. On this day at Bou Arada he must have reflected upon a scene that was beyond his expectations. It was only on very rare occasions that all the divisional artillery was together in one place. To have them there, ready deployed for action, and to be presented with such a rich target must have stirred his digestive juices to the limit.

The words "Uncle Target" have meaning probably only to gunners. They are in fact the code words given over the radio by the CRA to employ all the divisional artillery to follow his orders. It is a priority call and overrules anything else they might be engaged upon. The order is usually given in triplicate - "Uncle Target, Uncle Target, Uncle Target". That order, in triplicate, had already been given by Tiger; he had already given orders to the regiments of guns concerned to ensure that they were ranged on his selected area.

So advanced the German tanks. Leaving the road they launched themselves into the cornfields in front of Grandstand. They spread out across the valley and slowly they crawled towards Bou Arada. As they crept nearer they fired at various things that drew their suspicions - clumps of cactus, farm buildings, houses and such like. One or two buildings were set on fire yet nothing had happened to deter them. Then the grandfather of all thunder claps burst out: the combined decibels of close on eighty guns discharging 25lb shells together was something beyond belief. The noise was devastating. Tiger's uncle target was under way and scores upon scores of shells shrieked over our heads making an appalling din before they fell among the advancing tanks.

The area in front of Bou Arada had erupted in flames and smoke. The earth in the fields was flung in all directions. The tanks faltered and began to turn away from the centre of this destruction. Some of the tanks were set on fire; a small group taking evasive action moved towards Grandstand and got themselves bogged down in soft ground within range of some of our 'A' Battery guns. They were destroyed by those guns with just a few shots. Meantime, a column of German half tracks and motorised infantry came into view and began to run down the road towards the village. They barely reached their own tanks when Tiger switched the 25-pounders onto them. In no time the vehicles and half tracks were being blasted right, left and centre. They had no chance and were quickly put to flight.

Clearly the Germans had staked a lot on this attack. This was evident by the strength of their numbers and by the determined efforts the tanks were making. In spite of considerable losses, the surviving tanks were fighting back madly. They were raking Bou Arada and the surrounds with machine-gun fire and using their 75mm guns on anything they could see. They swapped shells with us with unnerving tenacity and so the battle continued with ferocity for some hours. The Luftwaffe then joined the struggle. Fighters, fighter-bombers and tank destroying aircraft were thrown in, a sure sign that the Germans were worried. Squadrons of Stukas came over and dive-bombed us again and again. The enemy artillery pounded us and tried very hard to silence our 25-pounders. The whole of the area in and all around Bou Arada was blasted and torn by shell-fire that day.

To add to this overall mayhem, the 51st Light Ack-Ack Regiment, also of our division, were present in large numbers and anxious to lend their support. They had spread their Bofors guns about the place in a generous fashion and in fact one of them was resident in my cactus and close to my HQ. When the waves of enemy aircraft began dropping loads of bombs and shooting up anybody they could see, our Bofors friends decided that it was clay pigeon shooting time. They pumped off their ear-cracking 2lb shells at everything within range and much more that wasn't.

At one stage, a party of some odd-looking aeroplanes came flying towards us. They were large, slow and somewhat clumsy in appearance. They flew over us quite low and circled once or twice during which time our near neighbours, in company with various colleagues, scored a couple of dozen near misses. These odd planes then set their noses down and prepared to deliver their cargoes. Our Bofors crew were off their gun platform in a thrice and disappeared underground.

The leader passed over us and dropped his bombs near the road beyond. Thus encouraged, the nearby team remounted their gun and boomed out a steady rhythmic thud-thud of tracer shells at the next approaching plane. With their fourth shell, they hit it smack in the tail and blew it off. It had no time to jettison its bombs and the explosion of bomber plus bombs was not easily forgotten. The occupants had no chance but at least it was quick. The bomber had crashed quite close by and we were treated to a series of volcanic eruptions from the burning plane. Ammunition was exploding constantly and black smoke belched from the carcass adding to the already smoke-filled surroundings.

Around mid-day, our own 26th Armoured Brigade came trundling along from El Aroussa behind us. It was the first we'd actually seen of our own tanks since we'd landed in Africa. Now here they were, Valentines and Crusaders so familiar to us from all the schemes in the UK yet pathetically armed with tiny 2-pounder guns. They were presumably here in readiness for our second assault on Two Tree hill which would now come as a counter-attack if it came at all.

Glad as we were to see the Armoured Brigade, I fervently wished that they would choose somewhere other than my cactus for concealment. They were easily spotted from the air and, although safe from bombs which didn't actually hit them, the same couldn't be said for us. Time and again the accursed Stukas came over and attacked us with their screaming dives. The ack-ack guns hammered away at them but were quite unable to prevent their determined assaults. There was a shuttle service of Stukas, Focke-Wolfes and Me109s going back to re-arm and returning to roar down at us. The ground shuddered and the air crashed like a very violent thunder-storm, and through all of this the flashes and bangs of the 25-pounders kept up a snarling exchange with the German guns. It was a spectacular scene and an incredible din.

Three Arab youths came running down the road towards El Aroussa, their eyes staring and their faces drawn with fright. Other parties of Arabs had made for the hills, some desperately driving a donkey or oxen before them. The men were shouting and children were crying. Army ambulances with large red crosses on their sides and roofs came bouncing up the road, and others, going rather more slowly, scuttled back to the first aid stations.

One gun detachment of 'A' Battery was buried by a Stuka bomb but were successfully dug out in time. Lieutenant Johnny Gaster was hit in the head but recovered to join my battery eventually. The Padre was hit in his backside as he dived for cover. After his quite famous wound had healed and he had rejoined the regiment, it became customary for the officers to greet him not with, "Good morning, Padre," but with, "Well, Parson, how's the arse?"

Everyone's nerves were getting frayed. The men around me were making forced jokes that lacked humour. After several hours of diving in and out of trenches midst this incessant noise and not knowing really how the battle was going, people grew restless and agitated. A large dog - there were usually a number hanging around rather than belonging to every Arab community - suddenly raced into our cactus grove barking loudly. Gunner Rowe who was usually a pleasant, even-tempered young chap, pulled out his revolver and shot it none too accurately. The poor creature yelled full throatedly before dropping. I turned on Rowe and cursed him heartily. Normally he wouldn't have done anything so pointless but this was not normality.

As the day wore on the battle grew less fierce. The Germans could obviously make no progress and, having suffered heavily, they began trying to extricate what was left. By evening it was all over and both sides ended the day in the same positions as they had started from. There had been acts of gallantry, men had bled, been shot, burnt and blown to bits - for what? As Sergeant Oakley put it afterwards, gazing at the scarred and torn hill-sides and the considerable number of burning military equipment, "I reckon those hills have got a bloody exaggerated idea of their own importance."

* * * * * * * * *

As darkness fell over Bou Arada the last gun fired a last defiant shell. The rations and water-cart arrived and equanimity returned. The only reminder of the day's battle-sodden hours was the occasional flaring of the still burning tanks. With the arrival of the echelons, rumours and counter rumours circulated, mostly to do with casualties on both sides and mostly exaggerated. But I think the Germans must have done a lot of counting that night. Eventually we pulled out our blankets and fell into a welcome sleep.

Two hours later I was being shaken and remember saying dimly, "Oh, bugger, what do you want?" It was Colonel Davidson. With apologies I scrambled from my blankets and learnt that I had half an hour in which to get my troop on the road. I was to join numbers 1 and 2 Troops of 'A' Battery and we were to make haste for the south again. It so happened that after we had left our comfortable road junction near Ouseltia, the relieving troops had been attacked by a force of tanks. The French troops and the anti-tank gunners had all legged it into the hills, leaving their guns without firing a shot. If these men had fought their guns to the last man, probably nobody would have heard of them. As it was, everyone heard, particularly those of more exalted rank. Colonel Davidson thought it a pity that I had not still been there. I reserved my opinion but privately congratulated the Germans on their timing. Meanwhile the French had understandably got the jitters. They had seen this group of tanks investigating one or two valleys and being hopelessly short of guns they had expressed their anxiety accordingly. Our small force was instructed to canter down to help in any possible way.

CHAPTER VI

ROBAA AND KASSERINE

Our destination this time was a place called Robaa situated in yet another valley about 12 miles to the south and separated from Bou Arada by a high and extensive range of hills. These hills were a sort of no-man's land, being patrolled by both sides and therefore unsafe to travel through. This meant that we had to make a detour back to El Aroussa, then south over a hilly, twisting road down to Siliana then eastwards another 15 miles to Robaa. A total distance of about 65 miles.

We failed to reach Siliana by daybreak so this composite battery, commanded by Captain Richard Duckworth of 'A' Battery, was put into a harbour while a reconnaissance party went forward to contact the French.

Siliana was rather congested with French troops all in a hurry to go somewhere but none of them able to throw much light on the situation. The four vehicles of our recce party pushed on from Siliana in the direction of Robaa in the face of a strong tide of retreating French army. Every car and truck in their possession was loaded way beyond capacity with troops; they were hanging on to tail boards, clinging to anything that offered a purchase including roofs. It made our journey hazardous and gave us no encouragement.

With considerable difficulty we did manage to reach Robaa, such as it was, and were directed into the mountains on the right to find the French general and his HQ. After an hour or two of dashing hither and thither we located him and were more than astonished to be greeted by his highness shedding tears, whilst all about us his lieutenants repeatedly uttered the words, "C'est terrible!"

This was rather new to us and nobody seemed quite able to open a conversation. We shuffled about a bit and finally Duckworth, prompted by Peter Heslop, began to ask the French general a few pertinent questions. The general confirmed what we already knew, that they were in retreat. He also confirmed what we had already guessed, that German tanks had been causing problems during the last few days. But what he wouldn't or couldn't confirm was where we were to make a stand. We tried vainly to persuade him to decide on a line that could be defended but since our French was lacking and his English was little better, it seemed that we were getting nowhere. It was decided eventually to fall back on Siliana for reasons that we could not understand.

Siliana was just a village with nothing to recommend it as a defensive position. As it was, the place was teeming with French troops, mostly Moroccan and Algerian, and they seemed to lack any direction or co-ordination. We wondered who the hell was supposed to be in charge. Certainly there was no sign of anybody attempting to establish a defence of any kind. The only thing that seemed to preoccupy them was the search for food. There were vehicles going round and round the village and troops doing the same, plus a fair sprinkling of mules neighing and braying. We were looking at all this and thinking we'd let ourselves in for a load of trouble when there came unexpected succour in the shape of a few Derbyshire Yeomanry armoured cars. We were never more pleased to see them and furthermore they were followed by some of 12th RHA's 25-pounders and lastly, eleven tanks of the 17th/21st Lancers.

We all met up just outside Siliana for a conference at which it was quickly decided to forget the French and go it alone. The little column of field guns, anti-tank guns, tanks, armoured cars and a few vehicles with extra food, water and ammunition made its way back towards Robaa. As darkness approached we stopped where the road split, one going north-east to Robaa, the other going south-east to heaven knew where. We formed a hollow square around this junction and settled ourselves down for the night. At dawn there was no sign or sound of any enemy so we formed a recce party of officers from the different units and went forward to try to discover what had happened to the Germans.

It was a lengthy reconnaissance for several good reasons. None of us knew this part of the country. Indeed we didn't even know where the French had been before they departed and we were not anxious to drive into enemy territory. Every time we rounded a corner or drove over a small crest, we stopped to scan the countryside through binoculars. We tried to note the likely tank approaches together with the features, or collection of features, that might lend themselves to form defensive positions.

Eventually we reached the small village of Robaa with the utmost caution. Still we had detected no enemy but we were pretty sure that the enemy held the high ground about a mile ahead and we knew that the road ahead, that swung north to Pont du Fahs, was in German hands. So we decided that this was far enough. As we faced the enemy, on the left of the road was open, rolling country with a few Arab dwellings or farm buildings dotted about. On the right of the road the country rose steeply and immediately into scrub-covered hills which extended for miles. This large area of hills provided excellent cover but was far too difficult for tanks except along the very few passes.

After a few nervous excursions into the hills, in an attempt to discover how far the enemy had followed the French retreat, we did eventually attract response from German mortars. It was something of a relief to know where the enemy was. Then, after minor adjustments during the next day or two, we established a very thin line or outposts in front of Robaa. There were no 1st Army troops either to our right or left for some miles at least.

My troop, being the only 'B' Battery troop, was detached from the remainder of our force and sent into the hills to prevent any hostile tanks working their way round behind the others down in front of Robaa. We deployed to cover the only junction of three roads or tracks in the hills above Robaa. The ground was a succession of steep-sided hills clothed for the most part in bushes and small trees. It was quite good for the concealment of our guns and very restricting for the movement of tanks. A troop of 25-pounders was also sent to deploy about one and a half miles behind my junction.

Siting my guns was easy enough but getting them into position was not. One in particular had to be man-handled by two detachments to get it up the side of a hill. The other two 'A' Battery troops were deployed down below on my left front. They were sited on either side of the Robaa - Pont du Fahs road, perhaps three or four miles away from my position as the crow flies. So far as enemy tanks were concerned, we of 6 Troop reckoned our position was pretty strong but our state was hopeless if attacked by infantry which was far more likely. It seemed we had cut ourselves off from the rest of the world and we could do nothing but wait for something to happen.

Two unhappy nights were spent with most of us awake listening and straining to hear any sound that might mean an enemy patrol. Yet strangely nothing passed our way. On the third morning a gunner from the gun furthest from my troop HQ came panting up to me saying that there were soldiers of some sort approaching their gun position. I rushed off to investigate and sure enough figures in extended line were picking their way towards us. The thing was, they were not coming from the supposed direction of the Germans nor were they coming from behind us, from the road from Siliana. The first thing I recognised was the shape of their tin hats. With relief I handed my binoculars to Sergeant Smith for confirmation and set off down the hillside to meet them. These were obviously infantry and I fervently hoped they had come to stay.

The coincidence that met me next was extraordinary. Making my way to the chap I rightly took to be the platoon commander, I hailed him with words of welcome. I was never more pleased to see a small body of British infantry and was expressing my delight when I stopped and stared. The young subaltern was undoubtedly the younger brother of one of my cricketing friends at home. They lived about ¼ mile away from me in Kent. After exchanging greetings I learnt that he belonged to the Buffs of 78th Division and that they too had been sent to do a rescue act. The rest of his company were down by the road with the two 'A' Battery troops. He had been told to find me in the hills and provide some necessary support.

Unfortunately, my friend and neighbour didn't stay long; he and his platoon were moved to join the others on the Robaa road. Compensation came with the arrival of a whole battalion of Americans. Clearly somebody was taking the threat of an attack in this out of the way spot very seriously. With the American battalion, the Buffs, the tanks, the 25-pounders and ourselves, we were growing in strength daily. A further coincidence came to light when I discovered that the troop commander of the 25-pounders behind my position was formerly a subaltern in my battery when we were at Cambridge and was also a friend of mine, his name was Tom Cracknell.

Of course we had no idea of what was going on in Tunisia in the course of overall strategy. We knew that the aim was to defeat the Axis armies and that the taking of Tunis itself was the key to that end. However, strategies have no place in the thoughts of the soldier who is actually doing the fighting. He is aware of nothing outside his immediate vicinity and environment other than his own family. He neither knows nor cares about what is happening in other parts of the world. He is concerned only with his day to day survival in the belief that nobody else gives a damn about him. Nobody, that is to say, except his fellow fighting comrades with whom he forges a fiercely close brotherhood. People talked freely during the 1st World War of soldiers and others sacrificing their lives. They still speak in the same way especially in church and in political discourse. The fact is that soldiers never did sacrifice themselves for a cause, they are sacrificed by others who see it as necessary.

We were therefore totally ignorant of any facts that had led to our occupation of the tiny track junction in the middle of a mountainous region of Tunisia. Much less did we appreciate what was in the mind of the German High Command. In retrospect, it seems that whilst both sides were building up their strengths as quickly as possible, the German Commander, Von Arnim, was intent upon keeping a wide corridor open from the coast to allow Rommel's Afrika Corps to reach the security of Tunisia. Consequently there had been a number of determined local attacks by both sides to occupy the few obvious, and less obvious, passes through the hills which were vital to both sides.

The Germans had tried the north, they had switched to Medjez el Bab, they had made a determined attack at Bou Arada and, although we didn't realise it, the next attempt to break through should naturally come at Robaa. The first hints of their intentions were given by their probing of the French positions with their tanks. As was so often the case, we had rushed assorted forces down to this hitherto unheard of sector, so had the Germans. No sooner had the Americans dug themselves in on the hills north and west of my road junction, than the Germans had similarly settled themselves on the hills on the eastern side. What had been a quiet peaceful and lonely area of this country had suddenly been invaded by a host of foreigners to the detriment of all concerned.

* * * * * * * * *

My troop HQ was on the hill just north of the junction as was the American colonel and his battalion HQ. I also had two of my guns tucked into this hill, the foremost of these was that which caused difficulties earlier. Further to the east there was a steep conical hill occupied by the enemy. These two hills were joined by a saddle which was no-man's land. To the south of these features and across one of the roads was another larger hill also occupied by the enemy. This hill rose between the two roads that met at the junction and directly to the west of this, across the second road, was the remainder of the Americans together with my other two guns. The distance between the opposing forces was probably less than 400 yards.

Each gun detachment had a sergeant in charge of the gun and responsible for its performance. In addition, each detachment had a bombardier who was second in command. One of these, Bombardier Brown, was a trumpet player in Billy Cotton's band before the war. This was one of the most famous dance bands of the late 30's. When we were making ready for our departure from Scotland, I stowed Brown's trumpet in my large valise for safety. We were all pleased and cheered whenever he had the opportunity to give us a musical session. Here at this isolated place, before the Americans arrived, he gave a small concert on most evenings. He also managed to evoke some cheers from the Germans, especially when he played 'Lily Marlene'. In such ways were spirits maintained in buoyant mood.

The Americans were new troops who were anxious to prove themselves. They were very well equipped and their confidence was brimming over. The fact that they lacked battle experience was no fault of theirs but its consequence was that whereas we suffered no casualties from shelling and mortars, they sustained far too many. Again, because their approach was somewhat naive, they were soon to suffer more extensively than they might have done.

It was obvious that the Germans were not here to exchange pleasantries, so it was reasonable to suppose that an attack would not be long delayed. The American CO decided to beat them to it and chose as his objective the conical hill in front. There was merit in this decision but none at all in his preparation. If the Americans captured the hill the other German position south of the road would become untenable, in which case we should hold a very strong and supporting position and could control this sector of the hills.

The Americans knew the whereabouts of the enemy, but they didn't know who they were nor had they any idea of their strength. They had not patrolled the area so they had no information about the ground over which they were about to attack. They didn't know for instance whether there was wire in front of the hill; if so, there would certainly be fixed machine-gun fire directed onto it. They didn't know whether there were any mines sown in front or around the hill. For my part, I didn't even know of the proposed attack and I had not even met the colonel.

As dusk fell on the evening before the American attack, I was walking back to my troop HQ having been chatting to George Notcutt who had made his daily visit with the water cart and rations. I could hardly fail to see a group of American officers standing in a half circle.

As I came close to them I heard a voice say, "... and the British anti-tank guns will go with the leading company to settle any counter attack by tanks." Since mine were the only British anti-tank guns in the vicinity, I decided to find out more. (NB, Unlikely as it may sound, those were the first words I heard the colonel say.)

The owner of the voice was the colonel who had summoned his officers for his final orders for an attack on the conical hill at dawn. Having introduced myself, I tried hard to conceal my fury at not being notified of these intentions and not being included in this order group. No attempt had been made to ask me what I could or could not do to assist in this operation. How could he expect my guns to be there when the bloody fool hadn't even told me there was going to be an attack? I just couldn't believe what I'd just heard but contented myself by telling the colonel, in front of his officers, that I could not accompany the leading company in the assault upon the hill with my guns as (a) I wouldn't know where to take them and (b) the gun-towing quads wouldn't get anywhere near the objective before being destroyed, and there was not the slightest chance of manhandling the guns across this country up to that conical hill. The best I could do was to get the guns up as soon as possible after they had secured the hill and even that might depend on the other hill on the right being neutralised.

It was clear that the Americans were not impressed by my offer and there were a few awkward moments. In the end, after I had actually refused to take my guns with the leading company, the colonel virtually accused me of cowardice by asking if it would be OK for me to join them after they had made the hill nice and safe for me. I returned to my troop to give them the news. I was unhappy and angry. I remember thinking that this was Alice in Wonderland and that I'd rather have young Gardener with his platoon of Buffs than three companies of these Yanks. Some hours later the semi darkness was split by the flashes and the silence broken by the opening broadside of the 12th RHA 25-pounders. In order to direct their fire onto the enemy locations it meant that the shells flew close to the crests of the hill we occupied. The noise these shells made as they hurtled past was quite frightening. Soon the first company of infantry set off down the saddle separating the opposing sides. They made good progress for the first 150 yards or so and then, as they picked their way forward through the rough scrub, the German machine-gunners began raking the slopes and their mortars opened a blistering fire.

The Americans retaliated with their mortars and the 25-pounders sent shells crashing all over the German positions. A number of American heavy machine-guns were also spraying the hilltop from our hill. The fire power was really intense but it was all very random because nobody could pinpoint the German trenches and gun emplacements at this stage. Eventually the Americans reached the slopes of Conical Hill and the battle seemed to subside. I couldn't find out the facts of the situation which was not surprising in these circumstances. But I began to wonder whether it was time for me to go forward to recce the hill for my guns. I believed the Americans had met with success at least on Conical Hill, though there was still a lot of firing coming from the enemy occupying the southern hill. Then the battle swelled again, smoke and dust was everywhere. Casualties began to be brought back, some on stretchers, some walking in various states of distress. There was a lot of shouting as the reserve company was pushed forward.

Mortar and gunfire increased from both sides and gradually it became apparent that all was not well. Soon there were more and more of the infantry coming back who were not wounded. Our own shellfire was falling on Conical Hill again, there was mortar fire falling just about everywhere and it was looking very much as though neither hill had been taken and that the Yanks had had a bad time.

In a little while the Americans were in full retreat, there could be no doubt about it. Groups were coming past us and numbers of them had flung their weapons away. This was a distressing sight to see those proud young men, who, having such hopes a few hours ago, had now lost all pride and were in complete disarray. They had so much believed in themselves and to have that belief destroyed so brutally was somehow inconceivable. The trouble now was that having decided to go, they didn't know where to stop. They picked up all the available transport, loaded some with wounded and simply disappeared away in the direction of the 25-pounders. Within an hour there were no Americans to be seen except for a section of a mortar platoon that was operating about 60 yards from my troop HQ. They were as bewildered as we were and came to ask me what they should do; their entire battalion had drifted away and they were stunned by the day's events and by grief. They decided to stay with us.

Amidst all this commotion my friend, Tom Cracknell, had been acting as forward observation officer for the 25-pounders. He had followed up the attacking infantry and had been sending back all the fire orders to the field guns. In other words, he had been responsible for the artillery support during the whole of the battle. I heard later that he had used a discarded German trench for an observation post. The Germans had been pushed off Conical Hill but had counter attacked fiercely. Tom had brought heavy fire down upon them but still they came on. Ultimately he was bringing fire down on his own position, so close were the oncoming Germans.

Tom got away with the last of the retreating infantry but in doing so he cracked up completely. He began yelling and screaming as he was taken back to his own gun area. I understand he was sent back to recover in hospital somewhere but I never saw or heard of him again.

* * * * * * * *

Since I'd received no orders to leave, I couldn't take my guns out of action. For one thing, the doctrines of the Royal Artillery were decidedly fussy about such matters. For another, I reckoned the Germans would not sit there and watch me taking them away. By way of reinforcing that view, they were sending mortar bombs over onto two of my guns from time to time. We could actually hear them giving orders to these mortars. This sort of situation is not in the text books and I vividly remember feeling not only abandoned but totally without hope. I kept searching the opposing hills through my binoculars expecting the Germans to follow up their success by sweeping across our positions. After all, there were only thirty of us plus five Americans.

Darkness began to fall and gave me the chance to call on my guns to explain what steps I proposed to take. I intended to shift two of them to where I might have a chance of making a dash if the enemy came with the dawn. One was an easy adjustment; the other was extremely tricky. The forward gun was the one we'd had to manhandle into its site but it had been taken most of the way with its quad. Our present predicament ruled out any possibility of taking a gun-tower along the road to fetch it. The only other way to recover it was up the enormously steep and rocky hillside to the top and then remove it by quad down the gentler slope the other side. We could now see some fires in the German hills. They were relaxing after the tension and, in many cases, the heartbreak of the battle and were cooking themselves some hot supper. I thought this a good time to attempt the recovery of the gun and accordingly I enlisted the help of the American mortar friends plus two detachments, making a total of 16 men. We attached what are known as drag ropes to the wheels of the gun. Six men lifted the gun trail off the ground (the long legs that brace the gun when firing). Then in the manner of a tug-of-war team, I gave orders in a whisper to enable the remaining ten men to pull together, one wheel at a time, "Together, heave; together, heave."

The going was exceedingly difficult in the dark and made worse by the rocks and bushes and, above all, without attracting the attention of the enemy opposite. This also was not in the text books. Nevertheless, in under an hour we had accomplished the task without so much as a bullet coming our way. Leading the quad up to the top from the other side was comparatively easy and very soon the gun was taken down the back way, as it were, and into its new position behind and to the left of a rough track that came from the direction of Robaa way below us. This had been quite an achievement and had cemented the relationship between the American mortar section and ourselves very firmly.

Our troubles were by no means over but I felt that I was now in a recoverable position to leg it with all four guns if I had to. They were now all accessible to

63

the quads and with luck we might get away with it. At first I thought we should all remain awake during the night because I felt sure that enemy patrols would come to discover what had happened to us. Then I thought that a few gunners would be a sacrificial offering for practised infantry. We had not slept the previous night and the day just ended had been exhausting, frightening and for a lot of the time we had been under fire. We were made additionally tired by all that had gone before, so I decided to defy logic and rules and ordered everybody to sleep with no guards to be posted. I felt that, if asleep, we were more likely to be captured, whereas, if awake and resisting, we were more likely to be killed. This may sound stupid but it is what I felt at the time.

In fact feelings at such times are not always easy to understand. There was relief at being alive so far, anger at being so deserted, fear at the prospects of the coming night and the following morning, and concern, yes concern, for the men who meant so much to me and who looked to me for their salvation. Those hours will never be forgotten yet I never mentioned them to anyone afterwards. I suppose I thought we should have been prepared to take on the German army by ourselves.

The night wore on and I wondered why nobody had come to see what had happened to us. Where was Duckworth and where was George Notcutt and his water cart? They must have heard the uproar of the day's battle. In spite of everything, I did eventually drop off to sleep and when Savage shook me awake it was already daylight on February 1st 1943. Savage said that he and Sergeant Oakley and a few others had been awake for a short while and one of them had seen movement out in front of us. I crawled to the top of the crest taking great care not to show myself on the skyline. Sergeant Oakley indicated where they had seen the movement but we could see nothing at this time. I scanned the opposing hillsides through my glasses and could see no movement there either; everything was uncannily silent.

After several minutes of searching I slowly rose to my feet and this brought no response. Soon we were a small group standing together on the skyline and were totally perplexed at the enemy indifference. Then we saw figures moving about 200 yards below and to the right of us. We flattened ourselves quickly and had a bren gun, a tommy gun and one or two rifles ready and waiting. Then one of the oncomers started waving a white cloth or handkerchief. In a short time two of the enemy had surrendered to us, my first prisoners of the 2nd World War.

The two Germans turned out to be Austrians and had crept out into no-man's land during the night. They had brought a few rations and a blanket each, then, after enquiring whether there were any more of them out there, I took them to my troop HQ. Savage began to make a brew of tea and to concoct some breakfast. I gave the two Austrian lads a cigarette each and a cup of tea and they promptly started sobbing. We learnt that at about the time we were striving with the gun up the hill, they had been ordered to leave and to go north in some kind of emergency. There were no Germans facing us at all.

The anti-climax was obvious in all of us, intense relief was an understatement indeed; it was a truly sensational reprieve. One or two of 6 Troop were shaking hands with one another, others were running about and laughing. Soon we could all hear Bombardier Brown serenading the world with his trumpet.

I wandered off alone after sending our prisoners back to the 25-pounders to send wherever they thought best. I walked through what had been the American lines and looked down at the saddle along which the Yanks had advanced and retreated at unhappy cost. Yesterday I cursed them for their performance and incompetence and for the fact that they had tried to drag my troop into the fiasco. We should have been completely written off - of that there could be no doubt. Today I felt differently about them; they had tried hard but just hadn't realised what faced them. It had been a bitter experience for them and they had lost a lot of good people. I didn't now mind very much that they had disappeared and left me, I just felt sorry for the whole business. I remember two things as I walked on those slopes where 24 hours earlier I would probably have been killed. One was that I said a prayer of some sort, partly for myself and partly for the Americans; the other was that, for some reason, I hummed and sang the song 'Pennies from Heaven'.

Meantime 6 Troop had not been idle but had turned bounty hunters. The Yanks had left behind a heap of good things. In a short space of time 6 Troop were re-equipped with a smart line in shirts, socks and underwear and so forth - including me. Then, after some food, I thought it now safe to leave Sergeant Oakley in charge while I went off to visit the others down at Robaa. To do that I had to go back past the 25-pounders to reach the road at the bottom of the hill. The 12th RHA gun position officer told me about Tom Cracknell which was sad but might have been worse. I continued on and back along the road through Robaa until I met Richard Duckworth's HQ.

Without giving me any chance of relating my fortunes of the last 24 hours, Duckworth shouted, "Follow me and I'll show you something." My driver, Bombardier Foster, and I followed on down the road for a short distance when, looking beyond Duckworth's vehicle, we saw a massive German tank. We'd never seen anything like it - although half off the road there was still only just room to get past it. Foster could think of nothing to say other than, "Bloody hell!" which he repeated several times. As we examined this leviathan we could see several 6-pound shot sticking into the sides and front and there was a split in one side.

The story was beginning to unfold when Stanley Edwards, No 1 Troop commander, joined us from somewhere. He was beaming all over his face and had not long returned from some medical post where he'd had a tooth pulled, but that was not the basis for the grins. The story began at dawn on January 31st, the same time that the Americans had launched themselves at Conical Hill. Enemy tanks were heard advancing from Pont du Fahs towards Robaa. The first sight of them came when this monster of a Mark VI Tiger tank trundled round the corner in front and on to where the Buffs were dug in on either side of the road. It was followed by two Mark III tanks in line astern.

The two 'A' Battery troops were dug in either side of and about 400 yards from the road. As the tanks entered their field of fire both troops opened up and stopped the Tiger tank and then destroyed both the Mark III's. There followed a hail of shelling from other tanks and guns upon the troop gun positions. Then, in the belief that the guns had been silenced, the enemy repeated the same tactics. This time both troops held their fire and allowed another Mark VI and two more Mark III's to proceed past the earlier knocked out tanks. Again the guns, which had not been damaged, opened fire and destroyed all three plus an armoured half-track that had followed. That ended the tank attack.

This was the first time that the new German Tiger tanks had ever been used in anger. We ourselves had no idea that they even existed and I could understand the elation expressed by Stanley. He told me that two of his four guns engaged the Mark VI's and hit them again and again before stopping them after something like 12 direct hits. That night the Germans put in a covering attack by infantry in an attempt to recover the Tigers. They wanted to prevent information on the tanks falling into our hands. They succeeded in removing the first of the two but the second was well into the Buffs' territory and they had to leave it. Within a couple of days the place was sprinkled with top brass, many of them flown from England especially to measure and record the particulars of this latest German super tank.

In passing, it might be worth recording that the total casualties suffered by those two troops were three gunners wounded. In the circumstances I felt it was hardly worth while outlining my own modest tribulations; there was very little to show for it unless you included some clean underwear and socks. Even so, I did point out that we'd had a battle and that, as a consequence, I now had no infantry at all. I was asked to stay put for a day or so while Richard tried to persuade a few of the Buffs to come and join me. With which slightly encouraging news I left them and returned to the hills. I called again on the RHA informing them of the activities in front of Robaa. They had seen nothing of the Americans and were as anxious about the situation as I was.

We spent another night in splendid isolation but during the following morning a convoy of vehicles announced the reappearance of the Americans. We naturally greeted them as did our mortar friends who were still with us. They couldn't believe that we had remained here since they had departed and their attitude to us changed perceptibly. Late in the morning I was requested to go to the American colonel and I wondered what he'd got in mind for me this time.

When I reached his HQ there was a large group of his officers already there and my heart sank in anticipation. The colonel was not one to stand on ceremony, he said simply, "I've called you here in front of my boys to apologise." He continued, "Before our attack I thought you lacked what it takes. I've changed my mind. We didn't do so good and my boys panicked, in fact they ran and left you. I will just say that it won't happen again." He then shook my hand and asked if I'd have a drink. Later we were offered various gifts by the Americans, in particular we received numbers of large tins of coffee, jam, sausages, sugar and lots more. 'Entente cordiale' was well established again. The whole of this episode in the neighbourhood of Robaa was reported by the radio and press in the following terms; "German armour probed our defences at Robaa and were

66

repulsed with losses."

We spent a few more agreeable days in the Robaa area with little interference from the enemy. During this time the regimental Padre paid us a visit. It was the first time I had personally seen him since before we'd left Scotland. He had recovered from the personal injuries sustained just below his loins and had brought us a few cigarettes. His infrequent visits to the sharp end were not the most encouraging of events, in as much as his visits seemed to coincide with, or provoke, enemy action. Had I been him, I think I should have worried a bit about the relationship with the heavenly boss. This visit was an exception to the norm. We were chatting and telling him about our recent experiences when, by way of celebration, a flight of Hurricanes flew over us quite low down. These were the first British fighters we had seen since the campaign began and we were much cheered by the sight.

They had obviously seen us because they swung round and came back towards us. We involuntarily began to wave to them until, unbelievably, they dived at us and let fly with machine-guns and cannons. No men ever launched themselves into trenches quicker than we did just then. The fighters came one close upon another and ripped the ground and trees to pieces around us. They were not content until they'd had several goes at us. The noise of bullets and cannon shells as they tore into the ground had a really blasting effect. Splinters of rock flew about and nearby trees were chipped and lacerated by the deluge of fire. It was thoroughly unpleasant and frightening.

The language of soldiers in action becomes more colourful and more explicit, if sometimes repetitive, as they feel themselves more than usually threatened. The Padre heard a few phrases which he should have found distressing but which could not have failed to impress him. This cavalier attitude by the airforce was a disgrace and happened too often. We could and should have suffered considerable losses from these Hurricanes, especially since we had made no attempt to take cover when they first flew over. On another occasion we were very heavily bombed by a crowd of Flying Fortresses which dropped hosts of bombs on the wrong area. Again in Italy one of my sergeants was shot to bits by a Mustang fighter which obviously didn't know one part of Italy from another.

When the Hurricanes left us it was a little while before we all climbed out of our trenches, just in case they had one more go. In that interval one of the gunners called out to a friend to ask if he was all right. The two of them were both Cockney Londoners and the response from the second was unexpected but none the less welcome. He replied in clear and exaggeratedly refined tones:

> "I wandered lonely as a cloud
> That floats on high o'er vales and hills
> When all at once, I saw a crowd,
> An 'ost of fuckin' daffodils."

Even the Padre laughed.

This relative peace was interrupted by messages ordering the 'A' Battery troops and my own to leave Robaa and to motor even further south to a village called Sbiba. To get there meant going back to Siliana, then south and west to Maktar in the forest, then west again to Le Kef - Sbiba road - altogether more than 100 miles and, of course, mostly in darkness. We never knew the reasons for all these frequent moves until we reached the other end, and often not even then. This trip was similar to others except the weather was improving; it was no longer as cold and certainly much drier. We were now in the middle of February.

* * * * * * * * *

Arriving at Sbiba we were met by the 2nd in command of the regiment, Major Burne. This was just as well since the place seemed to be in confusion, only this time they were Americans who were rushing about feverishly. We learnt that Rommel with his Afrika Corps had struck here in the south with panzer divisions and infantry. He had broken through and thrust on to the extent that he was threatening the 1st army rear supply routes. He was pushing up valleys in three directions. The centre of these was the Kasserine pass which had already fallen to the Germans. The northern thrust was the one with Sbiba at its head and where everyone was trying to set up a rapid string of defences.

Major Burne had already sorted out our roles and at once allocated the areas to be occupied by each of the anti-tank troops. My place was in the lower foothills on the left of the valley as we faced the enemy. As I moved forward with my four guns we passed through a thickly populated gun area. Our 25-pounder regiments were there and were accompanied by many American artillery units. All this was comforting as I set about the deployment of my troop; at least we weren't alone down here. My foothills were quite steep and there was plenty of cover and places to tuck the guns into. There were clumps of cactus and Arab dwellings all over the area of this valley.

The next day the expected attack arrived. We heard the German tanks pounding along some time before we saw them. In front the valley was flat for a few hundred yards, then it rose sharply in a sort of lip about 20 yards high. On top of the lip was a flat plateau that ran as far as we could see. The enemy tanks advanced over this plateau slowly and cautiously until the foremost of them reached the lip. Such moments promote all kinds of jittery feelings but they were nothing as compared with those recently experienced at Robaa.

We had been told to allow the Panzers to come right in close to our defences and accordingly we remained silent as the Germans were crouched over the brow of the lip. They were obviously searching through their binoculars and hoping to pick up either movement or recent diggings or vehicles etc. Presently a few of them began to machine-gun round and about and others sent their high velocity shells into various cactus plantations and farm buildings. After a time several of them left the others and ventured down the slope and began to make their way towards us. Unfortunately the artillery behind us thought this was far enough and a sudden deluge of shells exploded among these oncoming tanks. This caused the

Germans to scatter to either side and there followed some heavy shelling from both sides.

The Germans realised that this valley was well defended and turned to retrace their steps. One or two anti-tank guns opened fire including my No 3 gun. Sergeant Williams had a panzer in his sights and when it stopped and turned he decided he'd better engage it before it got away. He fired a couple of rounds and hit the tank. His gun was close by a small hut and the concussion of the gun firing burst one of Williams' eardrums. There was blood running down his cheek and he became very deaf but he was pleased that he could boast the scalp of one of the legendary Afrika Corps' tanks.

The German tanks withdrew most of their armour away from our artillery fire, leaving four or five tanks on the plateau. For some reason that I have never understood, there emerged from behind us half a dozen Churchill tanks which began to advance towards the lip of the ground in front. From my position I could see them very clearly as they lumbered up the steep slope. Equally, I could see the few enemy tanks on top waiting for them. It was awful not being able to warn them but I couldn't understand why nobody else had. There must have been countless people across the valley who could see what I could see and might have told those Churchills.

The first of those wretched tanks rolled up onto the plateau. There was a flash and a bang from the nearest panzer, another flash as the shell hit the Churchill which immediately burst into flames. The second and third Churchills crept up to help their colleagues. Both of these suffered the same fate within seconds of each other. There were three Churchills blazing, all to no purpose and the others could do nothing. Some of the crews got out but I believe that half or more of them were killed. Who sent them and for what reason are questions that should have been asked subsequently. Just what six under-armed Churchills were going to achieve against a panzer division, God alone knows. If they had stayed hull down at the top of the slope so that only their turrets and guns could be seen, they would have been in a much stronger position; they might even have knocked out some of the German tanks. The turret is the thickest part of a tank's armour and is obviously a small target to hit. After being pounded by our artillery the remaining panzers made off back to join the others of their division. That night both sides withdrew and by the following morning they faced each other some 20 miles apart. The armoured brigade of our division had managed to halt the Germans beyond the Kasserine pass at great cost to our people. Rommel had enjoyed some success but had failed to enforce a breakthrough and now he was running back to his starting lines. It had been touch and go and proved that the Germans by no means regarded themselves as beaten.

The 6th Armoured Division was now removed from the fighting zone as complete entity. There was a need to refit and re-equip the various units of the division. The tank regiments all needed new tanks. The British Valentine and Crusader tanks had proved to be totally inadequate in competition with the German Mark III and IV's and now, as we had discovered, the mark VI Tigers. Nothing in the allied armies was comparable with the Tiger but the American Shermans were equal to or better than the lesser German and Italian armour.

Now our armoured regiments were to be equipped with Shermans. The gunner regiments had been engaged with the enemy since November and were in need of rest and refit. The Guards Brigade were similarly placed.

We anti-tank troops returned to our regimental HQ area at Teboursouk, about 150 mile journey. Colonel Davidson had left our regiment just after Bou Arada to take over another regiment; he was killed a few weeks later. Colonel Slessor, our new CO, had been to see my troop at Sbiba and noted that we were in poor physical shape. We lacked outer clothing, most of what we had was worn and torn. Our boots were beyond repair in many cases, we had no razor blades, towels and so on. We should have been far worse had it not been for our self help from the Americans. He said we'd be able to get some sleep and change of clothes as soon as we reached Teboursouk.

During this journey we had stopped for a break and a brew of tea. A family of Arabs came along the road towards us. There was the man riding on his wretched hollow-backed donkey and three or four women walking along weighed down with huge bundles of sticks and other assorted goods and equipment. As they passed by, Bombardier Foster stopped the man and called one of the women, a young girl, towards him. He motioned the man to get off the donkey but without success. There was much rambling talk and gesticulating of arms until Foster drew his revolver and told the man to get off in obvious terms. This he did, whereupon Foster made the young girl relinquish her burdens and he put her on the donkey. He then made the man take up the large load of stuff and put it on his back and sent them all on their way with a wave of his gun. The other women were grinning and chattering down the road as they went. The young girl looked back at us smiling, the gunners all cheered and Savage volunteered, "You black bastard."

CHAPTER VII

SEDJENANE

Six troop were more than pleased to be making their way back to RHQ. Our excursion to the Robaa area in the southern hills had been a succession of events that were tailor-made to destroy our faith in allied assistance. We had been away from the rest of 'B' Battery since January 20th and it was now the beginning of March 1943.

We arrived at RHQ near Teboursouk for, we considered, a well-deserved rest. The following day we were issued with fresh clothing. We had lived and slept in our existing clothes since November without any possibility of a bath or even a proper wash. Added to the condition of our clothing and bodily hygiene was the general off-putting appearance of our hair. Apart from being matted with sand and dirt, the only attempt of cutting had been undertaken by myself when I had assaulted the heads of some of my troop with a pair of indifferent nail scissors. The results were not very picturesque nor, for that matter, very much appreciated.

That evening the colonel sent for me and told me that, regretfully, I must go with my troop and join my battery north of Beja. The Germans had begun to push through our defences in the north with tanks and paratroops. We were to move off as soon as we could get ourselves ready. I called my five sergeants together and gave them the news together with my own orders concerning the coming night march. It took a little while for the troop to pack up all its bits and pieces, to check food, water, ammunition, to hand in all the letters they'd all been writing to their families. Eventually the gun-towers were filled with petrol and we set off quietly on the 50 mile journey to 'B' Battery HQ.

Our journey north was slow but uneventful. Sometime during the night I found Major Hamilton's HQ and roused him from his sleep. I remember feeling a bit piqued at his lack of greeting, after all, he hadn't seen me for nearly six weeks and a lot had happened. I wasn't even offered a cup of tea; Ham merely said, "Oh, hello, Donald. Glad you got here." He explained that things were not going too well and I was to take my troop on further north through Djibel Abiod and on to an area just short of Sedjenane. Care was needed as no-one really knew where the front was or where the Germans had reached. Sedjenane was on the road to Mateur and Bizerta and, as far as I was concerned, was practically off the map.

Daylight had arrived when we came upon some of our troops. They were medium artillery guns and positioned just off the road on the right. Also, as I discovered, there was a group of anti-tank guns similar to mine about half a mile behind these mediums. They were all hooked up to their vehicles ready to move. I naturally wondered why I had been called from 75 miles away when there were already more guns available than I possessed. None of the troops in this area were from my division, so what was all this to do with me?

There was no information about where either our own troops or the Germans were. My enquiries from the neighbouring gunners didn't help. They thought that there had been an enemy break-through south of Sedjenane and also thought that our forward troops were retiring. The particularly disturbing news was that the mediums had been told to make ready to move back in the near future. Meantime they fired a few spasmodic rounds now and again in an unconvincing sort of way.

This whole area was heavily wooded but just in front of these guns there was a clearing in the woods either side of the road. The clearing extended about 200 yards to the right of the road and about 300 yards to the left. It extended about 200 yards along the road before low scrub and woodland closed in again. I quickly deployed two guns on the left of the road and one on the right; all three providing cross fire onto the road. The fourth gun I tucked into the woods some way behind, there being no space to do anything else with it. I thought after a bite to eat and a cup of tea I'd find the forward infantry and discover what was happening.

It was then that shells began to arrive, not in large numbers but intermittent shells landing here and there. They hit the trees splitting branches and trunks and sending jagged metal splinters whining in all directions. I remember well taking an instant dislike to this place. There was a keen sense of foreboding that persisted. Maybe this was because my information was so lacking or because those whom I had met so far were talking of leaving and retirements. My recent experiences at Robaa were still fresh in mind and somehow I felt vulnerable and edgy.

During the day, March 3rd 1943, the constant shelling prevented the medium guns from firing for the most part and kept us all confined to our slit-trenches for what seemed eternity. Some infantry turned up from apparently nowhere and dug in just to the rear of my guns. They said that our forward troops should be retiring through this position before long but they didn't know when. I asked them if they'd seen or heard any enemy tanks where they had been. They hadn't but they understood there were German tanks about up there somewhere.

I remember contemplating the position there. A handful of infantry who didn't know much more than I did and who looked past caring. They were clearly battle weary and low in spirits. A troop of medium artillery who showed every sign of bidding us goodbye before long, and my somewhat solitary troop of four anti-tank guns which could be overrun by enemy infantry as soon as they felt inclined. The prospect was bleak and I wasn't even sure that our presence was necessary. There was no certainty of tanks especially in this heavily wooded area and there were other anti-tank guns standing idle in the woods down the road. This struck me as a situation which was not only obscure and threatening to those present but one that completely lacked any authority, any conviction, any planning, even any awareness of what the hell was going on. It wasn't just me, we all felt the same. I think we felt akin to the sacrificial lamb, to offer ourselves as a temporary hindrance to allow others to establish some sort of position some way behind us.

This unhappy atmosphere persisted all that day to say nothing of the near misses from shells that a number of us suffered. That night the shelling subsided and the mediums began to pull out. I did the rounds of my gun positions and discussed our situation with them. As our neighbours the mediums were up-rooting themselves, we reckoned that this so-called section of the front was farcical and was getting worse by the hour. There was no question of sleep that night; we were too jittery and we feared the Germans might send patrols to find out where we were and anything else they fancied. It should be understood that we, as gunners, knew little about infantry tactics, perhaps about as much as they knew about ours. There was always a mutual anxiety and vulnerability in each of us in the absence of the other.

In fact nothing spectacular happened that night and March 4th arrived fairly quietly. We had some breakfast and the usual hot, soupy, oily tea and were able to attend to the wants of nature in comparative quiet and safety. For this we were always grateful since wanting to go urgently whilst being under fire was always an unhappy combination. I chatted a while with our few infantry friends who, it turned out, had occupied this position briefly some weeks earlier. I learnt among other things that an area that I had twice walked through had supposedly been sown with anti-personnel mines.

Sometime during the morning Major Hamilton turned up to see me, accompanied by an artillery officer from a field regiment. He told me that later that day all the infantry in front, between my position and Sedjenane, would be retiring through my guns and would be establishing a new line a mile or so behind me. I was to wait until these infantry had gone through and then I was to get my guns out of action and fall back to his battery HQ. In any case, I was to start withdrawing my guns not later than 1500 hours.

The friendly gunner officer was here to see if I wanted a smoke screen put down to mask the withdrawal of my guns. In retrospect I should have said yes, as it was I declined, thinking that the putting down of smoke was sure to arouse suspicion and would attract enemy activity. Hamilton accepted my decision and we talked about the ways and means of extricating ourselves. There were certain difficulties associated with the ground which in many patches was wet and boggy. The quads had 4-wheel drive but even so would have to avoid some of the worst areas that I had discovered through walking around.

The rear-most gun was easy and was virtually doing nothing so I ordered it to withdraw to Battery HQ by itself at 1430 hours. The three forward guns were a problem being deployed near the boundaries of the only open area. The quads would have to travel across this open ground and carefully at that, to collect their guns. I thought perhaps if they arrived together and moved to their guns at the same time, we might get away before the Germans had time to bring down any concentration of fire. That was my intention at about mid-day and I told Sergeant Oakley to arrange for the drivers to bring up the quads to a small clearing beside the road about ¼ mile back from the gun positions. I wanted the quads there by 1430 hours so that we could review the situation and make sure that the three of them would move up for the guns together.

At about 1300 hours, I set off on my feet to visit the three guns to explain to the teams that they must have their guns and equipment all ready to move. There are a number of stages needed to get a gun ready for action and a similar number to get it out of action and ready to be hooked on to its quad. In some cases the gun may have to be manhandled to a spot convenient for its vehicle to reach; such was the case with No 2 gun.

As I walked through the woods parallel to the road I heard one or two shells bursting somewhere in front but some distance off. I thought it maybe that the infantry had started their move back. I continued forward to our infantry who were standing in or sitting on the edge of their slit trenches. I explained to them my orders and my proposed movements, then I continued to my guns, this time avoiding the area of the so-called minefield.

By the time I returned to my troop HQ, it was approaching the time for the moves to begin. I walked to the little clearing by the road to await the arrival of the quads. As I waited, shells began to fall on the front of the wood and on the open ground. I grew progressively anxious about the coming operation. The idea of getting the quads across the open area and escaping with their guns before trouble descended seemed a vain hope already. I remember smoking one cigarette upon another and cursing my luck, in fact I cursed everything and everybody during those waiting moments.

In a little while the three vehicles turned and pulled off the road. By now the shellfire had increased perceptibly and the situation looked ugly. I realised that I could not order the drivers of the quads to go up as planned, so decided to abandon my former intentions and instead to take each quad up myself. I told the drivers to wait there with Sergeant Oakley and chose the No 2 gun quad to take first as it was the furthermost of the three positions.

I remember charging up the road the ¼ mile or less to the open area. On either side of the road there were two quite deep ditches. As I looked for a way over the left ditch, two shells burst not far in front of me; these were enough to make me wheel left and slam the vehicle at the ditch. It performed heroically and scrambled its way across and bounded on - I was bouncing like a ball in the driver's seat. Soon I had to stop because of the boggy ground, but I had got to within reasonable distance of the waiting gun team.

I jumped out and began to run towards them and, as I did so, one of the many shells fell beside the quad and knocked it out. I told the team that I would try to get some infantry assistance to get this gun nearer to the road and made my way back as quickly as events would allow. It meant pitching face down into the wet and muddy ground every few yards as by now the shelling was really fierce. Reaching the infantry I succeeded in getting one volunteer to help, a corporal as I remember.

We started off back to the hapless gun and after a few paces I yelled, "Down!" If a shell is going to hit, or land close, it gives practically no warning. This one burst right beside us and I felt hot air and cordite over me together with a thump at my side. The noise of the burst was hideous and deafening. I lay there unable to move and my corporal friend said - and I remember his exact words clearly - "I can't go on, sir, I think I've been hit." I answered that if he could make it he should return to his friends and I recall thanking him for trying.

The odd thing is that at that time I thought I was really badly hit but didn't think to say anything. The reason for this belief was that I was unable to move either my left arm or my left leg. I was sure that I had lost one or both yet I felt nothing. I stayed motionless for some minutes and was absolutely afraid to look at myself. I remember lying in the dirt with the howling and banging of shells and thinking, "I'm going to die here and I'll be found by the bloody Germans." In a very short time, that seemed an age, my self pity gave way to rage. I forced myself to look and discovered that both my arm and leg were still with me. The temporary paralysis was some kind of shock and I like to think that this was the cause of the tears running down my face. It was now obvious that the German gunners could see my position. There were hills around the village of Sedjenane, the nearest of them was perhaps less than a mile away and almost certainly they had observation posts on it. They would see any vehicles moving in my open area, in fact they would concentrate on it because everywhere else was shrouded in woods.

This thought did nothing to ease my anxiety but having to concentrate on the guns helped. So far I'd achieved nothing so I decided to fetch another quad and to have a go at No 1 gun which had easier access. On returning to the clearing I climbed into one of the two remaining quads shouting to Sergeant Oakley that I'd lost the first one and was going after Sergeant Harper's gun.

The run to the gun position was very similar to the first time. I jumped the ditch in the same place and made a dash for the remains of a building where the gun team should have their gun ready. Sure enough the detachment was waiting and hooked the gun onto the quad as soon as it swung round to them. The team leapt into the quad and Sergeant Harper put his hand on my shoulder saying, "I'll take this lot out, sir." He did so without delay, following the route out that I had taken. One gunner named Shamplina, didn't manage to get inside the vehicle but jumped onto the skirting of the gun shield and hung on all the way back as it bounced over the ground.

Once again I worked my way back towards the little assembly point. On the way I passed through the infantry positions yet again. There had been a few casualties from the shelling and I hurried past a group who were tending somebody who appeared to be holding his belly and contents in place with his hands. I couldn't help but reflect that that could easily have been my state only a short time ago and the prospect was still very much around. People say that those who are in, or facing, danger in war always think it will be somebody else who will get clobbered not themselves. This is not true, certainly not as far as I was concerned. The possibilities of physical harm overtaking my person were always apparent to me and in no way lessened during the next two years.

Arriving once more with Sergeant Oakley and the other drivers, I took my last quad to fetch the first gun. Again I dashed up the road and over the ditch; I made for the same building and hoped somehow that we could manhandle No 2 gun over to the quad. On the way up the road I saw Major Hamilton crouching behind a large boulder and he gave the thumbs up as I went past. Then, to my amazement, I saw Steve Lindsay waving to me with a broad grin. Steve was a troop commander in 'C' Battery and we'd always got on well together. He said afterwards that his troop had been deployed east of Beja. Nothing was happening and he'd heard I was in trouble and had motored up to see if he could lend a hand. Seeing him there at that moment gave me an enormous lift.

Reaching the ruined building, I swung the quad round for our escape and there followed a blinding explosion. The quad shuddered and bits of it flew in all directions (it wasn't even bullet proof let alone shell proof) and inside it was an indescribable noise. Shell splinters and other bits of metal flew past me and it was my turn to shout, "Jesus Christ." I almost fell out of the door and saw the front wheel flattened plus sundry other disfigurements, it was clearly hopeless and meant that I'd have to leave the gun. I spent a little while in a trench smoking a cigarette and trying to recover myself before giving instructions about disabling the gun to ensure it couldn't be used again.

I told the gun team to make their way back on foot and said I was going to No 3 gun on the other side of the road. For some time now the forward infantry had been making their way back through my area and had suffered casualties while doing so. Several long files of silent, haggard-looking men made their way along the ditches. They had lived and fought in front of the infamous Green Hill and Bald Hill to the east of Sedjenane. Their conditions were crippling mud, bitter cold and constant heavy fire, certainly one of the worst sectors of the entire Tunisian front. They had taken more than men should be expected to take. Now they looked as I felt, dazed and humbled. They did as they were bid and they were past caring, there was nothing else to do.

On reaching No 3 gun position I found no gun and nobody there - only men's equipment was lying about. I aimlessly picked up a rifle and slung it on my shoulder then I began to walk back towards the woods and, I hoped, safety. Still the shells fell and countless times I collapsed into ditches and holes. Once I lay in a hole and thought I'd just stay there until it got dark and the shelling stopped.

We used to use the expression "Bomb happy" meaning that someone was shell shocked. A good example of such a state was Tom Cracknell at Robaa. At this stage I felt that something of the sort would happen to me. The two lost quads had virtually been blown from under me; the shell that had forced my infantry corporal and myself to part company had singed the front of my hair. Another couple of dozen had fallen close and still the ground around me was being plastered. I remember thinking, "Christ - how much more?"

In the end I crawled out and joined the tail-end of the infantry. They said nothing and I said nothing but I recall their sergeant major down the road shouting at me to keep up. Then, in a little while, I was picked up by Sergeant Oakley who came looking for me in a quad. Back at Battery HQ, Ham explained that Steve Lindsay and Sergeant Oakley had collected the 3rd gun with a borrowed gun tower from the mountain battery whom we had met at Tebourba. They had lost their guns so their battery commander had generously offered the vehicle to help us. He was a fine man and I wish I'd made his closer acquaintance.

Meantime I had stretched out on a camp bed and, apart from shaking, knew nothing until the morning. In 48 hours 6 Troop had travelled through the night, occupied a tiny bit of Tunisia that could never have been defended, suffered something of a nightmare and extricated themselves with the loss of one gun and two quads but no loss of life. It transpired that Ham had stopped a British tank on its way back and persuaded the tank commander to try to retrieve my abandoned gun. The result was that they lost the tank as well in the boggy ground. The crew were understandably furious and poor Ham bore the brunt of their wrath.

CHAPTER VIII

A PIANO AND A FELONY

A hot cup of tea woke me on the morning of March 5th and a little later I listened to the stories from my troop concerning their individual and collective escapes from disaster the previous day. Between us we agreed that we'd got off lightly and I learnt from Major Hamilton that we were to go back to Beja to rest and to wait for the remainder of the battery to join us. 6 Troop prepared itself to move in splendidly quick time and by mid-morning we were on the way. The gunless detachment spread themselves among the other three quads and their occupants without waiting for specific invitations. We returned to Beja and crossed over a small bridge near Djebel Abiod on which the Germans laid mines two nights later. During this period of rest, which lasted a week to ten days, we missed the follow-up to Sedjenane. Our parachute brigade took over that sector and so clashed with the German parachutists. The fighting became extremely fierce with attacks and counter-attacks coming one upon another. 7 Troop of 'B' Battery was involved in all this and I had to send them one of my quads since one of theirs had been disabled. After some time, and in those circumstances a week can seem longer than a month, 7 Troop were relieved by the Sherwood Foresters and finally got out with the troop more or less intact.

In fact I was saddened by the news of one of my sergeants. A week or two before we were sent to Sedjenane, I was ordered to surrender one of my sergeants and send him to join 8 Troop who were operating in an area not far from Beja. At this time 8 Troop had been deployed behind me during our recent troubles and, as soon as they could be withdrawn, they were sent to join me at Beja. I learnt that Sergeant Agambar, whom I had sent, had been killed in his slit-trench by a shell. I have thought ever since that he might have been alive now if I had sent someone else. He is one of those I think of at every Armistice Day.

Meanwhile 6 Troop were relaxing at Beja which had been a rather attractive little town on a hillside. By this time it had been badly knocked about by a number of Stuka raids. Many of the houses must have been occupied by French people judging by their appearance and contents. Now the place was empty and stricken in countenance; the only signs of life were a small number of Arabs and a few dogs and cats. Inevitably the men set out to explore the place, mostly in the hope of finding some vino.

After one of these sorties I was approached by a couple of sergeants who told me that a piano had been discovered buried under rubble in a bombed house. They pointed out that the house had lost its roof and that the piano wouldn't survive long in its present state - could they collect it? I gave the matter scant consideration because the idea appealed to me. I'd always loved the piano and had strummed all the popular dance tunes at home whenever I was at a loose end. As an accompaniment to Bombardier Brown's trumpet this could be fun and a huge bonus when the battery was out of the line. Besides, to leave it would ensure its destruction, so I said, "Why not?"

Without further delay some 6 men set off in the troop's 3-tonner truck and returned an hour and a half later triumphantly bearing an upright piano in excellent condition apart from a few scratches. They'd not only exhumed the piano but had manoeuvred it down a small flight of stairs which were themselves covered with rubble. Of course we gave it a trial run and a few choruses of 'You'll Never Know', 'White Cliffs of Dover', and others rang out across those Tunisian hills.

Yet another quad was now taken from me. On arriving at Beja I had two of my own surviving quads plus one loaned by the mountain pack artillery. I'd sent one to help 7 Troop and now two men arrived with a message from the commanding officer of the pack gunners asking apologetically for his quad back. He had been given some replacement guns and now needed the means of moving them. I gladly returned the vehicle with a note of appreciation and thanks. But now I was left with my 15 cwt truck, a 3-tonner and one quad. This was a bit awkward when very shortly we were required to move with the whole of 'B' Battery to some place just on the Algerian border called Sakiet Sidi Yussef.

6 Troop struggled through the all night march from Beja with one quad, the 3-tonner and my 15 cwt truck pulling the guns, not forgetting the piano. We were allocated our space in an area that seemed all trees, and very wet, dripping trees at that. All we wanted was some hot food and then to be left to sleep for about a week. Instead I was ordered by the colonel to get my troop ship-shape and to prepare some convincing war-like gun positions for a demonstration to a Turkish delegation who would be accompanied by the usual brass hats. I think this was part of a broader entertainment designed to induce the Turks to enter the war on our side. Watching 6 Troop knock out dummy tanks with considerable flair and aplomb was, as it turned out, not enough to persuade the Turkish government that to follow our cause would be to their advantage.

Nevertheless this unexpected diversion served to shake up our spirits and to ensure that we washed away the outward muck of war. Meantime the regiment had arranged itself on a regimental footing. That is to say that there was an established cookhouse producing acceptable food, tents were erected so that everyone could eat and sleep in the dry. An officers' mess tent appeared which meant that, for the first time since leaving Ayr race course in Scotland, we were able to meet fellow regimental officers and to exchange experiences. We also learnt of the casualties among us. Then, not least, my piano was taken without my permission to the officers' mess. Ham was not a little surprised by its appearance.

It now transpired that the brigadier, Tiger, whom I have described earlier in the account of the Bou Arada battle, decided that some sort of concert would be good for the divisional artillery morale. He called for his brigade major, who is a kind of administration expert, and he called for his fiddlers three and told them to arrange something. He insisted that there must be talent among the four regiments, at which one of his advisors was able to inform him, with some enthusiasm, that the 72nd Anti-Tank Regiment had a piano.

I had it on the best authority, from the informer himself, that Tiger's response was electrifying. It seems there followed a number of messages flowing between his HQ and my regiment which resulted in first my colonel and then Major Hamilton presenting themselves before him. The gist of it all was that Tiger had very pronounced views upon looting, and an act of looting that had been instigated by one of his officers was something that brought him almost to phonetic paralysis. The outcome was that he ordered that I should be placed on trial before a court martial. I gather that my battery commander and my colonel had spoken as best they could on my behalf, but as yet I knew nothing about any of this. It was not until many weeks later that I heard the story.

The morning following Tiger's orders saw the arrival of a dispatch rider with a message for my colonel. The CO set off in his car for Tiger's HQ where he presented the brigadier with the message he'd just received. The message had come from the brigadier commanding the infantry battalions at Sedjenane. I'd had a few words with him during the withdrawal of my guns. Leaning on his walking-stick, he had offered me words of encouragement as I dodged about the place. It seems that this brigadier had written a few sentences concerning myself and the situation pertaining at Sedjenane. The message ended with his recommendation for my award of the MC.

Tiger was a proud man but was even prouder of his command. He expected all those under him to give of their best and to follow the traditions of the Royal Artillery. Some might say that he carried this philosophy too far, if anything went wrong he considered it reflected upon his overall group of gunners. Conversely, if anything went well there was a similar overall reflection. The fact that someone of his own rank, from another division, had sent that message, left him disarmed as it were. But he melted to the extent that I was never even reprimanded for the episode, though I remember I had to submit a report explaining why I had lost a gun and two quads. About four months later Tiger held a regimental parade in order to present awards to another officer and myself. As he pinned my ribbon onto my chest he said, "One military cross in exchange for one piano, you bugger."

Nevertheless, that piano survived the Tunisian campaign and was played consistently by me and by others in the course of time. It had been painted with the regimental colours in one corner, the name Sedjenane with the date in the opposite corner and my name at the top of the front, all in gold paint. It was used by one or two visiting American bands and concert parties in the interval between the African and Italian campaigns. It was also used by an ENSA party which included Beatrice Lilley when they came to Tunis. Tiger even gave permission for the piano to be taken to Italy but in the act of lifting it by crane onto a ship, it was dropped and smashed on Philipville docks. A sad end to a noble instrument.

CHAPTER IX

FONDOUK

In December 1942 the 1st Army comprised about half of one division: to call it an army at all was an absurd exaggeration. There was a part of 78th British Infantry Division, a very small part of 6th Armoured Division, some paratroops and a few Americans. These tiny forces were given the task of capturing Tunis and thus entrapping Rommel's Afrika Corps between the 8th Army in the south and us in the Tunisian hills in the north. Only somebody overlooked the probability of intervention by the other side. During the months of January, February and March both sides had been intent upon building up their strengths in anticipation of a show-down in Tunisia. At the same time they had been fighting to test the strength and disposition of the opposition and to secure essential passes and supply routes in preparation for the confrontation.

The so-called 1st Army relied upon long-distance convoys from the UK and from America for its growth and for its supplies, whereas the enemy were able to build their strength much more quickly by ferrying troops a comparatively short hop from Italy. Even when landed in North Africa, our lines of communication were hundreds of miles but the German needs of food, fuel and ammunition were close at hand and easily brought to the battle areas.

The consequences were that 1st Army had been almost entirely on the defensive, trying to contain larger forces which had far superior armament. In addition, our situation was made infinitely worse by our complete lack of fighter cover and consequent exposure to Luftwaffe attacks on troops and supplies alike. The Germans had hard-surfaced aerodromes around Tunis from which they could operate regardless of weather. There were no such blessings on our side; the streaming rain and cold, plus deep soggy mud, prevented all attempts to prepare ground for any kind of aircraft.

Now the situation was changing, for most of the above disadvantages were slowly being remedied. By April the weather had changed dramatically. Forward bases of aerodromes were constructed for fighters and medium bombers, large stocks of supplies were established not far from the fighting troops. Our numbers had been augmented to the tune of three British infantry divisions, two American divisions and a re-equipped force of French-speaking troops. The 6th Armoured Division had exchanged its few remaining Valentine and Crusader tanks for a complete set of American Shermans. Our three cavalry regiments must have numbered over 120 tanks between them, all of them at least a match for the German Panzers except for the latest Mark VI Tiger. For the first time the 1st Army was taking on the size and shape of an army and was beginning to flex its muscles.

After the collapse of Rommel's successes in the region of Kasserine, it was obvious that the Afrika Corps would drive hard for the coastal hills above Enfidaville. The only chance of preventing this was a break out by the 1st Army through the southern hills east of Ouseltia or Pichon, where Bobby Burrowes and I had gone to visit the French back in January. These hills constituted a steep wall and bastion extending south from the mountains around Pont du Fahs down to the Faid pass east of Kasserine, a distance of some 120 miles as the crow flies. Once the German columns reached the very formidable hills short of Pont du Fahs, they would be relatively safe. If the allied forces could burst through those hills and race towards Kairouan and cut the coastal road in the neighbourhood of Sousse, then the story might be different.

At the beginning of April, 'B' Battery was ordered to move south-east to the Kesra Forest again, not far from Pichon, to be grouped with the 26th Armoured Brigade. In fact, the whole of 6th Armoured Division was being assembled in that area, for what purpose we had yet to learn. The journey was memorable only for the choking clouds of white dust thrown up by the columns of vehicles and tank transporters. From the forest we were ordered to a forming-up area at a place called El Ala which, on acquaintance, was nothing but a collection of cactus groves in the sand.

By the next day most of the divisional artillery was in the same area. The traffic jams were unbelievable and the delays in marrying up one set of troops with another rivalled those experienced by fathers waiting for the delivery of their first born. Add to these distractions the fact that El Ala was the greatest source of deep, soft sand in North Africa, and you have the recipe for chaos. Every one who ventured more than a few yards off the road went down to their axles. All over the landscape the sand was flying off the shovels of despairing soldiers and really it would have been funny if the situation had been less urgent.

On April 8th the Armoured Brigade group was told that its job was to break through the Fondouk gap and to make all speed for Kairouan which was the Holy City of Islam, or one of them. Kairouan stood on a road junction and on one of the two routes available to the Afrika Corps retreating northwards towards Enfidaville. Fondouk stood, or rather sat, between two large dominating hills. One was to the immediate north and the other to the south; both of them were part of the long range referred to a little earlier. Between the two of them, running east and west through this extremely narrow valley or pass, was a deep wadi.

The intention was to launch a full-blown assault in this sector. To the north, which was our left as we faced the enemy, the Hampshires from 78th Division plus the French were to attack in the hills surrounding Pichon. The Welsh Guards from our division were to take the northern hill overlooking Fondouk and the American 34th Infantry Division were to take the southern hills. This would enable the sappers to deal with any mines and so allow our tanks through the gap and on to the east. The attack was to start early on the 8th in order to reach Kairouan by the 9th, otherwise General Alexander believed the Germans retreating before the 8th Army would escape. But due to the cock-up of formations of the division getting bogged down in the sands of El Ala, the Guards and Americans couldn't start until dawn on the 9th.

At Pichon, the Hampshires were going well and were pressing on beyond the village itself. My battery was moved forward into the plain facing Fondouk, taking its place behind our tanks. There we waited with many others for the signs that the two looming hills in front were in our hands. The battle of Fondouk was memorable in many ways and the first of them was my view of the Welsh Guards on that first day. They came past us in their open-sided transport, moving to their debussing point. They were not cheerful, they were not morose, they were singing.

81

We were sitting in our vehicles trying to keep warm, at this early hour it was very windy and bitterly cold. We were contemplating the coming day's events and knew that the Germans could not afford to lose those hills, yet the Guards were singing. The strange thing was that their singing was in unison. Succeeding trucks would be singing the same words of the same hymns as the one in front. We recognised the Welsh hymns even though we didn't know the words and there was an almost irresistible urge to join in, yet somehow it would have been intrusive to do so. Those were solemn and moving moments and the choking feeling that gripped me had nothing to do with the dust.

Soon our 25-pounders broke their silence and launched the softening up barrage. They were joined by the American artillery trying to flatten the hills on our right front. Heaven knows how many shells were screaming over our heads at any given moment but both hills in front were erupting in sheets of flame, smoke and flying debris. The noise was, to say the least, impressive. The nearest likeness might be to stand in the centre of a particularly violent thunderstorm for 20 minutes or so. Then, as the early daylight began to improve, we could see those guardsmen begin to climb the lower slopes of their objective. The barrage was still falling but now the gunners were concentrating on the higher part of the hill.

The guardsmen moved slowly in extended lines. As I looked through my glasses there didn't seem to be much cover for them, but there must have been hollows and cuttings in the ground because as one man left a certain spot another would take his place. Now there were spouts of earth in amongst the distant figures and the sound of the bursting mortar bombs followed moments later. To these were added the snarling rattle of machine-guns. I saw one man fall, then another and another. The barrage from our guns and the Americans' had stopped, so the Germans, who had been well dug into the hillsides, were able to sweep the slopes with their machine-guns with impunity.

The first outbursts of German fire had inflicted quite a few casualties on the exposed guardsmen. However, the others began to identify the whereabouts of a machine-gun or at least the direction from which the fire was coming. They would dart for cover behind a rock or fold in the ground and start to work in groups. Some would fire with intensity at whatever they had seen as the danger whilst a couple of others would dash for the next cover nearer the target. Sometimes it seemed they would make their dash when the Germans were firing at some other target. If one group of men was pinned down, another group would work round some other way. At times there seemed to be no movement by anyone, then suddenly figures would be scurrying upwards, sideways and even downwards all over the place. Our own mortar platoons came more into the action as German positions were positively located. Again the 25-pounders opened up, only this time onto specific targets. Their forward observation officers brought down concentrated fire on enemy machine-gun posts, or enemy trenches, or wherever it was needed. They blew hell out of everything that looked suspicious. All the time men could be seen falling when hit and a few dragging themselves towards their colleagues. Watching we felt helpless and angry.

Eventually the attacking troops could no longer be seen, some had reached the top, some had gone round the left hand side where there was more cover. The noise of the fighting continued but from different parts of the hills. Meantime, there was trouble with the Americans on the right. Instead of following in upon their artillery barrage, the infantry had not reached their start line. They had failed to send their troops into their preliminary positions and there was some confusion about the zero hour. Whatever the reasons, they attacked long after they should have done and when the Germans were prepared and waiting for them. Even then they swarmed forward in reckless fashion as if they were expecting a welcome.

The result was disaster; the Americans were new to warfare and it showed. They sent waves of men at those hills and, although they had plenty of fire power, it was as nothing compared with the fire the Germans directed at them. They were devastated and numbers of them were running back as numbers of others were running forward. The fighting was bitter but it was one-sided and by the end of April 10th the hills on the right or south of Fondouk were still in German hands. Fortunately for us, the Welsh Guards had done everything and more than expected of them. Their history may be swathed in glorious achievements but it's certain that they achieved greatness on this day. There were stories of single guardsmen, NCOs and officers charging German fortifications and machine-gun posts with tommy-guns or hand grenades. They lost so many of their number in that action but they inflicted huge losses on the enemy.

That night was spent still sitting in our trucks and reflecting sadly on the awful happenings of the day. The cold wind still swept through the gap in the hills from the east, dark figures passed carrying people on stretchers, motor cycles rumbled up and down and across the valley with messages. The German gunners sent over a few shells into this ample target but not many. The problem now was what to do about the southern hills? We rather assumed there would be a simultaneous attack at dawn by perhaps another of our Guards' regiments from the north and by the Americans again from the west. With our tanks to support them, we thought success would be assured. Instead, at dawn our 25-pounders started where they'd left off but there was no sign of an infantry attack. Too much time had been lost so our divisional commander was ordered to crash through with his tanks.

The second spectacle of this battle was then set in motion. The 26th Armoured Brigade led with the 17th/21st Lancers. They moved forward in their new Sherman tanks and I imagine that the crews were pretty keyed up since they too had witnessed the events of the previous day. As they closed on Fondouk, the leading squadron stopped and wirelessed back that they could see a massive mine-field in front. They were told to continue on and try to blow a path through the mine-field. And so it was, the tanks crunched their way into the mine-field and were blown up one after another. As one tank blew up, another behind would overtake it and deliberately drive onto succeeding mines in a kind of broad path. The crews were not necessarily hurt because, for the most, only the tank tracks were blown off. Nevertheless, as the crews climbed out of their disabled tanks they came under fire from the German positions. There was a difference though. The tanks still had their 75mm guns and heavy machine-guns left operational and they were used in reply whenever possible.

The great majority of the 17th/21st tanks were lost in that mine field (but most were recovered later and repaired) yet they had forged a way through and, just as importantly, had put the Germans on the hill to flight. The 17th/21st Lancers, having done their job, were replaced by the Lothian and Border Horse. They followed their colleagues' footsteps as far as possible until at the exit from the mine field they fell foul of a couple of 88mm guns. These guns were the scourge of our armour, they were not only very powerful but extremely accurate. The tanks couldn't get a crack at the guns without exposing themselves and being knocked out, so here was a problem. The 88mm's couldn't be neutralised by our guns because they were tucked in close behind the hills. There weren't any handy infantry to go in and sort them out, at least not until the Americans arrived in force. Nor was it known just how many 88s were dug in round and about. The Lothians saw one of these guns dug into the side of the wadi that ran twisting through the battlefield. They climbed carefully up and round the lower slopes of the hill to get to the right spot and then, a couple of shell bursts and the gun was smashed together with several of the gun crew. This incident was the secret of success.

Somebody in one of the tanks, I have no idea who, hit upon the idea of the wadi as an approach route to get at the other 88mm's and to get behind the German positions. Accordingly several tanks made their way along the bottom of the wadi; only the turrets could be seen above ground and sometimes not even that. The turret is very thick in armour-plate and so the tanks had the advantage. Amazingly, the Germans had omitted lay mines in the wadi. It was not long before the 88mm guns were dealt with and there followed a rush of squadrons of tanks pouring through the gap. The battle of Fondouk was over and the whole of the 6th Armoured was ordered through with all haste.

In our turn my battery moved towards the Fondouk gap; the scene all around was one of wreckage and havoc. We passed the dozens of 17th/21st Lancers' tanks, blackened by the explosions and some of them burnt out, others were still burning. We passed the pock-marked hills rent by shellfire. The whole area reeked of smoke and burnt earth. Then we passed rows upon rows of American dead; they were sewing them up in blankets and putting them in orderly fashion beside the road, presumably to be collected. It was a horribly morbid sight and none of us wanted to look at them. Poor sods, they never really had a chance and in a day or two they'd be forgotten except by their mates.

People talk and write about bravery in action. Just occasionally there are acts of bravery in war, selfless acts perhaps to help another, but mostly bravery is enacted where a person has little or no choice or, very often, out of sheer fury. There was a sergeant whose company was counter attacking a hill near Bou Arada. His comrades had been slaughtered all around him; as they neared the top the order was given to retire. He stood up yelling, "Fuck this - fuck this!" and rushed the enemy firing his tommy-gun all the way until they killed him. Similar scenes were enacted by the Welsh Guards at Fondouk, and at the end, the survivors must have wondered why? Men do not give their lives in battle for a cause, they do their bloody damnedest to stay alive. They are not interested in whether their actions will shorten or prolong the war so long as they are alive when it does end. The only men who look forward to a battle are those who've never seen one.

Beyond the pass at Fondouk the whole world opened up, or so it seemed. The northern hills spread gradually away from us leaving a wide open space. The southern hills ended as soon as we'd driven through the bottleneck; they formed a high rocky ridge going due south as far as one could see. Behind them was an enormous flat plain spreading for miles to the coast. That plain was a sea of wild flowers - it was totally different from any thing we had seen in Tunisia, it was wonderful.

* * * * * * * * *

The third spectacle of this battle was now unfolded. The job of our division was to race eastwards to intercept and destroy the retreating columns of the Afrika Corps. This obviously required tanks, it might and probably would require guns and, to be on the safe side, some infantry must be available. In addition there were all the necessary supplies, signals, medical services and so forth. We were about to advance deep into enemy territory and so would be vulnerable on all sides.

The division thereupon formed up on the plain to the east of Fondouk in a huge box. On the outside there were the Derbyshire Yeomanry armoured cars who were fast moving and the eyes and ears of the division. Next came the tanks spread across the front and the two sides - the Lothian and Border Horse and the 16th/5th Lancers all in their Shermans. (The 17th/21st had no tanks left for the operation at this stage). Inside the tanks were the gunner regiments; the 12th RHA on one side of the box, the Ayrshire Yeomanry on the other and the 72nd Anti-Tank Regiment across the front. The 51st Light Ack-Ack Regiment was scattered in various places, some of them in positions around Fondouk. Working towards the centre, there were the 10th Rifle Brigade, the other Guards regiments - the Coldstreams and the Grenadiers, then lastly came all the echelons of supplies in the soft centre.

It took a while to assemble this array of hardware and while we waited we looked about us at the reverse side of Fondouk. There were German gun pits, destroyed vehicles and guns, weapons thrown away, litter and personal effects of German soldiers. In the reverse side of the southern hill there was a very large dark cave. It had obviously been used as a head quarters and was capable of housing a lot of people. The Germans had left a fair number of their badly wounded in this cave. I suppose somebody must have found and seen to them but we had no time.   The order to move was given and the 6th Armoured Division numbering I don't know how many thousand troops, started to gather speed across that beautiful plain. Hundreds of vehicles, nearly a hundred tanks, about 150 guns and all the rest, were charging in box formation at 18mph behind the enemy lines. This must have presented the most impressive spectacle of modern warfare. I remember thinking what a mess we were making of the flowers.

During this cross country march there was no danger from enemy troops because we were leaving them behind, and anyway all those in the near vicinity were by now prisoners. The alarm bells must have been ringing loudly in enemy circles however. We expected and received maximum attention from the Luftwaffe. Stuka dive-bombers came again and again, screeching down on anybody and everybody. Messerschmitts swooped on us and their guns made a shuddering roar as the ground was torn apart by their impact. We had no cover and all we could do was to stop, wait to see if they were diving upon us individually and, if so, run like hell to one side. There were one or two tanks knocked out by the Stukas and, needless to say, quite a lot of vehicles set on fire. Even so, all of this did nothing to hinder our progress.

Kairouan was about 20 miles east of Fondouk. When we had reached within about 5 miles, and could easily see the taller buildings of the town, the box came to a halt. The armoured cars and some of the tanks continued south-east and others continued north-east. In a while there were sounds of gunfire and the familiar noise of conflict. Kairouan was declared an 'open' city and our tanks had caught some of the rear German columns late on this afternoon and early evening of April 11th. The rest of us were parcelled up to harbour for the night. We anti-tank gunners were required to deploy ourselves to protect the soft centre of the division against attack from any direction. At last we were able to cook some food and brew some hot tea, the first hot food for two days. That night there were a number of fires burning a few miles away; they were some of those caught by our tanks and armoured cars. But we'd been too late to catch the main columns of Rommel's army. We were off again at dawn of April 12th, this time heading due north along an axis running parallel to the road to Enfidaville. Sometime in the late morning the leading tanks met opposition and 'B' Battery were told to deploy on the right to protect the flank whilst the armour could deal with the problem ahead. We troop commanders were hurrying and scurrying about getting our guns in position and all the while the enemy were lobbing shells at us. It's easy to say so and so was being shelled, or we were being shelled and then to dismiss the fact as being just a nuisance. In fact, being shelled is both frightening and very dangerous; nearly all our casualties, and there were a good many, were caused by shellfire. Personally I would rather be bombed because you could see what was coming and you knew as soon as it was over.

Although there were enemy tanks two or three miles to our right, they did not venture towards us. I think they were there to protect the remnants of their escaping forces making for the hills. We came out of action at dusk and Ham asked me to take the battery to a map reference near a farm at Bordj at the base of the hills on our left. He was going ahead to find out what was wanted of us in the morning; he went off in the direction of the hills and with a request from us to get the kettle on.

* * * * * * * *

By the time the battery had recovered all the guns and formed up on the road, or track, it was dark. We moved off, as always without lights, with me leading and went along nicely for a while, then the track came to the edge of a deep wadi. We couldn't cross there so I had to make a trip on a motor cycle along the bank of the wadi until I could find a suitable place to cross. This done, the battery followed dutifully and crossed the hazard successfully. After that we could find no sign of a track to follow and decided to set off across country.

Very professionally I took a bearing from my map to our destination and then worked out the special calculations to be made for my compass to relate this bearing to the stars. I had to run a sufficient distance from our vehicles to take any bearings otherwise the metal would distort the compass readings. We had been told all about this sort of thing back in the UK but this was quite another

86

matter. I had a strong impression that, had I taken a vote, it would have been one of 'no confidence' in my navigation. Fortunately I had other means at my disposal which I did not disclose immediately .

The contretemps encountered by the armour during the day had left a number of tanks and other vehicles burning on the field of play. I'd noticed a couple of bonfires in the far distance before we crossed the wadi, which were roughly in the direction I thought we needed. Accordingly I steered a course for these fires as faithfully as the ground would allow. Our progress was slow and there were sundry diversions for various reasons. My optimism was eventually rewarded when we came upon a road where we turned right and, after a further ¼ hour, we were met by Ham who had no idea why we'd come from the direction I pointed out. We were much relieved since we had no idea where the enemy were. Ham took us to a kind of basin in the ground which he had ear-marked for our night's harbour.

We distributed the guns around the rim of this basin by way of protection and rolled our blankets on the ground. We lit our tins of sand to make ourselves some tea and, being more than a little weary, we were soon asleep. Weary or not, our sleep was short-lived. Suddenly there was a hellish banging and crashing that caused all of us to leap to our feet. The firing of guns was accompanied by the sound of tanks moving and came from a couple of miles up the road to the north. We stood by our guns in readiness - we could see fireworks and tracer ammunition flying all over the place. This shattering shindig lasted for less than ½ hour and then gradually subsided into occasional explosions.

We stood to for perhaps another 3/4 hour then, doubling the guard, the rest of us returned to our blankets. It was about 2.00 or 2.30 in the morning when I felt someone shaking me. The reason was that, in defiance of all that was reasonable or possible, Ted Newman had arrived with rations and the water cart. How in the name of absurdity he had traced us to our harbour, God and Ted alone knew. If I'd been taken ten miles away I should have been unable to find us again. Ted had come twenty miles and possibly more, and he had brought mail with him. Father Christmas could not have equalled this feat and we were appreciative. I cannot remember a time when Ted failed to reach he battery with his supplies and it was something of an achievement.

Soon after 3.00 am we once again wrapped ourselves into blankets. At daylight we looked around whilst others were preparing some breakfast and found some dead Germans not far away. We buried these unfortunates and I happened also to find a pair of 10 x 50 Zeiss binoculars. These I used for the rest of the war and brought them back to England when I returned. (I eventually sold them in Bideford, North Devon, in 1951 when I was on my honey-moon.) Our breakfast was interrupted by a Sherman tank approaching from the plain in front of us. I went to meet the tank and was greeted by a lieutenant troop commander who appeared to be dressed in blue. He climbed out of his turret and jumped down; he was wearing pale blue silk pyjamas with a silk scarf around his neck. He asked me if I'd be good enough to tell him where the bloody hell we were. I did my best and invited him and his crew to have some breakfast.

Once again we formed with others into the box and began to advance northward. This time the box was smaller and must have split into two because our tank force seemed to be only the Lothian and Border Horse; the Lancers were probably working further to the east with the remainder of the division. We passed the place where, last night, there was this private battle; there was plenty of evidence of German trucks and tanks which had been knocked out. We learnt that, in the darkness, we were not the only ones to have become lost, some of the Lothians had been wandering about and one squadron had followed another to a harbour area in the foothills near us. When they got there they discovered they had been following German tanks. The Germans drove in and dismounted, the Lothians promptly shot them up, hence the display.

We were following the long range of hills that were mentioned earlier and which extended south from the Pont du Fahs area, only this time we were on the other side of them, behind the German lines. It was a disquieting feeling for us not knowing what was going to come from where but it must have been a pretty sobering thought for the Germans. A large number of them were taken prisoner and they couldn't understand what had happened. They thought we were the 8th Army having reached this far much earlier than expected. They were not as far wrong in their belief as was generally thought.

Our progress was slow and faltering and the columns of soldiers kept trying to light their brew cans, but before the tea was ready the order to move would assuredly come. The dust of tanks hurrying here and there could be followed and disruptive bursts of shells would fall among us from time to time. Presently we were told to deploy the guns as of yesterday. We had to protect the right and rear of the force. The tanks had come up against some firm opposition and wanted to free all the available armour for the purpose of clearing it.

After the guns had been settled in their positions, I wandered off to take a look at an Italian tank that had been knocked out in the recent encounters. My curiosity was partly because there was something almost irresistible about viewing, at close quarters, a formidable enemy weapon that hours ago was being used to destroy you. Whereas before, it was a symbol of a powerful and ever-threatening enemy, it was now reduced to a shoddy blackened hulk of steel and wreckage that represented nothing that ever evoked a sensation of awe or respect. It was a bit like laying a ghost and it made you realise that the enemy was just as vulnerable as we were.

The inside of this tank was a mess and I didn't investigate too closely. Then, as I walked round to the other side, I saw human brains scattered on the ground beyond. Suddenly the scene became personalised. I left hurriedly wishing I hadn't come.

In fact we stayed in our positions for the rest of the day and were dive-bombed fourteen times in six hours and, to add seasoning, we were strafed by Messerschmitts in between times. Some time in the afternoon we saw trucks and armoured cars approaching from behind. As they got nearer we could see, through glasses, they were different and all motoring along the road. Soon a cheer went up and they and we ran to meet each other - it was the 8th Army.

We celebrated with much hand-shaking and back slapping. We exchanged packets of cigarettes because we had nothing else to offer. There was a good bit of verbal cross-fire; they wanted to know what we were doing here, and did we want them to shift the Jerries while we made them a cup of tea? Our people hoped they'd had a good time paddling in the sea and enjoying overlong leaves in Cairo, Alex and Tripoli.

88

In the late evening we were ordered back to Bordj, our division had been told to break off the battle and to hand over to the 8th Army. The next day we spent watching the 8th Army's yellow trucks moving up towards the hills. In point of fact, that was as far as they ever reached. The following day the 6th Armoured moved back to Fondouk and thence to the Kesra Forest again. From there my battery returned north to the El Aroussa area which was north-west of Bou Arada. We came to rest on the side of a very pleasant sunny ridge and here we were issued with KD (khaki drill). Fondouk had been an experience, a sad experience, an exhilarating experience and a proud experience. I learned too that Peter Heslop of 'A' Battery had been hit by a shell at Fondouk and lost a leg.

ENCOUNTER at ROBAA (Chap vi)

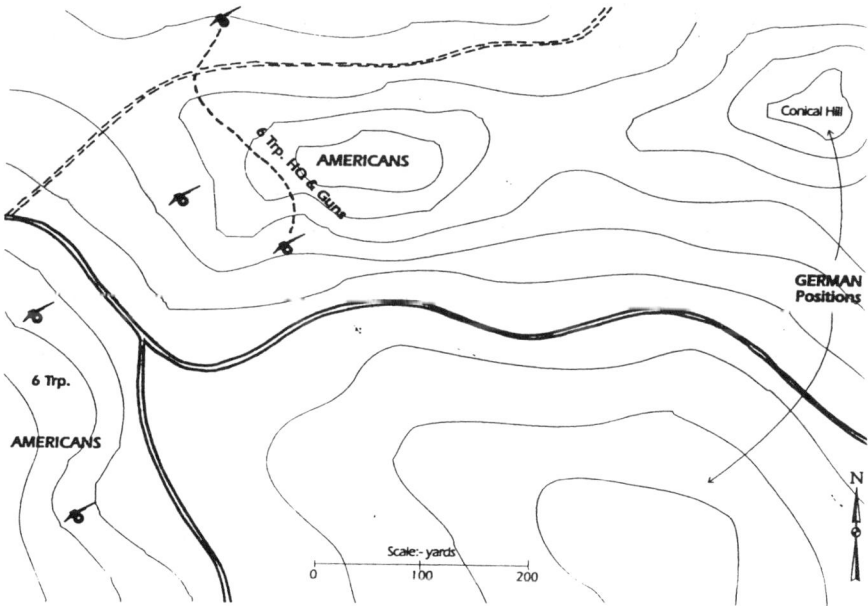

CHAPTER X

DJEBEL KOURNINE

Khaki drill was a pleasant change of clothing but it had certain drawbacks: it was obviously cooler, the weather was getting hotter every day - and above all it was clean. However, the knee length socks, which were part of the guise, were not impervious to flies. Nor, for that matter, were our bare arms and knees. The flies which concentrated upon us and upon our food whenever we tried to eat, looked very much like the common house fly at home; the principal difference being in their armament. They were tough and carried a lance which when properly directed would penetrate army socks without difficulty. Some would say that their powers of penetration rivalled those of the 88mm and they correspondingly inflicted a flesh wound that was not to be despised. Such were our problems during the next few days as we sat and slept and wrote our letters home and thought our private thoughts.

On one of those days Ham brought a young lieutenant from our paratroops to see me. He left us to talk and the visitor explained that shortly he and his chaps were going to drop on the Tunis airfields. Their task would be to destroy enemy aircraft and blow up buildings, ammunition and anything they could make a mess of. They would certainly have to fight their way out and back to our lines even if they didn't have to fight their way in. There was a definite limit to the quantity and weight of arms and ammunition they could carry with them and this was always a problem. He was on the scrounge and Ham had told him that I had acquired a small supply of German machine-guns and ammo during my travels. This was true and they had been used to let fly at low flying enemy fighters and Stukas. I wished him well and said I didn't think I'd change jobs and gave him the two machine-guns that 6 Troop had captured plus two long boxes of ammunition. The point was that they reckoned they could find more ammunition for the guns from the airfields and other places during their exploits.

During this first half of April there had been a general flare-up along the Tunisian front. The 1st Army was wrestling frantically to secure the launching sites for the final offensive on Tunis, Von Arnim's army and the Afrika Corps. Both sides knew this and Von Arnim was still being reinforced from Italy, in addition to the divisions from the Afrika Corps which had now joined him. Practically every square mile of German-held territory was fashioned by nature with defence in mind. The Germans were determined to give nothing away and saw no reason why they should not continue the Tunisian war indefinitely.

One of the keys, probably the most important and certainly the strongest, to opening the way to Tunis was Longstop Hill on the Medjez - Tebourba road. The hill where, back in December, 6 Troop had been the sole tenants for one night. The prospect of Longstop was daunting enough in itself, but there were a whole number of hills to be taken along the ridge to which Longstop belonged before the latter could be contemplated. Some of this was now achieved. While 6th Armoured was operating through Fondouk, the 78th Division was locked in a savage contest over those hills. It was hand to hand stuff with awful consequences to both sides. These were some of the strongest defences in this whole theatre of war and the subsequent stories of gallantry were many.

Perhaps the only alternative to an advance up the Medjez valley was a breakthrough in the Goubellat plain and on to the Pont du Fahs - Tunis road. This eventuality had not been overlooked by Von Arnim and the hills guarding this approach were also heavily fortified. Even so, 6th Armoured Division was concentrated south of Medjez el Bab in order to attempt another breakthrough. The start of this battle was delayed by the Germans beating us to it. Our two 25-pounder regiments had been deployed in the area of Banana Ridge in readiness for the coming tussle; our 'A' Battery anti-tank guns were also there to protect the 25-pounders.

The enemy attacked 24 hours before we were due to move with the 26th Armoured Brigade yet again. They came very close to our gun positions but were chased off finally by our own infantry. Then, while our 46th Infantry Division attacked at Bou Arada, a little to the south, and 78th Division were attacking to the north of us, our tanks wended their way through the hills south of Medjez towards Goubellat and the plain. It was April 18th and there was no preliminary bombardment for an infantry attack, since we already held these hills from which we were soon to emerge. Apart from the appalling dust from the tanks and following trucks, the scenery was singularly beautiful. The drenching winter rains and the cold had given way to hot sun; the result was a profusion of wild flowers and, in the plains, corn growing rapidly.

After an hour or so we had descended to the lower ground and the Goubellat plain opened out to our right. Our leading tanks were now about a mile ahead and had fanned out across a broad front. So far the advance had been peaceful enough and, significantly, we were not being bombed or strafed. The desert airforce and our RAF fighters had by now established air bases sufficient to ensure reasonable air cover for the first time and this made a welcome difference for us poor mortals on the ground.

All four troops of 'B' Battery continued to move forward slowly but not far behind the tanks. We had to pick our way carefully as we rode our vehicles and gun-towers across country - there were ditches and rocky outcrops to be negotiated. Whereas the tanks could scamper about as the mood took them - this was what they were built for - they behaved for all the world like packs of hounds let loose in the countryside. This, of course, was too good to last and before long there came the bangs of guns followed immediately by the exploding shells among the tanks ahead. We knew these first arrivals were not enemy field guns - there was not sufficient interval between bangs and explosions. They were almost certainly 88mm and, at once, the tanks scurried for cover.

The diagnosis was right but they were not 88mm anti-tank guns as such, they were two Mark VI Tiger tanks which carry 88mm guns. These two Tigers were hull down on the crest of a hill in front. The expression 'hull down' means what it says; the tank's hull is down behind a hill leaving only its turret above to enable it to fire. These two kept the whole of our tank force at bay for two or three hours. They could easily out-gun our Shermans and their armour-plating was so thick that they were immune to armour-piercing shells except at close range. Their vital statistics were as follows: weight 56 tonnes, 4 inch armour plating, length 20 feet 6 inches, height 9 foot 6 inches, width 12 foot 6 inches, armament two heavy machine guns 7.92mm, one 88mm gun which alone weighed 1½ tonnes; each round of ammunition was 3 feet long and weighed 33 lbs.

Eventually this difficulty was overcome partly by our 25-pounders concentrating fire on the Mark VI's, partly by our fighter/bombers giving them a nasty time, but mostly because our tanks out flanked them and threatened to get behind and cut them off. So once more the division moved on and this time it covered several miles before meeting the real resistance. The plain changed its nature to low undulating hills separated by flat areas and, here and there, a steep-sided outcrop of rocky ridges. The tanks had reached the mountainous region that was the main line of enemy defences. I use the term mountainous because the range of hills now facing us were far too large and menacing to be described as hills. In particular, straight ahead of us there rose, directly out of the plain, a twin-peaked massive rock structure with sheer rock face supported on either side by lesser hills which themselves were formidable. Further behind and more to our right was the huge forbidding mass of Djebel Zagouan, the highest mountain in Tunisia.

As we drew gradually nearer to this huge range of hills, we were all thinking that whatever came next was going to be both suicidal and bloody impossible. The twin-peaked monster in front of us merited a name to itself; on the map it was referred to as Djebel Bou Kournine, to all those who faced it unwillingly on our side it was known as Two Tittie Hill. By now things were getting warmer, the tanks were firing to our front, to our right and to our left. Shells were coming back at us from various directions and, as usual, nobody knew what was going on. My battery split into two groups, 5 and 7 Troops were put onto a sort of pimple on the left, and 6 plus 8 Troops were fanned out on the plain from where we were able to do precisely nothing. There we spent the night having dug some impressively deep trenches.

The night passed noisily with tanks lurching about all over the place creating chaos and a certain amount of panic. Added to this were the gratuitous offerings from the German artillery and a helping of bombs from the Luftwaffe. A few vehicles were hit during all this and those set on fire only served to encourage the Germans, but, considering the amount of transport that was spread around, we came off very lightly. Early next morning my troop, with 8 Troop, were moved forward to occupy a low rounded hill on the right. We moved under darkness and sited the eight guns of the two troops in a sort of hedgehog. We spread the vehicles as much as we could behind the hill and hoped that they were not in view from the German positions. Daylight found us still digging ourselves in but we had completed the difficult part of the operation. It was then I noticed that slightly behind our hill and further to the right was a large lake and beyond that a smaller one. They were in fact salt lakes, and we were quite pleased because they guarded our right flank.

We could now see that ours was the last undulating ridge before the German defences; we were separated by a flat area of plain and the distance between us was barely 2000 yards. There were no forces on our right until you reached the Bou Arada sector about 5 miles further south. Behind us over the left shoulder was more flat plain and more undulating ground on the left. Both those areas were pretty stiff with troops which was just as well, had it not been so we should have been blasted out of existence. The next day or two saw our tanks probing here and there, exchanging shots with the German guns and with some of their tanks. We did nothing but cling to our slit-trenches because we were shelled morning, noon and night. It was worse than usual because the German guns were not their normal field guns but much heavier. They blew dozens of craters in our little hill and on one afternoon our only medical assistant was nearly written off.

We had one doctor for the whole regiment and he had one assistant, Bombardier Postles, who naturally worked with him at regimental HQ. On this occasion we had Bombardier Postles with us for the first and only time. He was huddled in a trench about 50 yards from my troop HQ during one of the sessions of heavy shelling. Suddenly there were shouts amid the crashes of the bursting shells. Bombardier Postles had been three parts buried by a shell burst close to his trench; he was soon freed by the nearby gun detachment but was obviously shaken by his experience. He was very popular with our regiment but was never allowed to forget his short stay with the 'boys at the sharp end'.

On that same day something rather similar happened to my HQ personnel. We were also in our trench, the inhabitants of which included my troop sergeant, my driver, my DR Rowe, my batman Savage and myself. We were crouching as low as possible and from time to time we had earth and stones raining on top of us. It was customary on these occasions for Savage to express his feelings on the war in general, on Arabs, on Germans in particular and their lineage, to offer his resignation and his sympathy to the war workers at home. He was in full flow and had delivered himself of a few 'Bastards' of assorted descriptions when he augmented his outburst with a throaty bellow. To be accurate he bellowed several times concurrently and with increasing volume.

I was wedged to his immediate rear in the trench and was very much aware of the near miss we had just encountered. From the noise coming from Savage I thought he had been hit. He lost no time in explaining his circumstances and the fact that he had received a red hot splinter down the back of his shirt. I thrust my hand down his back and managed to grasp the jagged piece of metal. I promptly burnt my fingers and dropped it. He sent out further distress signals until I'd made a second attempt with better success. Having dropped the hot splinter to the bottom of the trench to be recovered later, I pulled Savage's shirt up and saw several red patches where he'd been burnt, but not too badly. I myself had a tender hand from pulling the blasted thing out, but Savage was in no mood to offer any thanks. The splinter was about one inch long and ½ inch wide and was not something to be easily forgotten by Savage.

* * * * * * * * *

Somebody decided that, to break the deadlock, the Guards should give a repeat performance of their attack at Fondouk, only this time instead of the Welsh it was to be the Coldstream Guards. Two troops from 'C' Battery were to go with the Guards and the objective was to occupy the hills and ridges either side of Djebel Kournine. Following that, a fighting patrol was to scale the Djebel itself to subdue the OP's on or near the summit.

Everything went wrong. The column of guardsmen and the anti-tank guns went off in absolute darkness past my position and out into the plain. Out there they lost their way and lost contact with their neighbours. They took hours to sort themselves out, by which time a heavy mist or fog had enveloped the whole area including my hill. At dawn the attack hadn't started and should have been aborted; instead the gunners were trying to dig themselves into rock and the guards were trying to do the same in the early slopes of the hills. At about 0600 hours the sun began quickly to lift the protective mist and the whole force was revealed to the Germans from their defences very close by. In a very few minutes the expected onslaught broke out. Rifles, machine-guns and mortar bombs were directed at the exposed guardsmen and gunners. Their vehicles were systematically set ablaze, the guns were obvious targets and, all in all, it was catastrophic.

There was only one course of action to be taken, that was to get out. Those who could grab a truck, that was a runner, set off for home as fast as they could go. Each vehicle was laden with soldiers and many of them were carrying wounded. The remainder were making their way back on foot and it was a sorry sight. After a while we saw a man, walking upright but dragging one leg, coming towards our hill. Two or three gunners ran to meet him, he was only about 150 yards away, and helped him in. They took him to Bombardier Postles who did his best to make him fit to travel back to the nearest forward aid post. The guardsman was smiling broadly not withstanding that one of his buttocks was practically shot away.

The two troops of 'C' Battery were pretty badly knocked about; I don't know the extent of their casualties, only the officers. The battery commander was quite badly wounded and did not return to the regiment. Of the two troop commanders, one was killed at the foot of the hills, the other was Steve Lindsay, who had come to see me at Sedjenane.

Steve had brought some of his people back in a gun tower and then had decided to go back to collect a gun. This was not only ridiculous, it was suicide. This was not done out of any sense of duty, it was his way of showing the enemy, and anyone else, that he was not given to running away and that he was a match for any bloody enemy. He drove across that plain and reached close to where the gun had been left. Then the quad was hit and set on fire. I hope Steve was killed at that moment, but later they found his remains in the driver's seat and identified him by a ring still on his finger. I was numbed when I heard this account. I am sure that if I had been at hand, I could have stopped him. It's a pity he wasn't wounded in the first place, it might have saved his life.

The next day the 1st Armoured Division from the 8th Army came to take over from 6th Armoured. Again there were expressions of rivalry between the two armoured divisions but the newcomers got no further than our leading tanks. That night I had to go back to meet the troop commanders who were going to relieve 8 Troop and my own and to bring them to our gun positions. I went in my 15 cwt truck with Bombardier Foster and Savage. It took me some time to find the relief party in the overall melee of trucks and tanks of two divisions and in darkness. However, we eventually met and had a chat about the general situation and the behaviour of the enemy in particular. We scrounged a cup of tea from somebody and set off back to the gun positions. Soon we heard aircraft overhead together with a host of light ack-ack shells bursting upstairs. We drove slowly along, winding our way be tween all the trucks and trying to find places of recognition. Bearing in mind the return journey I had made mental notes of features, burnt out vehicles etc.

There were frequent stops during this return journey. Sometimes I pulled up beside a friendly tank for protection against impending bombs, sometimes I stopped to explain to the others the points of recognition so they might find their way with their guns later on. In spite of caution we were caught off balance by one enemy plane. We heard the bomb falling before hearing the aeroplane. Foster and I both leapt out and flattened ourselves on the ground whereas Savage got as far as the tail-board before being helped on his way by the blast of the bomb. It exploded about 40 yards away on our right and I'm bound to say, sent our heads reeling; it also ripped a number of holes through my 15cwt truck. We walked over and inspected the sizable crater made by the bomb; it had thrown quite a bank of earth around the rim. Amazingly no-one had been hurt by this bomb which had fallen in quite a congested area.

On the last 3/4 mile forward to the gun positions we passed a number of burning vehicles and one ammunition truck that gave us a bit of trouble as it blazed and exploded its contents in all directions. At last we arrived at our hill and our friends were shown the defence system that we had evolved. We then had to wait for them to make haste to collect their guns and return to complete the relief. At least they had trenches already dug which would provide some safety for them. The change took practically the entire night and we were relieved in more senses than one to get out and away before daylight. Fortunately we were not shelled during the actual take-over, but we heard later that those who took over our positions on that little hill suffered heavily in the subsequent week. They lost most of their officers and many of their gun teams in the pernicious shellfire. They had used three troops in place of our two and were that much thicker on the ground. Even so, I feel sure they must have shown themselves much more than we did; if they had stayed in their holes I doubt that their casualties would have been so heavy.

CHAPTER XI

MEDJEZ AND BEYOND

Throughout this inadequate story, I have attempted to confine myself to facts as nearly as I can remember them and to resist the temptation to turn events into more exciting narrative. For example, I might have dwelt more fully on the plight of the Americans at Robaa. They had gone and their dead were left lying about in the saddle between the hills. I had wondered what on earth to do about them before the Americans returned. It would have been an unhealthy place to be if the bodies had been left much longer. Yet, having been left stranded by them, I didn't fancy the task of turning 6 Troop into a party of grave diggers.

It would not be difficult to decorate this account with lurid pen pictures from time to time. But this is not a whole-hearted story of war, it is merely a tale of events as experienced by one troop of gunners and by me as their troop commander. Having said that, I think it appropriate to say something about feelings, including those between battles.

It has been said that war consists of short periods of fear and long periods of boredom. This may be true of many but in our case the fear and the boredom were about evenly balanced. Apart from the spell when 6th Armoured Division was taken out of the line to Sakiet Sidi Youssef in the second half of March, the intervals between the times spent under fire were never longer than a few days. Those few days were spent catching up on sleep, writing letters, doing some washing if we had enough water and such matters. All the time our ears were tuned in for the sound of a gun or a mortar being fired. You may be well out of range and you know this perfectly well, yet you can't prevent yourself from being nervously alert.

Similarly, we never recovered from the attentions of the Luftwaffe during the first 4½ months of the Tunisian Campaign. Scarcely a day had passed without us being bombed by Stukas or shot up by Messerschmitts. The whole of Tunisia was littered with burnt out trucks resulting from these constant attacks. The outcome of this was that even when we were not actually in a battle area, we nevertheless dug slit-trenches as soon as we settled for any length of time, ie, if we were staying longer than a few hours. There must be thousands of tons of earth, stones and sand shifted by hand in every area of war.

Apart from this nervous tension there were two things on our minds constantly: one was the ever yearning for mail, the other was the next battle. The only thing that really lifted the morale of all troops was the arrival of mail. Letters were read over and over again, any snaps of family or girlfriends were brought out of pockets continuously for another look. These were our lifelines and our last hold on normality.

Against that there was the ever present unease and speculation about our next move. This was a wearing down process because the longer we survived, the more apparent it became that survival was partly luck and luck was certainly exhaustible. The law of averages was not particularly kind and was apt to exact its toll. I can only quote statistics for our regimental officers, but, of some 30 of us of all ranks who left Scotland originally, 10 survived the Tunisian campaign. That is two-thirds of them were killed or badly wounded and didn't return and a couple of them were taken prisoner. In addition, there were other reinforcement officers who were lost, but I can't remember how many - a few of them I never even knew.

In the course of being in action it is inevitable that one meets with distressing circumstances. Most of these can be shut out of one's mind but not all. I remember being furious at the knowledge that some of the dead had been dug up by Arabs in order to rob the corpses or take clothing off them. It was disgusting but not something to dwell upon. On the other hand, the Welsh Guards' assault at Fondouk stays with me still. Even today I get a lump in my throat whenever I hear the Welsh singing those same hymns. A year later, in Italy, I took my turretless Sherman tank along a track north of Cassino. There were mines along the track so I drove through a hedge to get past them. On the other side of the hedge was a very small paddock and part orchard with longish grass. I just stopped my driver in time to prevent us driving over the body of a British soldier. As I looked I could see the place was full of bodies; you could see that they had been recently killed and were lying grotesquely in that lovely glade. I had to shift one or two in order to allow the battery to get through. They seemed very young men and must have walked into machine-guns; they sprawled just as they fell. Only recently, on Remembrance Day, I was driven to tears thinking of that episode - it being one of those I cannot forget.

These digressions from my main story are in order to explain to anyone interested that, during this somewhat lengthy account of one anti-tank troop in North Africa, there were things going on that formed a different fabric from the plain continuity of events. I want to show that, interwoven with the facts of incidents and places, there were feelings for others as well as oneself. There was laughter as well as awful fear. Yet I think I have not been able to convey the loneliness of being in action and the absolute dependence on fellow soldiers around you.

Most of the time we did not know what the rest of our battery were doing and we practically never knew where the rest of the regiment were, much less what they were doing. The family spirit forged within the troop was as essential as it was indestructible.

* * * * * * * *

At the end of Kournine, the battery returned to an area south-west of Medjez el Bab. There we found things very different from when we left it in December. This time the whole countryside was filled with troops, vehicles, tanks and guns. During the past month the 1st Army had been launching attack after attack along the whole of the Tunisian front. The Americans were now altogether in the north facing Mateur and Bizerta; the French were in the southern hills and with new equipment. The enemy had been given no chance to redeploy their forces since they had been fully occupied keeping our pressure at bay. All this general and fierce fighting had been eating into the German defence positions in order to establish footholds from which to launch the final onslaught. Now the spring was being coiled in readiness to fling the combined weight of 1st and 8th Armies at Von Arnim's army plus the Afrika Corps which had joined him (Rommel had returned to Germany). It could be said that loins on both sides were well and truly girded.

General Alexander had taken over as head of a new army group; he had combined the 1st and 8th Armies to form the 18th Army Group. He had moved formations about and now had three armoured divisions at his disposal and about a dozen or more infantry divisions; in addition were the Americans and French. Such a concentration of troops with such fire power would not have been known in the 1st World War. Then, with the weather hot and flying conditions perfect, the softening up process began by our air force. Wave after wave of bombers crossed over us for two or three days. Hundreds of these medium bombers with their fighter escorts flew to and fro continuously and the only retaliation was the infrequent dash by a Messerschmitt or two from Tunis. These enemy excursions with their fighters were short and perfunctory and showed a distinct nervousness. So much were the tables turned that, whereas in the earlier months in Tunisia we could not travel in daylight without more than considerable risk, we now roamed about openly watching hosts of Spitfires patrolling over our lines and beating up anything seen over enemy country.

Nevertheless, although so much had changed for the better so far as we were concerned, we all knew, or thought we knew, that the worst was yet to come. For five months we had been defending a thinly held line. We had been outnumbered by the enemy in everything except guns. The guns had broken up many infantry attacks and driven off many tank attacks. This in no way detracts from the simply magnificent performance of the 1st Army infantry formations.

The exploits of those battalions have been recorded and described in a number of books and they should be regarded as some of the finest troops ever. There has always been a readiness to bestow battle honours on regiments which have distinguished themselves in prominent and successful battles - though without the prominence and the success, the interest and recognition is not very apparent. This comparison could equally be made with higher formations, eg 1st and 8th Armies.

Alamein will always be celebrated for its success in turning the tide in North Africa. It has become the symbol of the 8th Army's outstanding and meritorious advance from Alamein to Tunisia. Yet during all that time the 1st Army, or the earlier elements of it, were fighting without respite and very little to show for it. The victorious 8th Army's advance came to a halt as soon as it made the acquaintance of the Tunisian hills. It would never have gained its reputation had it been fighting in those hills instead of the open desert.

During this campaign we anti-tank gunners had fired fewer shots in anger than any other of the fighting agencies, yet no front line in Tunisia could have existed or been held without us. The infantry could not form a secure defence without the anti-tank guns. The essence of every position was for the anti-tank guns to form the centre piece and the infantry to deploy their platoons in accordance with the gun layout. The enemy had possessed and used many tanks and the gun was the only answer; so much so that the tanks would withdraw as soon as they were engaged by anti-tank guns but were prepared to brazen it out with the 25-pounder field guns.

Our difficulty had been that there were not enough of us in the early days; everybody was shouting for us including the French and the Americans who seemed to be ill-equipped in this respect. Thus my modest troop of four had travelled hundreds of miles up and down the Tunisian front in response to the constant demand. A fact that the divisional commander, General Keightley, remarked upon to me when he visited us.

Now, suddenly, it had all changed. The whole army had prepared for the coming offensive and was now ready to smash its way through the enemy fortifications. The infantry divisions were to attack in the hills, with the main thrust towards Tunis to be made in the Medjez el Bab valley by the 6th and 7th Armoured Divisions. These two renowned divisions were both jealous of their reputations and each reckoned themselves to be the cream of all the armoured formations. The 7th, known as the 'Desert Rats', had made their name in desert fighting and wore a Desert Rat for their identifying insignia on the outside of the upper arm. We of the 6th Armoured, wore as our insignia a Mailed Fist which is now the emblem of the Royal Armoured Corps.

Nevertheless, neither of these divisions could be launched until the foremost enemy defences had been breached and the sappers had swept routes through the very extensive minefields. So the stage was set and tens of thousands of troops were standing in their trenches, making last minute checks to the vehicles or tanks, checking ammunition and other necessary articles of haberdashery, scribbling short letters home and not knowing what to say nor how to say it. They couldn't say how they felt. The last message that many hundreds of families would receive from a husband or son was complaining of the heat and cursing the flies. "Had little Vera got over her measles, had Tommy started to walk yet? Thank you for the socks, they come in very handy. That's about all for now. Love - SWALK." Two days later he was lying blackened in the corn-fields; now the flies were all over him but he didn't mind at all.

* * * * * * * *

'B' Battery now found itself with a new battery commander. Major Hamilton had gone to regimental HQ as second in command and he had been replaced by Major Howard Hillier, newly promoted from Tiger's HQ. He was not an anti-tank gunner and was the first to admit that he had a lot to learn. He had not in fact been in a fighting unit in action but had performed outstandingly well in an organising capacity at Brigade HQ. We troop commanders were surprised and suspicious of this appointment and really, although he was a likeable man, we could have no confidence in his ability to handle the battery. Making mistakes when you're playing at soldiers is part of learning but those same mistakes in action can have very unpleasant consequences. As it transpired, it made little difference for the short remainder of the African campaign. Later in Italy, during Howard's brief command of the battery at Cassino, his lack of experience showed itself in one or two hair-raising episodes.

Waiting now for our role in the coming battle, we learnt that, as usual, 'B' Battery was under command of our 26th Armoured Brigade. Two troops were to go forward with the tanks and the remaining two were assigned as divisional anti-tank reserve. We drew lots for the dubious privilege of running with the armour (remember that none of our vehicles had any protection from shot and shell and troop commanders rode in ordinary 15 cwt trucks). 7 and 8 Troops drew the short straws leaving 5 and 6 as reserve.

We had all expected a huge set piece battle like a repetition of Alamein, with preparatory barrage, infantry advance, tank thrust and all hell let loose. In fact it wasn't like that at all. Alexander had the enemy in a vice and was turning it tighter every day, indeed this had been going on for some time. It was thought that the German defence systems grew stronger as Tunis was approached. They had had months to prepare them and to augment natural defences with inter-supporting fortifications. Even so, no-one can withstand unremitting attack indefinitely, especially if under constant air attack and with the added problem of having supplies reduced.

The will to fight is as important as the ability to do so. Alexander reckoned that sooner or later the walnut would crack and the plans were made for that eventuality. How long before that crack appeared was not easy to assess - after all there were a quarter of a million enemy troops dug in behind those defences. It was clear that they were not about to give up their strong holds; we learnt afterwards that they didn't think we could break through at all. It seems that Von Arnim expected the main thrust for Tunis to be made by the 8th Army from Enfidaville. Failing that, he thought the next likely area would be from the north-west, from south of Mateur and through Tebourba.

To encourage this indecision one or two feint attacks were launched. Attacks and counter-attacks were going on throughout the whole of the 200-mile front but special attention was given to the northern and southern extremities. Then gradually the pressure along the Medjez valley was stepped up. 78th Division, with their battleaxe insignia and who had fought with the 6th since the beginning, were now asked to do the impossible yet again. They attacked along the mountain ridge that formed the left hand wall of the valley as you faced Tunis. This was a huge escarpment of steep-faced hills each of which had to be taken in turn, and from this wall there sprang the most famous hill of all, Longstop. It is futile trying to describe the achievements of these men and in any case I was not an eye witness to those deeds. Suffice to say, the valour displayed on those hills is legendary and was the turning point of the final phase.

With the taking of Longstop the guards were sent in against other features that stretched across the valley. They took Grich el Oued, a village to the right of the Tebourba road, and moved on to other obstacles. The battle was now well and truly on. On May 6th the gunfire became intense, something like 400 guns brought fire down onto the German strong points. These were not vastly obvious defences, with the exception of Djebel Bou Aoukaz, they were small hills and clusters of dwellings and mosques but they were interlocking and well prepared. The whole area was now erupting in smoke, dust and noise. Nobody could possibly tell what was happening in this bloody turmoil. There were a thousand private and local battles being conducted.

The participants in all this had no idea what was going on to their right or left or in front and behind. The smoke and flame in the valley ebbed and flowed, abated briefly and burst out again in one place then another. The hills and mountains on either side were equally blanching under the pock marks of shell bursts. Scores of machine-guns, theirs and ours, competed to make the most devastating noise and effect. The corn-fields which before had given the impression of beauty, serenity and timelessness, were now providing a protective cloak for hundreds of dead and wounded. Many of them were marked by upended rifles stuck in the ground by their comrades.

Under the supervision of the sappers, flail tanks went into the mine-fields in front of Medjez. These were tanks with a large revolving drum between two long steel shafts in front. Attached to the drum were several rows of very large and heavy chains and, as the tank advanced, the chains were brought over and forward, flailing the ground in front. They were very good at setting off the mines even though the chains suffered in consequence. The sappers double checked the roads or tracks thus swept and marked the lanes accordingly with white tapes.

So it was that later on May 6th, the 6th Armoured Division roared its Shermans through the mine-fields and onwards towards Tunis. A similar way had been secured away to the left to allow the 7th Armoured to launch themselves likewise. In a matter of hours these tank formations had outflanked or neutralised the opposition in their path and had driven past the bulk of the German defences. Such was the speed of the armoured regiments and their armoured car recce squadrons, that the enemy were bewildered and hopelessly demoralised. They didn't know what had happened and whether their other defences had collapsed. They didn't know which was their front and which their rear. We had outdone the Germans at their own game and they began to panic.

There were sundry pockets of fanatical resistance but, in truth, they didn't matter any more. That night 5 and 6 Troops were called forward, and a weird journey it was. We set off along a dusty mine-cleared track which called itself 'Toc' and seemed to go on for miles across country. Out on our flanks things were burning all over the plain. Tanks, trucks, stores, petrol dumps, half-track vehicles, bren gun carriers, and every now and then we'd come up against a party of our infantry with a group of prisoners. At the same time the war was continuing on all sides. Firing was constantly breaking out all over the place including behind us.

Our orders were to protect Tiger's HQ and since he, as usual, was intent upon keeping abreast of things, we were obliged to over take practically the whole of the division before we caught up with his HQ. In fact we managed to deploy our two troops as dawn broke on May 7th. I'd managed a slender breakfast and was engaged upon the usual exercise of trying to find out what was going on, when I saw a troop of

25-pounders approaching. As they drew near I recognised, to my amazement, the troop commander with his head out of the roof of his truck. It was John Sibbald who had been a fellow subaltern in my battery when we were at Cambridge. We used to go out on Saturday nights together. He had got himself posted out to the 8th Army and was now part of the 7th Armoured Division. We had a few brief words before he drove on with, "See you in Tunis."

Soon we were driving forward again and by now we had left the battle behind. Later, as we drew nearer to Tunis, we encountered a quad in a ditch beside the road; it had originally belonged to 8 Troop of 'B' Battery and had been lost at Tebourba back in early December. Later this day our Derbyshire Yeomanry armoured cars entered Tunis and, with them, similar cars of 7th Armoured Division recce regiment. The tanks followed on their heels and not only did Tunis fall but the enemy forces were split in two. The tanks had advanced 30 miles or so from Medjez el Bab.

Von Arnim's plan had been to hold as long as possible, then to withdraw from Bizerta and the north. If necessary he would withdraw further into the Cap Bon peninsula and its hills together with the hills south of the peninsula. This was mountainous country that was capable of being held for months, providing supplies could reach the troops. Some of the enemy's finest formations were in those hills, eg the German 90th Light Infantry, most of the remains of the 10th and 21st Panzer divisions and others.

Thus, just when we thought our war was over, the 6th Armoured was pulled out of Tunis and sent with all possible speed to the south-east and ordered to break through Hammam Lif at all costs. Hammam Lif was a relatively modern town built in the narrow gap between very high hills that extended almost to the sea, and the sea itself. With this door closed there was no way into the hills or the peninsula other than by sea.

After a long day of fighting and pursuing the enemy with the ultimate prize of Tunis, the armour had to race 12 or 15 miles to this further task that should, by all the laws of modern warfare, be impossible. The town was laid out with roads either parallel or at right angles to one another. General Keightley, decided to attack by night. The road from Tunis ran through Hammam Lif and on across the base of Cap Bon peninsula straight on to the sea at Hammamet on the far side of the peninsula. Hammamet and Nabeul are now the haunts of tourists and have probably changed their appearance.

This last battle of the Tunisian campaign was probably the most difficult that the Division had been asked to carry out. The Division was to attack a bottleneck that was very heavily defended. There was no room to manoeuvre, the place was full of 88mm guns and the hills and town full of snipers and other infantry. As one author has put it, in his account of the African campaign, "The subsequent march of the 6th Armoured Division must place it and its general in the very highest place in the military history of the war."

On reaching Hammam Lif, it was found to be stiff with guns, mines and tanks hull down behind walls and such like. There were anti-tank guns and other equipment in the hills above the town which clearly prohibited a straight forward frontal attack. General Keightley had to wait until the next day to send in the Guards under heavy artillery barrage to take the hills just above the town. This took all day to achieve but success was gained by the evening. Next day, the tanks tried to get into the town but were repulsed by the enemy guns and tanks. In a desperate bid, Keightley switched all the divisional artillery onto the town as the daylight ended. Then, with the moon rising, he sent in the Lothian and Border Horse regiment of tanks. The difference here was that the tanks carried a cargo of Guardsmen. At all the road intersections Guardsmen were dropped off and fanned out down all the roads, with grenades and bayonet. Any machine-gun post was blasted by a tank and gun positions were dealt with by either Guardsmen or tanks or both. In a few hours it was virtually over and the division began to pour through. Our guns had engaged one or two targets in the hills including an anti-tank gun. It must be a novelty in war for one anti-tank gun to exchange fire with another.

May 10th saw the 6th Armoured motoring full blast along the road to Grombalia and beyond. On the way we passed all kinds of enemy machinery. There were guns of various sorts and sizes abandoned or knocked out; there were workshops, petrol and ammunition dumps, some complete, some on fire. There were air fields and suddenly we came upon what looked like very large tanks; they were Panthers with extremely thick armour and very steeply sloping fronts. Above all it was the start of the collapse of the German and Italian armies.

The fact was that the enemy didn't know where we were. They found they were firing in all directions and wherever they could see there were British forces rushing by. Their generals were unable to give any lucid orders because they no longer knew what was happening. The enemy didn't know which way to turn let alone which way to go. They were completely surrounded and there was no prospect of them getting anywhere near the boats that had been promised, even if they existed.

As we travelled down this road we were subjected to some air burst shells but without any consequence. Then the floodgates were opened and hordes of figures could be seen coming out of the hills towards us. Frankly we were not too happy with this prospect, since 6 Troop with its 35 men were soon faced with a couple of hundred fully armed enemy. We told them to dump their arms in a heap off the road and to walk towards Hammam Lif. Some German officers came down a side lane in a French motor car complete with their kit. I took some pleasure in kicking them out and making them walk with the others. So it was that the cavalcade of enemy prisoners grew and grew. It was an incredible sight and experience to see a whole army giving up so suddenly. It was an absurd anti-climax after so many months of combat to see such disintegration.

'B' Battery pulled into a field near Grombalia and almost every man began to write home with the news that he was alive and the war in Africa was over. As I wrote a motor bike arrived and I was hailed by its rider, "Donald, you bugger, how about a cup of tea?" It was Barry Rintoul, who was a friend I'd found on my course at Larkhill OCTU near Salisbury. We had been commissioned together but he had found his way into an artillery survey unit. He later went into the church in spite of his greeting to me then. How he had found me on this occasion and at this time only he knew.

The next day 'B' Battery moved on towards Hammamet where I first saw oranges and lemons growing - alas they weren't yet ripe. We came to a halt at Nabeul at the sea's edge and in no time all of us had plunged into the sea. It was as though we were purging ourselves of the senses of war. Nearly 300,000 prisoners were taken in the next few days plus unknown quantities of tanks and equipment but we cared nothing for that. Now everywhere was quiet, we could look on the sea with our thoughts and we too were quiet.

103

Extract from 'Legion' journal of the British Legion, dated November 1990:

'November 11th'

I speak for the dead, the dead of all the wars,
They were our parents, our children and the friends of mine and yours,
I speak for those who perished, who died for the common good,
Doing what they had to, in the only way they could.

Don't say that they were heroes, that they sacrificed their all;
They went because they had to, not to answer Britain's call.
And they didn't give their lives away; they were slaughtered where they stood,
Doing what they had to, in the only way they could.

No knight in shining armour, defending what was right;
They were ordinary mortals, often petrified with fright.
But the highest place in Heaven, if the Lord is truly good,
Is for those who did what they had to, in the only way they could.

F.Lacey

PART TWO

ITALY

BATTLE of CASSINO - Showing River Crossings

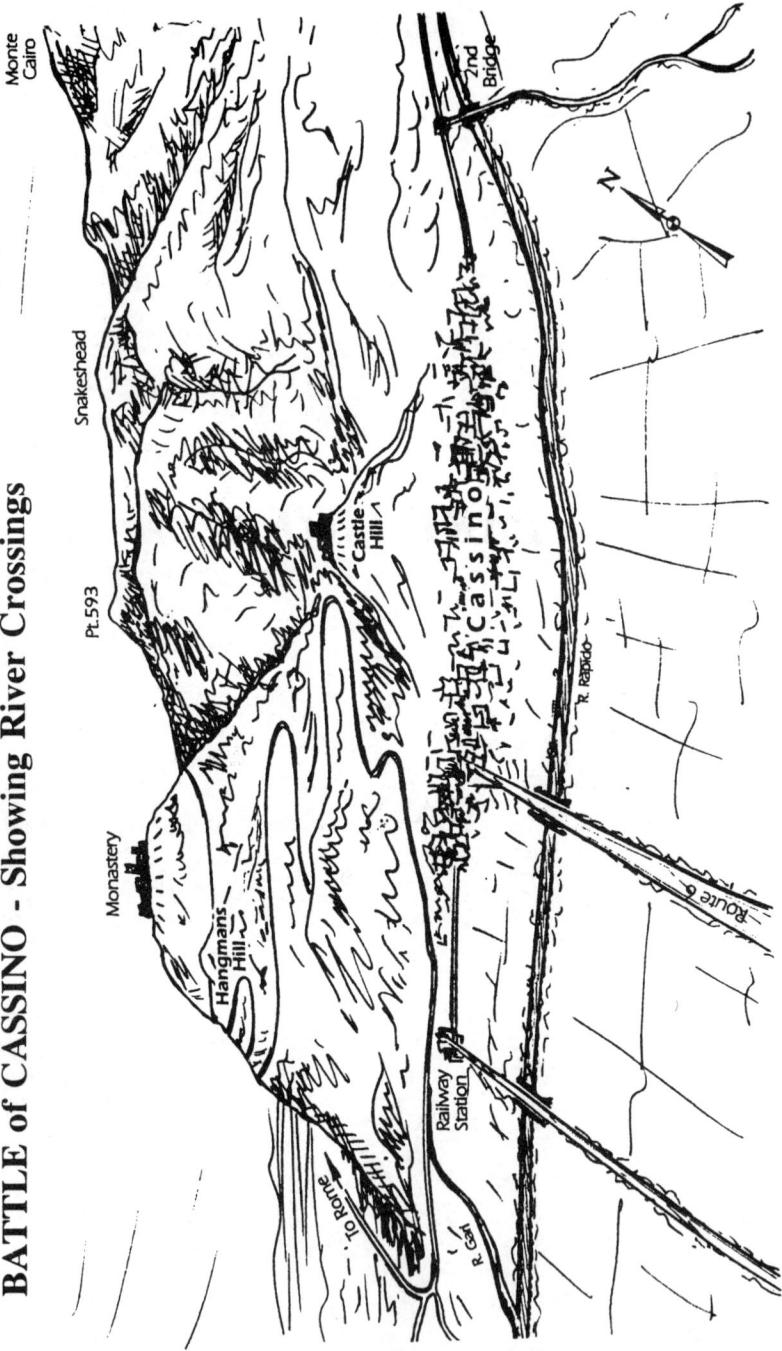

Monte
Cairo

Snakeshead

Pt.593

Monastery

Hangmans
Hill

Castle
Hill

Cassino

R. Rapido

2nd
Bridge

N

Route 6

Railway
Station

R. Gari

to Rome

CHAPTER XII

INTERMEZZO

With the conclusion of the Tunisian campaign, the various divisions of the 18th Army Group were dispersed in different directions. Some remained in Tunisia to assist in sorting the confusion and mess left behind after 6 months of war. Some returned eastward to take care of Libya and Egypt and that end of the Mediterranean. Some, including the 6th Armoured, moved westward into Algeria. Many of the formations lost a number of their officers and NCOs who were returned to England to offer some expertise to the armies at home. We didn't realize it then, but, although 6th Armoured was eventually sent to Italy, it never again fought in the way that it had done in Africa, as a single unit. Because of the nature of the country and of the war, the division fought more in independent units as and where required.

Meanwhile the summer of 1943 was remarkable for reasons other than the conflict itself. The 72nd Anti-Tank Regiment found itself in an undistinguished-looking valley somewhere southwest of Philippeville, the coastal town west of Bone. The valley was fairly steep sided with the inevitable olive groves covering its sides and a rather slothful stream meandering along the bottom. It was about 30 miles inland and, although featureless, it nevertheless bore the name of Robertville.

Its native population comprised approximately 35 million flies together with 5 million mosquitoes and a small selection of lizards and praying mantis. The average temperatures of that summer ranged from hot to stifling.

Now began a period wherein we assumed that we would be dusted down and polished for the next theatre of war. The problem was where? Our hopes were that we should be sent home for some leave and, we supposed, an eventual merger with the 2nd front forces into France. The alternative choices were a landing in Italy, a landing in Southern France, a landing in Greece, a journey down the Red Sea to India and thence to Burma.

A few weeks elapsed and the full Summer's heat fell upon us. It brought with it a number of thoroughly unpleasant afflictions. I suffered the distinction of being the first of the regiment to succumb to malaria. Captain James, the regimental doctor, was more than pleased with this event. He had been reading up all the symptoms and wanted confirmation that he could diagnose the disease when confronted with it. I had pride of place on his sick-list and was visited by him several times daily. He viewed my raging temperatures and shivering body through benevolent eyes, but with a certain satisfied expectancy, as if he had discovered the antidote and couldn't wait to prove it. Very soon he had other candidates claiming his attention, and later still the hospitals were being filled with malaria victims. Many of our number were very ill and, sadly, a few deaths were recorded.

The second plague to befall us, and the most unpleasant of the selection visited upon us that Summer, was that of dysentery. Everybody has heard of dysentery, but to experience it is to suffer in the proper sense. It was so contagious that there could have been very few in the regiment who managed to avoid its miseries. Having no wish to describe the effects in detail, nor to dwell too heavily upon its consequences, I will say only that it was an everyday sight to see men crawling on hands and knees towards the latrines. The latrines were pits dug about 4-5ft deep and with a structure of poles to hold the fly nets over them. New pits were dug continually during the Summer months, to cater for the never-ending demand. The trouble was that there seemed no immunity, people were being reinfected constantly; so much so that anyone contracting the disease more than three times was sent home to the UK. There were many among us who did their best to qualify.

After a few weeks of this kind of epidemic, the regiment looked a sorry sight. The average man had lost several stones in weight, and some were in a dreadful state of emaciation. Doctor James despaired of all the acknowledged methods of treatment as recommended in the medical books, instead he embarked upon his own cure. It was simple and certainly more effective, if somewhat violent; it was a hefty dose of Castor Oil. Castor Oil in conjunction with dysentery was a never-to-be- forgotten combination, in essence one could say that the resultant coupling was highly volatile. Let us leave it at that.

As the Summer progressed, and just to ensure that everyone had every opportunity of hospitalization, we were subjected to a lively outbreak of jaundice. The infections of this isolated valley were nothing if not virulent, and it was as a result of this particular malady that I found myself in one of the local hospitals. There were two mobile hospitals attached to our division and one or two others. They followed us in action and remained with us when we were in between campaigns as it were. These were the Canadian and the 4th British, on this occasion I was in the Canadian hospital. These places were naturally entirely under canvas but quite elaborately fitted out. Being army orientated, the officers had separate wards, not better but separate. We used to try to obtain special privileges and demanded of the matron that she assign to us the prettiest nurses. Such requests were always, or nearly always, sternly refused.

During this stay in hospital there were two things that stand out in my memory. One was a visit by Tiger, the Brigadier. He talked to various people as he made his way down the ward, then, on inquiring who I was, shook my hand and sat on my bed. He then told me calmly how he had ordered my Court Martial about four months ago, but relented in order to support my recommended MC. I didn't know quite how to react to this piece of news, but hoped he wouldn't mind my thanking him for making the right decision.

The other incident took place one evening when our personal reveries were interrupted by screams from somewhere away from our tent. One or two of us, who were able, left our beds and went to investigate. As we reached the entrance to the tent, a nurse came hastening towards us shouting for help. She explained the emergency in a few short sentences.

The nurses had their own latrine in a tent; it consisted of a large box, with one side removed, positioned open side downwards over a prepared pit. The opposite side had a suitable hole cut out with a lid to cover the hole. Thus the appliance represented a primitive W.C. but with out the water. This nurse had gone to use this 'convenience' and, on sitting down on the box, had heard something moving or making some sort of noise down below. She had jumped up and shone her torch down into the depths and there looking up was a moving snake. She had recoiled with a yell and raced towards our tent.

So, wearing our Sir Galahad pyjamas and armed with sticks, three of us made our way to the ladies' loo. With a borrowed torch, a long-handled shovel, the sticks, a lot of laughter, a quantity of advice and considerable luck, we succeeded in ejecting the snake from its commode. The snake was about 2½ feet long and of indiscernible colouring, not surprising in the circumstances. It started to make off but somebody belted it over the head with a large piece of rock and its unhappy experience ended there. We returned to our tent to claim, in vain, our well-earned reward of a kiss from the nurses. They might well have paid up but for the close proximity of the Matron's tent.

To complete the catalogue of environmental anxieties there was the inescapable heat; when the Sirocco wind blew from the Sahara, it rose to 121°F in the shade. This heat was disabling to the extent that we could do nothing during the day, except in the very early hours and in the evenings. The hours between were spent lying naked under mosquito nets and doing very little other than sweating. We became more lively at night but darkness didn't lend itself to much constructive activity. In fact some of us spent many nights, indeed weeks of nights, trying to comprehend the niceties of playing Bridge under the Padre's instruction. We had a new Padre now, whose name I can't remember. He figured more prominently later on in Italy, but he was well liked and quite a character.

Not even the Padre, with his acts of supplication, could prevent the constant, insatiable attentions of the flies. Our only escape was under a mosquito net and, bearing in mind the dysentery prevailing in this valley, it was small wonder that we all fell prey to desert sores. These sores developed wherever the flies pierced the skin on our exposed surfaces, and they very quickly festered and became thoroughly unpleasant.

However, there were redeeming features of this long hot summer, principally the nurses at the Canadian hospital. Those of us who had spent a little time in hospital, together with those who had made strenuous efforts to visit friends so interned, had somehow made the acquaintance of numbers of the nurses. It seemed only natural and neighbourly that we should visit them socially, or so we thought. Then, because of the conditions I have already described, the Colonel gave permission for each battery to send swimming parties to Philippeville. A convoy of four or five 3 ton lorries were loaded with soldiers and departed for Philippeville every afternoon.

In a short time there were those of us who borrowed some smaller and less uncomfortable transport to travel the 30 miles or so to the coast. To be more exact, we detoured to the Canadian hospital to pick up a few nurses who were as eager to bathe in the sea as we were. Arriving at the miles of sandy shore in the early days of this practice, and having no swim suits, we put a suitable distance between us in order to undress and swim. However, such modesty was short lived. Soon we were undressing and bathing together without a blush to be seen, and enjoying it all the more. It should be noted that mixed nude bathing in public had not been sanctioned in those far off days.

There were other progressions arising from these swimming trips. The nurses were able to reciprocate by running dances within the hospital precincts. Even the Matron gave her blessing readily, and probably thought, wrongly, that her nurses were at lesser risk when they entertained the young officers in this way. During those hot nights it was to be expected that young couples should wander outside to seek, among other things, cooler surroundings. These were all welcome interludes in an otherwise depressing outlook. We were still wrestling with thoughts of the future, because we had all rather expected that there would be a landing in France during these months, but nothing had happened. So what was to become of us?

* * * * * * * *

The immediate future offered distractions enough as our regiment was totally reorganized. First, we acquired a fourth battery; second, we reduced each battery from 4 to 3 troops, thus there were still 12 troops in the regiment. Third, the batteries were renamed; instead of A, B and C, we became 111, 112, 113 and 327 batteries. Why we couldn't have 114 battery I never understood, but I've no doubt that somebody at Army HQ was given an MBE for creating this piece of deception. Fourth, our equipment was changed; 111 and 112 batteries were to become self propelled with 3 inch high velocity guns mounted in a sort of tank. 113 and 327 batteries were each to retain 2 troops of 6 pounder towed guns and a third troop of the new 17 pounder guns. These latter were large and powerful and had been used towards the end of the Tunisian war with some success.

By this time I had been promoted Captain and consequently had surrendered 6 Tp, which had become Fox Tp. Our battery (112) now comprised Dog Tp, Easy Tp and Fox Tp. Howard Hillier was our Battery Commander, Ted Newman our Battery Captain and I was a new appointment with the title of Recce Captain - working with the Bty Cmdr. Our three Troop Commanders were John Berryman 'D' Tp, Johnny Gaster 'E' Tp and John Latham 'F' Tp.

Very soon the sergeants, the gun detachment drivers and the troop officers of 111 and 112 Batteries, plus myself, all motored off to a nondescript area of trees near the port of Bone. There we found a large contingent of Americans, together with an assortment of equipment and armament, large and small. We had joined our American friends in order to receive our new self-propelled guns which were, needless to say, American built. It was an outstanding fact that, throughout the 2nd World War, Britain could and did produce some superb fighter aircraft and bombers, but utterly failed to provide the army with a tank that was half as good as the German Panzers. Even our anti-tank guns were soon outdated and their replacements were a hotchpotch of ordnance - neither one thing nor another. Still, the American Sherman tanks had done a good job so far and we now looked forward to this new equipment.

The first thing that struck us about this American camp was its comparative comfort and hygiene. All the tents were spacious and all had excellent nets which efficiently excluded the flies. The mess tent was large and well appointed and the food was outstanding, including plenty of fresh fruit and vegetables, though it took us a while to accustom ourselves to jam and honey on eggs and toast for breakfast. Also, wonder of wonders, there was ice available to plop into our fruit juice. The ablutions were equally impressive, with plenty of water available for washing, and rows of aluminium bowls set out on long trestle tables for the purpose. We were unanimous in our determination to prolong our stay as long as possible.

Very soon we were introduced to our reason for coming. The self-propelled guns were known by the Americans as Tank Hunters. Their technical name was M10, and that is what we always called them. Strange really because all the different tanks had their own names; the self-propelled field guns were known as "Priests", yet our M10's were never christened. They had the appearance of a tank but were different in certain respects. The body was a Sherman, but the turret and gun had been removed and replaced by an open-topped turret with only 1 inch thick armoured sides. This special turret was in order to accommodated the more powerful gun which fired both armour piercing and high explosive shells.

When we saw these M10's we were impressed by their size and appearance. By today's standards they would not have turned any heads, but in those days they looked formidable. Certainly they were capable of dealing with any of the enemy armoured vehicles. They were designed strictly as tank destroyers, hence the single powerful gun, plus a heavy machine-gun mounted on the rear of the turret for anti-aircraft purposes. They were powered by two radial aeroplane engines, one to each of the tank tracks, and it was our business to learn how to drive them. The trick was not only to learn how to manage the two big levers, which were really outsized handbrakes operating on the tracks, but to ensure that each engine was operating at exactly the same speed as its twin. If the engines were not properly synchronised, then one track would move at a different speed from the other, which would undoubtedly incline the machine to become self-willed.

It took about a week for the members of our party to accustom themselves to their new SP guns. We drove them over some excessively steep and bumpy country, to test our skills and their ability, and we all expressed ourselves more than content with their performance. In addition, we were more than content with the Americans' hospitality. The food, which was always of enduring concern to the average soldier, was different but excellent. There were cinema shows in the evenings, there were drinks to be consumed free, since we were their guests. There was a kind of shop with clothing available and I purchased a marvellous pair of brown boots. Soft leather, comfortable and with thick crepe rubber soles that lasted me the rest of the war. They were especially good when clambering over the M10's; the latter, having a smooth metal surface, were slippery to the ordinary boot.

We were genuinely sorry to leave our American friends in their woodland camp, where the air was much less stifling and creature comforts were considered quite important. They were a jolly lot and we had all enjoyed our stay with them, only wishing it could have been longer. Journeying back to Robertville was something of an anticlimax, except that on arrival there was much excitement at the sight of these M10's.

* * * * * * * * *

Next followed a period of training anew with our strange equipment. We also had three new Troop Commanders and it was my job to arrange and supervise training exercises for all three troops. We set off every day to different situations where we were attacked by imaginary enemy forces in varying circumstances. Thus we evolved different tactics more suited to the size and performance of these self-propelled guns. A little later each one of them was submitted to the regimental Light Aid Detachment. This was a body of men who were mechanics and expert in the ways of guns and vehicles. It was they who recovered our M10's, when they came to grief in battle, and repaired them. Now each gun was modified by certain installations to enable it to perform as a field gun, like the 25-pounders.

With these introductions we reckoned our value would soar in the estimation of others. In our view we would shortly become indispensable. Able to take on and destroy all known enemy tanks; able to engage distant targets with high explosive shells in support of the infantry and able, because of the greater velocity of the gun, to outrange our own field guns. We felt that no-one could really afford to be without us.

There remained a difficulty to this achievement though; at the time only Colonel Slessor, one officer in 111 Bty, Ted Newman and myself knew the intricacies of field gunnery. I was trained as a field gunner before being posted to an anti-tank regiment. It is a complicated business to land a shell from a gun, tucked behind a hill, onto a target perhaps 8 miles away, particularly if that target is a small one. So it was now necessary to introduce the gunners, NCOs and officers of the two SP batteries to the magical sophistications of field artillery. We sent officers and NCOs to the 12th RHA and the Ayrshire Yeomanry to undertake instructional courses. In addition we established ranges where I took small but regular groups to learn the art of shooting the M10's from an OP (observation post). For this we used live ammunition. Altogether there was frantic activity in our area during the months of Autumn 1943.

Although the daytime temperatures had abated so as to allow plenty of opportunity for this training, the rainy season seemed impatient and anxious to hinder our best intentions as early as it conveniently could. Soon our tented accommodation and surrounds were presenting a dreary appearance. It became necessary to dig little ditches round the walls of tents to collect the rain and channel it into other ditches which, in turn, conveyed the gathering waters to larger ones. So the system developed, until there was a collection of streams running down the hillside into the swollen stream in the valley.

All this brought about a desire to improve our living conditions. A number of methods of tent improvisation and types of fireplace were experimented with, in the pursuit of dryness and warmth. Each battery designed and built a small clutch of huts for the different ranks of the users. These, it was hoped, would prove robust and weather proof as well as being exciting and cosy. They were constructed of large biscuit tins filled with earth and bonded together with mud. In like manner there were fireplaces with chimney pots in a variety of shapes and sizes. The roofs were angled in accordance with local preference and a combination of chimney requirements, updraught or downdraught or whatever. The dominant considerations were weather-proofing and comfort. There was an undoubted pride and competitive side to these efforts, and the whole had more than a passing similarity to a shanty town of Peter Pan and Wendy houses.

constructed of large biscuit tins filled with earth and bonded together with mud. In like manner there were fireplaces with chimney pots in a variety of shapes and sizes. The roofs were angled in accordance with local preference and a combination of chimney requirements, updraught or downdraught or whatever. The dominant considerations were weather-proofing and comfort. There was an undoubted pride and competitive side to these efforts, and the whole had more than a passing similarity to a shanty town of Peter Pan and Wendy houses.

Those winter months passed slowly and were not the most comfortable. Christmas came and went with very little to commend it. I played a few carols on my piano and there were a number of sing-songs that accompanied the ration of drinks distributed through out the regiment. We were entertained by one or two concert parties who were pleased to borrow my piano, and altogether we made a pretence at enjoying ourselves.

Now that we were into the New Year our thoughts naturally turned to Italy where some of the divisions we knew, together with others we had yet to meet, were slugging it out in the mud and mountains. They had done well and had not only put the Italians out of the war, but the latter had elected to help us and, where possible, to fight against the Germans.

Meanwhile the advance had come to a halt at a place called Cassino.

Author and driver with M10 and Jeep

CHAPTER XIII

INITIATION

It was March before we received the order so reminiscent of many months past, "Prepare to Move". In good time the regiment made its way, battery by battery, to Philippeville docks. Only one thing of note happened at this time, the loss of my treasured piano. Because of its history, permission had been obtained to transport it to Italy, but, in lifting it onto the ship, it slipped out of its sling, crashed and burst into pieces on the dockside. I had entertained vague thoughts of getting it back home after the war and thus my hopes and sentiments were dashed together with the piano.

Our voyage to Africa, 16 months earlier, had been a pleasant and memorable cruise in a splendid liner that was, for the most part, comfortable, stable and privileged in essence. Our journey to Italy was in stark contrast. It was undertaken in a vessel called a Tank Landing Craft (TLC). These were the ships that looked rather like small oil tankers. Their front ends, or noses, were hinged to enable them to open and drop a draw-bridge onto a beach in order to discharge their cargo. To accomplish this it was necessary for them to have a suitably shallow draught. They were capable of carrying a host of tanks and other equipment, but everything had to be chained down and very carefully stowed; the reason was obvious once we reached the open sea.

I make no pretence to knowledge of nautical matters, only that I'm somewhat fascinated by them. Nevertheless, common sense suggests that the deeper a ship sits in the water, the more resistant is should be to the movement of the surface waves. Conversely, a ship with no visible means of support beneath, and which sits virtually on top of the water, must be very susceptible to any prevailing disturbances. That being so, it will be no surprise to learn that our journey to Italy was never without incident. This wretched TLC struggled with its heavy load through some forceful seas; it plunged, pitched, lurched and rolled like a barrel. We, its unwilling passengers, had no choice but to follow its every movement. Progress was slow and, for the majority of those present, unpleasant. I spent much of the time avoiding the close proximity of my fellows, the consequences otherwise could be nasty.

During the 2nd night of our voyage we were moving somewhere to the north of Sicily and noticed a red glow away to the south east. As time passed this glow increased in brightness, with frequent showers of fountain-like lights. We learnt that it was the volcano Stromboli erupting and, considering that it must have been 80 - 100 miles away, the display to those in the vicinity must surely have been breathtaking.

The journey into the next day continued in its drunken, pedestrian way. At times our TLC was not so much ploughing through the waves as harrowing its way up and over them. Eventually, with some relief, we saw the distant and emerging shapes of the Italian mainland. I suppose we all felt pleased and excited at the prospect of exchanging the deprivations of Africa for the beauty and imagined temperance of Italy, although we had no desire to hasten our introduction to the Italian front. As to temperance, we had a lot to learn about the Italian climate.

On a lovely sunny day round about 20th March, we arrived at Naples. The famous bay was sparkling, lively and looking every bit as Neapolitan as we had hoped. Vesuvius overlooked the scene with an age-old forbearance, though it was further from Naples than I had expected. These first impressions, as we entered the bay, were entirely encouraging. Then, as we approached the quays of the harbour itself, we passed a number of half sunken ships and others battered but still afloat. The scars of war were evident and the only healthy ships around seemed to belong to the navy, but this couldn't spoil our enthusiasm for this new country. Some ass quoted loudly, "See Naples and die", which many others thought in bad taste.

As at Algiers, it took ages to unscramble the battery from the far reaches of our Tank Landing Craft and to coax the M10's from their berths without driving one or two through the side into the harbour. At length the battery formed up above the quayside, less the M10 and vehicle drivers, and began a long march from the docks to a transit camp on the way to Caserta. It was dark when we began to climb the steep hill away from the bustle of the ship-yards. Some of the battery found that the firm ground, after many hours of pitching and tossing in the TLC, caused them to stagger appreciably as they began to walk. This only added to our elation at having arrived safely in a country where we felt much nearer to home, where we already felt more akin to the local people.

After a short stay at the transit camp, we collected our transport and made our way to a village some 30 miles or so to the north. To be exact our collecting area was adjacent to the picturesque village of Piedimonte d'Alife. As everyone knows, there is a long range of mountains running, like a spine, the length of Italy from the Apennines north of Florence to the foot of the country. Piedimonte d'Alife snuggled into the lower slopes of these mountains; it was beautiful and its inhabitants friendly. We were pleased to have left the restrictions of our miserable valley at Robertville in Algeria, and more than pleased to have exchanged them for the fresh, clean and green countenance of our new host country. Everything was so different; the people, the roads, the fields and rivers, the houses, the mountains and the climate. We had become so acclimatized to the dust and remoteness of Africa that it was, in a sense, bewildering to be scooped up and whisked way into this new environment.

One thing that was familiar though, was the presence everywhere of olive groves. Once again we spread ourselves, our tents and vehicles in between and, where possible, under these eternal olive trees. Very soon there arrived a strong visitation of young women. They were received with acclaim by 112 Battery as a whole; and the fact that they had come seeking to do our washing, in no way dampened the enthusiasm. This was good news because our clothes were not only anything but spotless, but mostly in glaring need of repair. Within a couple of weeks my young signorina had labelled all my shirts, underwear and socks with my name and had repaired and patched everything according to more civilized standards. It was a great improvement on one's lifestyle and did much to restore our sense of well-being once more.

Now that we found ourselves in Italy, we immediately began to take interest in the whereabouts and happenings on the Italian front. Until now many of us had

113

remained unconvinced that we were to join the Italian campaign. The battle for Sicily had come and gone and likewise the landings and advances on the mainland. Yet still the 6th Armoured had not left Africa. We had felt for some time past that there would be a landing in Southern France, and that it was more likely that we should be sent there. Such an expedition would go hand in hand with the Italian war and the one would be likely to assist the other, so we thought. Those doubts having been resolved, we addressed ourselves to the pleasure of becoming better acquainted with this new set of circumstances.

We discovered that the Italians, who had been our enemies until a few months ago, showed an unexpected friendliness. We sent truck-loads of men into Naples by way of recreation. They were nearly always entertained by the local people and often too much so. The soldiers also lost no time in fraternizing with the local girls and families of the village. They smuggled tins of food and sugar in exchange for bottles of vino, to their mutual satisfaction. The young Italian men were mostly in the army, or prisoners of war, but the remaining men were kept happy with the supply of packets of cigarettes from time to time. It seems likely that rapport has been established between strangers by such methods since prehistoric times.

Another form of recreation, that was freely available, was the exploration of the surrounding hills. Ted Newman and I spent many hours walking and scrambling over this gloriously mountainous area. There was a large lake or reservoir high up in the hills above Piedimonte. From this lake there flowed, through large pipes, a deluge of water down steeply to a generator. From there the over-flow of water swept through the village, and provided an everlasting washing machine for the local people as it ran through a stone walled enclosure built for the purpose.

The hills in this part of Italy seemed almost continuous. There were valleys, but few flat areas between the west and east coasts. When examining the countryside, it appeared that the hills were so formed that the peak of one was inevitably overlooked by the summit of the next. In between all of them was an assortment of streams and rivers beside which and over which the infrequent roads meandered. At every crossing of these waters, where the banks were particularly steep or the crossing difficult for any reason, the bridge would be blown by the retreating German army. To accompany this, the banks on either side were usually sown with mines. The unfortunate sappers and others who had to bridge these gaps were, in many cases, subjected to machine-gun and mortar fire whilst they were so engaged. Somebody should have taken a count, but certainly there were more bridges blown than there were towns in Italy.

One night I was woken in my tent by the sound of a distant thunder storm. There were constant rolls of thunder but no rain, neither could I detect any lightning. After a while my curiosity drove me outside where the source of the noise became apparent. Although some 40 miles away, there could be no mistaking the eruption of Vesuvius. The red molten showers of rock could be plainly seen and lit up both sky and surrounding country. The display was inspiring in its magnitude and the roars of every explosion must have caused consternation in that area. The light in the night sky was somewhat similar to the

114

initial bombing of London, but the concentrated power could be felt as well as seen. For the first time I could appreciate how Pompeii had been overcome and submerged. The ferocity of Vesuvius during the following days was both primeval and magnificent. I was thrilled to have seen it.

* * * * * * * * *

Throughout this first month we devoted all our working time to our M10's. Quite apart from driving them on confined and difficult roads, the crews needed to become familiar with many mechanical functions to do with maintenance, coping with some electrical faults, changing a broken track and such matters. Further courses were held for the sergeants and troop officers by the 12th RHA, plus endless instruction for the radio operators, and reserve operators, on transmission and maintenance of the radio sets. Then, to test our competence, we undertook a few exercises with our infantry using live ammunition. We put down barrages and engaged targets close to the infantry at their request. This not only gave us confidence in our skills, but equally demonstrated to the infantry that they could rely on our performance as supporting artillery.

On 19th April 'D' Tp of our battery was required to relieve a troop of 111 Bty at Cassino. This news brought us down to earth at long last.

It was the news we knew must come eventually, but hoped would be postponed indefinitely. Not only 'D' Tp but the whole battery was brought to a state of readiness by this development. A general feeling of edginess invaded the troops and once again the familiar feelings of apprehension began to establish themselves.

There were newcomers to the battery whose reaction was slightly different, and who confessed to slight waves of excitement coupled with natural unease. Two of the three troop Commanders were new, Johnny Gaster being the exception, and, together with Howard, lacked battle experience. They naturally had questions which were not always easy to answer.

The journey northwards was picturesque but wet. Route 6, the road to Cassino and Rome, twisted and wriggled its way past miles of stores and dumps of ammunition. There must have been many shiploads of stuff hidden under the trees along the lower slopes of the neighbouring hills. Then a large hill appeared to block the way. Mount Trocchio is a huge hill, made to look more so because it is not part of a range as others are. It is somewhat isolated, and stretches for one and a half miles, north and south, half across the Rapido Valley. The road was forced to bend acutely round the northern end of Trocchio, or to the right hand end of the hill as we travelled, and the valley beyond was completely obscured until one reached that bend in the road.

On turning the corner of Trocchio the great expanse of the valleys of Rapido, Garigliano and Lire open before you. The view is of a broad flat plain, soft and fertile in appearance, extending far to the south-west. The right side, or north-east, is soon closed in by the mountains that stretch to the Adriatic. But the sight that snatches the attention from all else, is that of Monastery Hill and the mountains beyond Cassino. Route 6, having made its drunken way for many miles, suddenly surges forward and runs absolutely straight for the last two and a half miles into Cassino. The Monastery, sitting on top of that towering hill, strongly resembling a fortress rather than a place of refuge, overlooks the entire scene.

112 Bty found its new temporary resting place a mile or two north of Route 6. We made our way there as dusk fell, and with caution steered our M10's along sunken lanes to the new area. We learnt at once that this was a place where no-one moved about in daylight. It became second nature for us to move about only after dark; indeed the army at Cassino became a nocturnal army. Even then such movement had its dangers. Any noise would bring response from the opposing artillery, and, during the last 5 months or so, both sides had acquired a shrewd idea of the other's dispositions and supply routes; such areas were subjected to harassing fire practically every evening and sometimes during the night.

'D' Tp was obliged to move to the 'A' battery positions by vehicle and then by foot. Because the site of the two guns was so uncompromisingly close to the enemy, they were to take over 'A' battery guns rather than replace them. To reach this place the River Rapido had to be crossed by Bailey bridge, often under fire, or waded. On reaching the road beyond, you turned right and continued past the old barracks. In due course one of the several tracks leading off left took you across a field or two and then began a steep and difficult climb. The track wound round the edge of this particular mountain until it reached a kind of shoulder of Monte Cairo. This was a long and most awkward climb even for small vehicles, and made worse by the precipitous drop from the track of some hundreds of feet.

At the top of this mountain track were the two M10's to be manned by 'D' Tp. They were in an anti-tank and close support role, which entailed sitting under regular mortar fire. This, due to the rocky ground, was particularly nasty; even so the crews had other anxieties such as trying to distinguish between friendly and hostile patrols. Everyone up there was so nervous that any thoughtless noise or rash move was apt to start somebody shooting. The troop suffered only one casualty and thought themselves lucky.

* * * * * * * * *

One afternoon during the tenancy of the Mount Cairo positions, Howard Hillier decided that he and I should visit John Berryman and his gun teams. There was nothing untoward about this announcement and I assumed that Howard meant that we should conduct our visit after dark. My surprise then, when he declared his intention of starting at once, was perhaps self-evident. Now I have already emphasised that the survivors at Cassino had achieved that position not least because they had conscientiously observed the local rules about daytime movement. They had been at pains not to arouse the enemy's curiosity nor yet offend his dignity. Howard's proposed trip would undoubtedly provoke both of those senses and a good many more.

My natural leaning towards survival prompted me to challenge the wisdom of

116

a mid-afternoon visit. Pointing out the obvious risk of being summarily expunged, if he persisted with this front line inspection in a jeep at 2.30 pm, did not dissuade him. Howard felt that the darkness would deny us the opportunity of viewing and comprehending the circumstances of the M10 positions. He summoned his driver and explained our intended mission and told the Sgt. Major that we might be gone some time but not to expect us for at least three hours, "If at all" added the driver.

At 3.00 pm the three of us set off in Howard's jeep. The jeep was a remarkable American run-about born of the war. It was very small, open topped, with sides no more than 12 inches high. There were two front seats and a sort of seat behind, designed more to carry a few bits and pieces than a passenger. It could convert from 2 to 4 wheel drive and possessed a number of gear ratios both forward and backward. It was simple, powerful and could go almost anywhere. In spite of all these virtues, it had no means of eliminating the revealing plume of dust which accompanied every kind of truck that moved along the churned up lanes. This unfortunate fact was very much in my mind as we motored off in sprightly fashion heading for Cassino.

There were two bridges which the Allies had pushed across the Rapido at Cassino. One was a replacement for the main Route 6 bridge, the other was at the northern end of the town near the hills. The first was permanently hidden under a heavy smoke screen put down by our side. I suppose this was to deny the Germans a clear view to their artillery and mortars, but it meant that the area around the bridge was in permanent fog. The major part of Cassino was beyond this bridge and to the right or north of it. The town itself was shared by the two sides, what was left of it.

The Germans held the section of the town nearest to Monastery Hill and, of course, the high ground behind. They no longer held Castle Hill overlooking the northern end of the town; this had been taken by the New Zealanders before we arrived. The Allies held the rest of the town and the two sides were cheek by jowl among the line of buildings that divided them. Sometimes they actually shared the same building for brief intervals, and for long periods they were within stone throwing distance of each other. The buildings, so called, consisted of large congested heaps of rubble for the most part, with a few skeleton buildings here and there. Many of the roads had, for practical purposes, disappeared under these heaps because there was no opportunity to clear them. Cassino bore a very strong resemblance to a long contested town in the 1st World War. Its state was one of devastation and included the pervading stench of decaying bodies within the town. There could have been no greater contrast imaginable than between the beauty of the Italian countryside and the pitiful desolation of Cassino.

Our journey to John Berryman's two guns entailed a 20 minute drive along narrow lanes in a gradual descent toward the town. During all of this time we set up a wake of powdery dust behind us and I reckoned that most of the troops in the vicinity must be watching with disbelief. As we approached Cassino we aimed for the northern Bailey bridge and we passed some of our infantry who surfaced

117

to see who was motoring abroad at this time. Howard seemed unconcerned about our advertised progress towards the Rapido crossing; for my part, I could feel several hundred pairs of eyes following our fortune, and I imagined most of them wondering when to pull the trigger. By now we were well within range of German soldiers who might feel inclined to test their skills.

We reached the Bailey bridge and the noise made by the jeep rattling over its loose planks was akin to a machine-gun operating not far away. I could not believe what was happening as we gained the far side and turned right. The road ran at the foot of the steep-sided hills that ranged away N.E. and north from Cassino and all this time the driver and I were expecting someone somewhere to shoot at us; we simply must have been noticed by the Germans, so why were we not stopped? Whatever the reason, we completed that journey without mishap and I maintain that it was a unique occasion and one that I would not have believed possible. The fact that the driver and I were never quite the same again is, I suppose, of small importance.

We reached John Berryman's position after climbing the mountain track amid mortar-bombs dropping by way of escort, they fizzed past us and mostly dropped into the ravine below. The noise of our jeep, as it clambered over the loose surface, had attracted the mortars and we were not thanked by the infantry on arrival at the top. Popularity or no, we spent a few hours with and around the M10's, trying to see the enemy positions and trying to discover the whereabouts and extent of our own forces.

The environment in this area of the front was just about as hostile as one was likely to find in this scale of operations. Not only were the hills incredibly steep, but they were essentially rocky and therefore resistant to the digging of protective trenches. The effect of the shell and mortar bursts was correspondingly more deadly, since they sprayed their splinters when bursting on the rock surface. The Germans were expert at preparing defence systems, both interlocking and mutually supporting, and had been preparing these positions for may months past. In addition, after each major attack, they had made the necessary adjustments to any doubtful chinks in the system. They had successfully repulsed a number of determined and heroic attacks launched earlier by the Americans and later by the Indian and New Zealand divisions. Now the Poles, led by their General Anders, were taking over this sector, and were to give a magnificent account of themselves in the coming weeks. There had been a horrifying loss of life in these hills and ravines, especially along the so called "Snakeshead Ridge" culminating in Pt. 593 which overlooked the Monastery.

Meantime our small party began the return journey to our battery HQ. It was now dark and we could make as much noise as we liked, the reason being the uproar of the evening barrage. It was at this time that the valley came to life, both in front of Monastery Hill and behind it. Rations and other supplies had to be brought to all the hundreds of soldiers no matter what their country of origin. Some of the paths leading to the forward troops in the mountains were too difficult even for jeeps; for these areas only mules were capable of maintaining the essential lifelines. The artillery chose this time as the most likely to repay their efforts.

On reaching the road at the bottom of the track we turned right to retrace our steps. Travelling towards Cassino it soon became clear that we were not going to return across the bridge. The whole area, including Monastery Hill, was under intense fire, and I couldn't resist pointing out that the route we had used earlier that afternoon was now emphatically a no-go area. A short distance on we found a way down to the river on our left. Here it was fast running, full of boulders but rather less than 2ft deep. Having little choice, we engaged the 4 wheel drive and drove into the river, but we managed only a few yards before the jeep lodged itself between boulders. We all stepped out into the water and lifted the jeep's rear end clear of the obstacles and tried again. This procedure was repeated about four times before we gained the other bank. We didn't mind getting wet because we were more than glad to keep our distance from the town. Our eventual return to our HQ was a moment of surprise to the others and great relief to ourselves.

APPROACH to Monte CASSINO (Chap xiv)

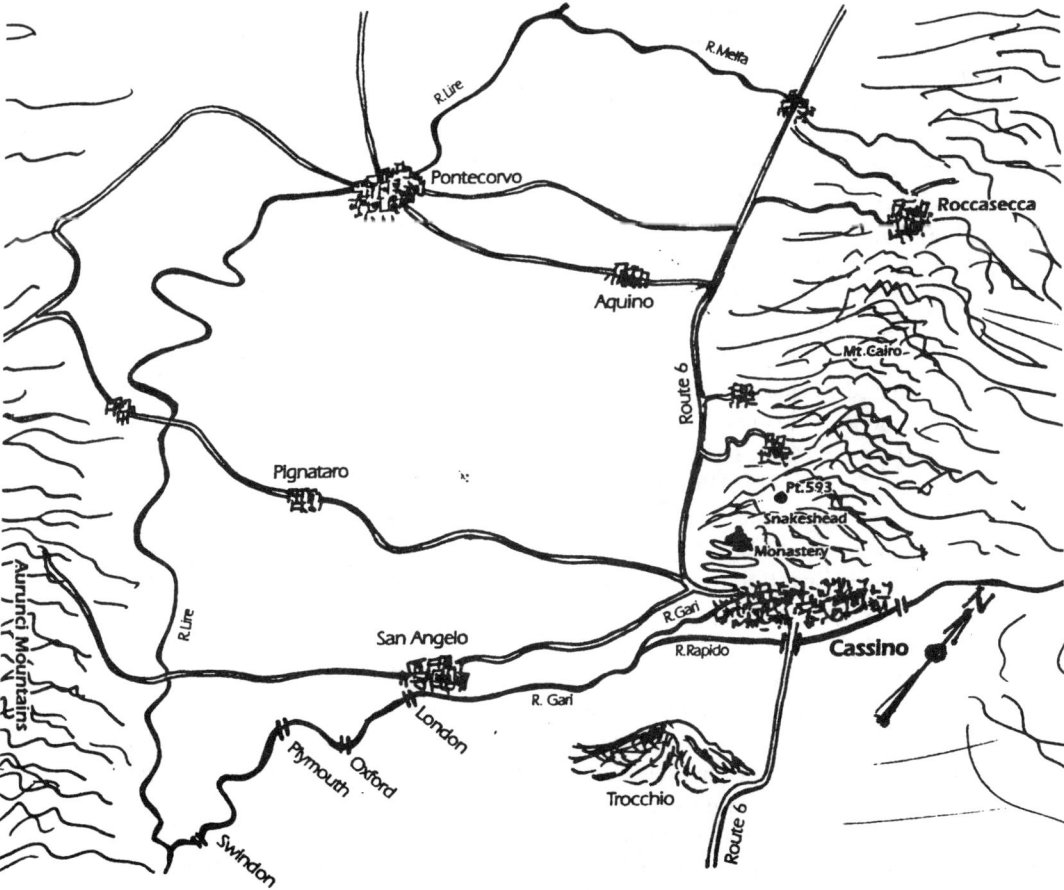

CHAPTER XIV

CASSINO - DIADEM

On 28th April 'D' Tp was relieved by Polish anti-tank gunners. During the next two weeks we received, and executed, a range of conflicting orders concerning the regrouping of all the forces along the Cassino front. This task, entailing the movement of regiments of tanks, regiments of guns, battalions of infantry, together with supporting troops of signals and engineers and others, was a process that had been continuing for some time past. Naturally, all movements had to be undertaken at night. New routes had to be found and made available to withstand the exceptionally heavy traffic of a modern army. They had to be marked and taped so as to be clearly identified at night to enable formations to find their new positions and ultimately their battle areas.

This shuffling was a major exercise and so much depended on everyone being in the right place at the right time. Extra formations and divisions were moved from the 8th Army on the Adriatic Coast, and much effort and care was directed to the cause of deception. Imitation tanks and guns sprang up in their dozens to replace all those which had been moved to other, hopefully secret, locations. Some guns were moved in to take their place, and they were required to fire with great vigour every evening to convince the enemy that nothing had changed. The Germans knew that an attack was coming, but it was in all our interests that they should not know where the main thrust was to be, and especially not when.

Within and under the ruins of Cassino lived the infantry and a few tanks crews, plus some thriving neighbourly rats. Both sides had constructed a number of strongholds by the strategic placing of a tank inside the remains of selected buildings. In a well known magazine entitled 'The Sphere' there appeared some photographs, in the issue dated June 3rd 1944, showing some action shots of the town and surrounding places. One photograph shows a few British soldiers in the chapel crypt of a convent before the fall of Cassino. According to this magazine, this refuge had withstood 99 direct hits before these particular troops occupied it and another 15 hits subsequently. Such circumstances illustrated the difficulty encountered in ejecting determined opposition from the chaos that was Cassino.

As the River Rapido left Cassino, travelling southwest to join the River Lire from the direction of Rome, it was first joined by the smaller River Gari which ran out of the hills north of the town. Thence the Rapido became the 'Gari', deeper and slower and more twisting. About 4 miles downstream on the northern bank of the river stands the village of San Angelo. Today the road to S. Angelo passes the British Cemetery and not only is the latter in a beautiful setting, with trees surrounding the multi-patterned rows of graves, but it is well sited historically.

Resting about halfway between Cassino and S. Angelo, and with the Monastery still near enough to overlook the scene, the cemetery is not far from the village where some of the most savage fighting, in the crossing of the river, took place. It was strongly fortified by the Germans and, perched on a knoll beside the river, it could command a large stretch of the approaches to the Gari. Many of those lying in the cemetery along the road, are there because of San Angelo. Today it is a delightful, picturesque and serene village that has long since healed its wounds and, with them, the tragedies that had unfolded all about it. Those few miles of the Gari river and the countryside to the west of Cassino, looking tranquil now, broke the hearts and the bodies of thousands of young men in 1944. This last battle is commemorated by a dark marble column which stands on the river bank at S.Angelo and is inscribed with words referring to the occasion. The battle is additionally remembered by the annual public holiday at Cassino on the anniversary of its liberation.

* * * * * * * * *

Looking objectively at the overall Italian situation, things seemed to have reached something of a stalemate. After a good start during 1943, the Allies had reached Cassino that October and had been unable to make any further progress. This was partially due to the bitter cold, snow and rain of the winter months, but also to the steadfast attitude of the Germans defending these exceptionally strong positions. It had been proved that this section of the front could not be breached by tanks, so it would rest with the infantry to force a way through the well-tried defences. The Anzio landings had established a substantial bridgehead but had failed to break out, and it was clear that the Germans were not going to be forced out of Cassino by that threat.

General Alexander had seen the effects of the American attacks across the river in the earlier months, and similar attacks in the hills, directed at the Monastery. He'd seen the further attacks by the Indians and, more recently, by the New Zealanders in February. All of these had proved costly ventures without much success to show for them. He couldn't afford to launch a big offensive unless he could be confident of the result. If Cassino fell, then Rome would surely follow and, with it, a large slice of the German divisions in Italy. To have a chance of cracking the Gustav Line here, the infantry would need overwhelming odds in men and guns and perhaps in tanks as well. Even so, they couldn't all be used at once no matter how concentrated, so there would remain a gamble to some extent.

Alexander eventually produced 2-3 divisions to throw at every one of the German divisions. On the right he sent the Polish Corps to tackle the hills and work round to the north of the Monastery and Point 593; thence to cut off Cassino and those hills, and cut Route 6 behind them. To the left of Cassino he sent the British 13 Corps, to cross the Gari in the neighbourhood of San Angelo, and to thrust onwards along the line of Route 6 and link up with the Poles. On the left of the British was the 5th Army, with the French Corps on the other side of the meeting between the rivers Lire and Gari and extending beyond in the Aurunci mountains. They in turn had the American Corps on their left working through the Aurunci mountains and the coastal plain.

This historic battle for Cassino, code named "Diadem", was due to begin on the night of May 11th 1944. As one of the many thousands of actors on that stage, I can say that we were the last to know when the curtain was due to be raised. However, on May 11th this information did filter through to 112 Battery who had moved about a bit during these early days of May. At first we were going to add to the preliminary barrage; then we were to give cover to so and so while they did such and such; no, we were to come under command of a tank regiment when they crossed the Gari; now we were to support the Rifle Brigade, and so it went. Our new equipment meant that until the end of the war we didn't know what role we should be given next. The choices were anti-tank guns, field artillery, close support guns and occasionally as second rate tanks.

In the event we were sent to join the Derbyshire Yeomanry, who were to work independently as soon as the assault divisions had gained a bridgehead sufficient to accommodate the additional fighting units. The Derbyshire Yeomanry were the reconnaissance regiment of our division and had been equipped with armoured cars in Tunisia. There we had seen little of them, and had never worked with them in action. Now, like us, they had been given different weapons, namely Sherman tanks. In consequence it was inevitable that they should be used as another tank regiment instead of an armoured recce regiment. Just what our purpose was in marrying up with the D.Y. we didn't really know. Still, we had become accustomed to being pushed around in Tunisia, apparently Italy was to be no different.

At 11.00 pm on May 11th, or 2300hrs as the army would have it, there occurred a sudden shock of noise. For a few hours all had been quite along the front, the evening harassing fire had been faded out after a short spell and Cassino seemed unnaturally placid, even pensive. It is said that along the whole front there were 1600 guns of assorted sizes on our side. What proportion of those were gathered behind our local positions opposite Cassino and along the Gari is not disclosed, but something like half would not be an exaggeration. Whatever their number, a multitude of guns sent their thousands of shells over and into the hills and the valley. They sought to destroy all the known German positions, and to render the opposition ineffectual, by fear and sheer weight of noise and destruction. This inferno continued for about three-quarters of an hour, during which time the country before us gave the appearance of being ablaze. Towards the end of that time the barrage had moved away from the river to allow the infantry to get close and to bring up their small boats in readiness.

By midnight the assault troops were on their way. The Gari was about 9ft deep and with a strong, though not fast, current; it was only some 20yds across but, at that, was a formidable obstacle. The Germans, being no fools at this business, had long ago ranged their guns and mortars onto many probable crossing points of the river. They had registered all the likely approaches and of course had managed to sow many hundreds of mines on both sides of the river.

Our barrage may have looked and sounded devastating, but it had failed to neutralize the mortars and machine guns that began to rip into the hapless infantry. Many of the fragile boats were holed and sank, some were carried away before gaining the far bank. Such an undertaking with men and equipment would have been difficult in daylight without enemy action. To commit hosts of men, most of whom were not familiar with the vagaries of boats and currents, in darkness and under raking fire, is to invite trouble and chaos. There was plenty of both.

The early stages of this battle raged throughout the next day and night and on into the second day. By then the British and the Indians had severely dented the enemy line, they had established a wide bridgehead and penetrated a couple of miles. It had been cut and thrust, hour by hour, with an endless succession of well-prepared defences each to be taken individually with rifle and grenade. Any ground that lent itself to stalking unseen was inevitably mined or crossed with trip wires attached to booby traps. One wondered how anybody could survive conditions such as these.

After two days and nights without rest, and with friends and mates being shot and maimed all about them, the leading troops had fought and cursed and shivered with fright, and butchered other men they'd never previously seen, in order to claim a couple of miles of the Lire valley. They were hungry, cold and dirty; some had wet themselves or worse, some had cried in despair, most had sworn at the remains of the Monastery which was still just beside them, or so it seemed. Certainly they were overlooked from that hillside just as they had been before. It seemed that Monastery Hill was going to exert its influence to the bitter end. On the right the Poles had suffered a bad time, just as the others had before them, their losses were unacceptable, and they had been forced to ease off until 13 Corps could get behind Monastery Hill and on to cut Route 6 and the supply tracks to the hills.

* * * * * * * * *

Early on May 14th 112 Bty was drifting with a tide of traffic along a very dusty road with the intention of meeting up with our friends the Derbyshire Yeomanry. Our progress was much hindered by what appeared to be the remainder of the 8th Army choosing to use our designated route at the same time. Every road, lane and track that wandered about this valley south of the river was choked with all conceivable types of army transport, including tanks, like ants on an away day. Howard became restive in his anxiety to reach the D.Y. and I had difficulty in dissuading him from overtaking all those in front. Such a move with our M10's would have been the equivalent of damming a river.

There was nothing to be done but move, snail like, with other traffic and hope that things would improve. We knew that eventually we had to cross the river via Oxford Bridge, one of four Bailey bridges thrown across by the sappers. "London" was hard by San Angelo, "Oxford" was perhaps half a mile further down stream, "Plymouth" was another half a mile on and "Swindon" was way beyond near to the confluence with the River Lire. I presumed these bridges, together with the routes serving them, were one-way systems; if so, there must have been connecting tracks from one bridge to another through the mine-fields.

I suppose it must have been about midday when we made contact with the D.Y. We were perhaps 3/4 mile from the river and, in the course of time, began another ponderous move in the convoy with some elements of the D.Y. This time there was ample evidence of what had gone before; we were passing through the forming up areas of the infantry which the Germans knew perfectly well. It had been reduced to a wilderness of shredded trees and cratered fields by shell and mortar fire. Soon we would enter the area of the random mine-fields.

Our way was taped to ensure a safe passage, but we had long since learned that recently cleared mine-fields were to be treated with suspicion and caution. On this occasion I had been reminded of this when I wanted to have a pee. I walked only a few yards along what looked like a recently trodden path which was just short of the marked mines area. I passed a stump of a tree and beside it a boot; showing inside the boot was the grey distorted bulge of a foot. Discouraged by this I retraced my steps forth with and with greater care.

On a stop/start basis our column made its halting way towards the river. Not only were our self propelled guns very different from the guns we'd had in Tunisia, but so was much of our transport. The Troop Commanders had the small American 'Honey' tanks for their HQ vehicle, and the Bty Commander, with whom I rode when we were in action, was provided with a specially adapted Sherman.

It was a Sherman tank with the turret removed and had provision for several wireless sets, it had no guns and was essentially a communications vehicle. In this HQ Sherman we were following one of the D.Y. tanks; behind us there was an armoured half-track, this had wheels in front and a shortened version of tank tracks in place of rear wheels.

We were all travelling slowly along the route marked on either side by tapes and doing our best to follow in the tracks of the people in front. I was sitting on the turret rim directly over our right hand track. My purpose was to assist our driver to place our tank as nearly as possible in the tracks of the Sherman in front. This was not as difficult as it sounds. We were doing nicely until suddenly there was a deafening bang behind accompanied simultaneously with something the size of a large wheelbarrow flashing past my head. So close was this object that I felt the breeze of it and my hat fell off.

Looking round and feeling slightly shocked, I saw the half track lying blackened with its nose on the ground. Two of its occupants were standing up and grinning, they looked like a couple of black minstrels. The missile that had nearly taken my head off was the front axle of the half-track together with its surviving wheel. A whole crowd of vehicles had passed along that track and the mine that had destroyed the half-track had been gradually uncovered. Our Sherman had run right over it, but the heavy wheel of the half-track had been pushed through the surface onto the mine. The men were saved by the length of the engine of those vehicles. Usually the drivers and front passenger of any trucks setting off a mine would suffer at least their legs smashed, and often much worse.

This distraction caused delay for the column until, with the help of the tanks, we pushed the reminder of the half-track off to the side of the track. Thereafter we studied the ground with even more caution as we made our way forward. There was a long low ridge running parallel with the river and about 150 - 200 yds from it. This small ridge allowed us to approach thus far with out being too easily seen, but the ground from there to the river was absolutely flat and open. Any bushes, trees, vines or hedges had long since been blown away. We felt very exposed as we trundled in crocodile formation towards Oxford Bridge, and I recall slipping off my perch into the protective custody of our Sherman. This move was precipitated by the arrival of some mortar bombs,and due to the noise of the continuing battle, it was impossible to hear the plop of the mortars being discharged in the distance.

Oddly, the river here was called the Gari and had been since the meeting of the Gari with the Rapido. But we were so used to referring to it as the Rapido that it remained so as far as we were concerned.

So at last we rattled our way across the bridge and, along further taped tracks, began to move up the slow gradient on the other side. It was now into the evening and a haze was forming along the river valley. Already we were glad of the comparative safety of the M10's and our Sherman, because there were plenty of shells and mortars exploding over the valley. The evidence of battle was everywhere. The ground was littered with discarded ammunition boxes, wrecked vehicles, clothing, battered defensive posts, trenches, temporary graves and goodness knows what else. The whole area was naturally scarred with shell holes and the place had the smell of scorched earth and rottenness.

There was confusion everywhere, not least about where we were to go and what was our objective. The course of the battle dictated the objectives and consequently the latter changed from time to time. It was difficult to move formations about in restricted areas, where the enemy was still active and where mines had been sown anywhere and everywhere. There were very few lanes and farm tracks that had not been visited by the mine layers. Some of the fields and vineyards were sprinkled with anti-personnel mines and other kinds of booby-traps were concealed and set off by trip-wires or wires stretched between vines etc. The verges of the lanes and tracks were favourite spots for the anti-tank mines, and all of these formed part of the first line defence for the Germans in Italy. It was all extremely nerve-racking because one couldn't trust any piece of countryside to rest in or walk through.

The night of the 14th and the day of the 15th was spent in wending our way cautiously through a maze of little lanes and tracks that wound past vineyards and olive groves. It was slow going and, being now close to the current battle area, there were a number of alerts and alarms. The valley was dotted with farm houses and buildings, many of these had been converted into gun positions or machine-gun nests. Lots of them had been, and were still being, engaged and destroyed; others had yet to be dealt with and all were under suspicion. During this uncertain advance we passed by some of the dead of both sides. One wretched German had been killed by the side of the lane and had been run over by a tank, presumably at night.

Late that afternoon we harboured in the lee of a slope which gave concealment from the enemy. There were sunken lanes and hedges everywhere which meant that we could move about without being seen, this was quite a novelty after weeks before Cassino. Howard decided to go off on a reconnaissance and wanted Johnny Gaster and me to go along too. We set off in separate jeeps, nipped round the side or our protective hill, and headed for the enemy.

Howard wanted to find out what was going on and how far away was the front line. We had not gone far, perhaps 500 yards, before we caught up with a lot of banging and small arms fire. This suggested that, in answer to his second question, the front was very close. This was confirmed when more than one

German machine-gun spurted its very rapid fire in our direction. The bullets were not close to us, but made a crackling noise as they hit various objects about 100 yards to our right. Johnny and I decided that this was far enough to take our jeep and promptly parked it in the lane under the hedge. Howard, on the other hand, shot off down the lane in front of us, not even waiting to see if we were following. We were both astonished at this and wondered where the hell he was going. I said we'd wait a minute or two because undoubtedly he'd be back even faster than he went.

After some 7-8 minutes Johnny and I thought we'd better walk forward to see what had happened to Howard. There was still quite a bit of firing being exchanged together with a similar exchange of mortars. In short, it was unpleasant if not down right dangerous to be walking abroad. We managed to get a further 100 yards and then slipped into a ploughed field on our left where we hoped to have a better view of what was going on. The view that we had away from the hedges enabled us to scan the ground in front in the hope of seeing something of Howard. This still limited view was not reserved for us, it was also shared by the enemy. All at once came an incredible noise, rather a succession of noises, such as I'd never heard before. The nearest likeness that I can think of, is that ridiculous whooping made by a naval destroyer when it sounds off salutations to somebody.

Johnny Gaster and I both stopped and listened, then we flattened ourselves into the field. There followed half a dozen huge bangs with heaps of earth flung everywhere and over us. They were like miniature eruptions. These explosions were close, far too close, and, as we picked ourselves up, there came the sound of more being discharged. We dived into one of the craters made a few moments earlier and immediately heard the approaching whoosh of the next batch. Another 6 of these things fell with enormous crashes all about the spot where we'd been standing before. Cringing in our crater the two of us were covered with earth and stones and the reek of burnt earth was very strong. We decided to risk one further dose by staying in this same crater and then, as soon as the next bursts had arrived, we'd make a sprint for the cover of the lanes and hedges.

So it was, a third clutch of these bombs, or whatever, roared over and ripped the field apart about 20-40 yards from us. The craters were more than 3ft deep and had a diameter of some 6ft. We fled with very commendable speed and gained the nearest lane as the next whoops signalled more on the way. Simultaneously there came a voice calling "Johnny, Johnny". Looking round, I saw two small brown faces grinning from holes in the bank under the hedge. They were little Gurkha soldiers of the Indian Division, renowned for their bravery. There were others similarly dug in along this lane, and it didn't take five seconds for Johnny Gaster and me to share two adjacent holes with our Gurkha friends.

We waited, thankful to enjoy the comparative safety of those trenches, until the heat was off. Our little friends couldn't speak our language any more than we could speak theirs, so we parted with smiles and a pat on their shoulders. Our jeep was as we had left it and, there being little else to do, we made our own way back to the M10's. At least we could tell the others what was happening a few hundred yards ahead, and we were in no way comforted to learn that they had been listening to the explosions that we had been dodging. We subsequently learned that the cause of all this disturbance was a new weapon called a 'Nebelwerfer.' It was a six barrelled rocket launcher, each rocket weighed 75lbs and had a range of 7,300 yards.

Meanwhile I was worried about Howard, and I was trying to decide how I was going to find him. Savage had left me to become a wireless operator and his place had been taken by gunner Jones. Jones was a small but always cheerful soul who adopted a philosophical attitude to active warfare. He was not born to be a soldier but he was prepared to do his bit, to brew some tea, dig holes and such like; but he was willing to leave the firing of the M10's to others and was grateful if people didn't start any thing. His maxim of 'live and let live' was not one that could easily be reconciled with the concept of war, but he did his best. Now he offered me a welcome cup of tea with the sound advice that, "It doesn't do to push your luck too far, Sir".

Within a few minutes, Howard's jeep turned into our field and he stepped out looking flustered but pleased. He explained that he'd intended to find out from the infantry how things were going, in order to assess the situation from our point of view. Unfortunately he ran into crossfire and was obliged to take instant cover. He didn't know where he was and obviously couldn't continue with his quest, so he'd waited for a lull in the storm and dashed for home, so to speak.

In contrast to what had been happening a few hours before, as darkness began to fall I saw numbers of tiny bright green coloured lights flying about. They were quite plentiful in the hedges and it was not until I finally tracked one down that I realised they were fire-flies. It appeared that those little bright insects were not allowing their normal way of life to be interrupted by the noise of a war, nor was the nightingale which was in operatic flow.

* * * * * * * * *

During our hesitant approach to the river 24 hours before, I had been called to an order group given by our force commander, Maj Norman Brundell MC. It was with his squadron of the Derbyshire Yeomanry that we should be working for the foreseeable future, and certainly for the first days of the coming battle. Major Brundell was known always as Eager Brundell; I don't know why this was, but I didn't know his name was Norman until many years later. He was a most popular man and rightly so, always considerate, dashing in the nicest way, with a charm and humour. On this occasion he outlined our task and warned that it would almost certainly change because the other side of the river was all confusion. He told us to keep our heads down, "Because there will be rather a lot of grape flying about".

The day following our abortive recce was May 16th. We were supposed to be forging on past Pignataro and to Pontecorvo beyond. But Pignataro was still in German hands and there was stubborn resistance from a few places around the village as well as the village itself. The Colonel of the D.Y. was Col Peter Payne-Galway. He had the task of taking a low ridge where enemy machine gunners and others were holding up our infantry and giving the latter a bad time. He had told Eager to take the hill as soon as possible. The squadron was to rush the hill and sweep the enemy off; our Infantry would follow to occupy the ridge and secure it.

Eager protested that the place was full of snipers and the tank commanders, with head and shoulders out of their turrets, would be extremely vulnerable. The attack had to proceed, so Eager ordered all his tank crews to keep down inside the Shermans out of harm from small arms fire. He himself rode with his upper half outside his turret in order to see and control this local action. He led this attack and reached perhaps halfway to the top of the objective when he was shot and killed by a sniper. Col Payne-Galway, as soon as he heard, came to the scene and, enraged by the loss of Eager, took his place and rushed the hill in his Sherman, firing a Tommy gun madly all the way. The squadron chased after him and the Derbyshire Yeomanry roared onto that hill and beyond hitting everything in the way.

The fighting during the next day or two continued to be fierce and ugly. These were the last defences of the Gustav line at Cassino. Pignataro stood on a rocky ridge which was host to a number of caves; these lent themselves readily for natural defences and the Germans were skilled in blending them into their scheme of fortifications. The battle in this area of the valley was exhausting and costly. We brought the M10's up in case the enemy tried a counter attack with tanks; but the country was so close with vines and olives, that we couldn't see far in any direction; and we, like the tanks, were vulnerable to anti-tank guns, mines and Bazookas. At length the Indians, with tanks supporting them, took the important village of Pignataro on the 18th May.

On that day, although we had no knowledge of it at the time, the Monastery and Cassino fell. That night the Poles, who had occupied the Monastery, were letting off flares to celebrate a conquest that had the grimmest of all stories to tell. The Gustav line was cracked and it collapsed. That line, with Cassino as its pivot and its heart, had withstood battles throughout history. It had been a bastion denying the Allies the road to Rome for the last 7 months and, in doing so, had become a legend and a graveyard.

There were thousands of casualties before the last battle, 'Diadem'; the first battle cost the Allies between 10,500 and 11,000 casualties, but the published casualty figures for the fourth and last battle were:

American	18,000		
British and Poles	15,000	Germans	38,000
French	11,000		
Allies	44,000		

Eager Brundell is in good company in those acres that embrace so many, half-way between San Angelo and Cassino.

CHAPTER XV

MELFA TO PERUGIA

The fall of Cassino was more than a milestone in the Italian war, it was symbolic in the struggle between the gladiators in this contest. It was a public announcement that there was now nothing that could prevent the Allies from occupying the whole of Italy. This must be only a matter of time and time was on our side. We knew there was another line of prepared defences to be breached a short distance behind Cassino - this was the Hitler line, but we felt that the worst was over. The hope was that there would now be a breakout from Anzio which should turn the achievement of Cassino into a mighty breakthrough.

Our optimism was blunted soon enough. We made progress towards Pontecorvo but were shelled and bombed heavily for our trouble. It was a time of no respite, with enemy resistance revived in a sort of desperation. As Eager had prophesied, there was plenty of grape about, but during one lull in the happenings I was talking to Sgt Mortimer, a sergeant on our battery HQ, he was a most popular man with a large sunny face and disposition to match. Although a butcher by trade, Sgt Mortimer looked as though he should have been a farmer.

As we chatted he suddenly collapsed onto the ground beside me; in reply to my question he said he'd been hit and was clutching his side. I undid his battledress top and pulled up his shirt, sure enough there was a bullet hole in his right side below his rib cage. He was very grey with shock and in some pain, but we got him onto a stretcher without difficulty and so on to the back of a jeep. I told him he'd be all right and he answered "Will I, oh good" He then began the journey back to the nearest forward aid post and thence on to hospital where the bullet was removed. A couple of our chaps were able to visit him in hospital and he proudly showed them his bullet. Two weeks later he died in hospital.

Shortly afterwards we were slowly making our way along one of those little lanes that criss-cross the valley, when I saw in front a destroyed Bren Carrier which had clearly gone over a mine. I could then see signs of mines in the lane beyond, so decided to bypass that spot. I drove through the left side hedge with my Sherman and immediately stopped the driver; in front was the body of a British soldier and we had almost driven over him. The small paddock had longish grass and, as I stood on the Sherman, I saw that the place was filled with bodies. These poor devils must have run onto machine-guns, because there were so many.

It was a distressing sight and I had to move one or two to allow the battery to get through. I don't know how many were lying there but there seemed to be a body every 4 to 5 yards.

Meanwhile Pontecorvo fell and we switched north to Aquino which we reached by the 21st, then worked our way parallel to Route 6. By the 25th the Derbyshire Yeomanry group was approaching the river Melfa, and on this day Howard Hillier was posted to the newly formed 61st Infantry Brigade where he had some special job at Brigade HQ. Major J Mclennan, who took over the re-formed 5 Troop way back at Medjez-El-Bab in December 1942, was now our new Battery Commander. Mac, as he was known, was a small but gutsy man and I think he was rather surprised to be taking 112 Bty.

Mac had an unhappy initiation as Battery Commander because, at the moment of joining us, we were trying to force a crossing of the River Melfa. The battery was supporting 'B' Sqdn of the Derbyshire Yeomanry together with a company of the 10th Rifle Brigade and a battery of the 12th Royal Horse Artillery. At first we were told to try to cross not far from the Route 6 blown bridge. Then, overnight, the plan was changed to move further west where there was a better chance. We started at 0430 hours on the 26th, by 0500 a DY tank and an OP (observation post) tank of the RHA had both blown up on mines. This caused an hours delay to find a new route. A new start was promptly followed by 'F' Troop's Honey Tank breaking down and John Latham was obliged to transfer to one of his M10's. 'E' Troop, with Johnny Gaster, joined the leading tanks and reached the sought after crossing to find it occupied by the Canadians who were burying their dead. The DY and 'E' Tp returned to explore the area where we had been ordered to go in the first place; here we found a small bridge intact.

The Melfa was a relatively small river feeding into the Lire from the hills to the north of Route 6. It was quite fast running and had cut a very steep gorge throughout this part of its course. The tanks and 'E' Tp deployed either side of the approaches to the bridge and searched for signs of the enemy. All looked quiet and one of the D.Y. Troops together with 'E' Tp crossed the bridge. The last M10 to cross was machine gunned from our near bank with the result, due to our open turrets, that one of the gunners was killed.

'F' Tp plus a second troop of the Derbyshire Yeomanry then probed along the river bank towards Route 6. John Latham's gun exchanged fire with a German 88mm gun on the other side. They both missed with their first shots, the second from the 88 hit the M10's gun and smashed it, the third slammed into the M10 which burst into flames. The driver was killed and John Latham, Sgt Harper, Bombardier Bullock and Gunner Rowe, all my old 6 Tp people, were all badly burnt. They jumped out of the open turret, but in those few seconds they were enveloped in flames. They went to hospital for many weeks and Lt Latham never returned; Sgt Harper rejoined the battery eventually and I'm not sure of the others.

The Rifle Brigade were unable to cross the river so, although the tanks had reached the top of the ridge rising from the other side of the river, they couldn't stay there indefinitely; and the M10's were especially at risk from infantry either firing into the open turrets or lobbing grenades into them. We decided to withdraw the armoured vehicles before nightfall. The first M10 to start across the bridge was knocked out by the 88mm and set fire to the bridge. The casualties this time were two gunners killed, another gunner, the sergeant and the bombardier wounded. Both the sergeant and bombardier died later in hospital.

During all this we had taken some prisoners, some of them by accident. The Germans were dug in along the deep banks of the Melfa, and one of our M10's, in crossing in the first instance, had unintentionally knocked the heavy machine-gun clamped to the rear of the turret so that it swung and pointed down along the river. To the gun team's surprise, a group of Germans popped out of the river bank with their hands raised. We made these prisoners carry our wounded back across the river, which they were quite happy to do.

The D.Y. Troop and the 'E' Tp guns had to be abandoned since they had no means of recrossing the river. We managed to retrieve all the men, which was some blessing. Having lost 5 of our 12 guns, and with the depletion of the DY Sqdn, we were ordered back and replaced by 111 Bty and others. The Rifle Brigade remained by the river and I took the remainder of this force back a mile or so to harbour for the night. It was now dark and the Luftwaffe came out to find us. They dropped flares lighting the whole area and could quite easily see the clouds of dust thrown up by the M10's and Shermans. The aeroplanes began to drop more flares over us and I thought it prudent to take cover.

There was a fair-sized wood on the right and I made for a lane that took us in that direction. The lane went alongside this wood and , by driving to the far end, almost all of our column was able to stop under the concealment of the trees. The aeroplanes circled above us and concluded we'd gone into the wood; they began dropping their bombs all over it, which suited us well since we were parked along the edge of it. Twenty or more bombs were dropped without inflicting any casualties on us.

Next day our infantry crossed the River Melfa without trouble, the enemy having left during the night. I went to the burnt our M10 of 'F' Tp and found it still fairly hot. Inside I found the sickening remains of the driver whom I'd hoped to bring out in order to bury him. I was unable to do this and felt guilty about leaving him there, but there didn't seem much choice.

We salvaged one of 'E' Tp's guns and used it to make 'F' Tp up to strength, we now had two complete troops, 'D' and 'F'. These two were deployed as field guns and put down a large dose of harassing fire on Arce, the next small town to be overcome. By the end of the month we received new M10's for 'E' Tp plus the necessary reinforcements. Lt Clifford Betts joined us to take over 'F' Tp in place of John Latham, he was the second Troop Commander for my old 6 Troop since I had left them.

Today, if you visit the River Melfa in October and look along that gorge from the bridge over what was Route 6, you will be dazzled by a continuous carpet of wild flowers that grow like bluebells. I don't know their name, but they have the colour of strawberries and custard mixed, and grow about six inches high. The nearest I can venture to describe them would be small wild cyclamen.

* * * * * * * * *

To digress a little more at this point, I'd like to refer to our Padre for a moment. I spoke before of him trying to teach some of us the game of Bridge during the long Algerian nights at Robertville. Now, in Italy, he busied himself endeavouring to help in whatever way he could. I only wish I could remember his name. From a letter I wrote in those days I learn that the Padre had been abroad for longer than most of us but remained uncomplaining; on the contrary he was, "A jolly sort of man yet very sincere, and what a talker", that was how I described him at the time, but had also talked about his qualities. I was particularly impressed, and glad, when, after the Melfa river, he turned up

131

promptly, but out of the blue. He said without fuss "I've brought a few crosses along Donald, thought you might like them for your chaps." He made off and collected the bodies of those killed, something that I had always found difficult to do, and saw to their graves and burial, and other things one has to do. Going through a person's private papers, to return them to the family at home, requires tact, sensitivity and a strong stomach, sometimes those papers may be torn and bloodstained and might be better not sent.

It was strange how the Padre must have followed the course of battle and its everyday consequences. On most occasions, when we had suffered more casualties than usual, he would arrive, clap his hand on my shoulder and say something like, "Hello Donald, I hear your battery has had some more bad luck." "I am afraid so," I answer, "Yes - Yes - rather - Yes, well - hmmm - beastly - right - poor chaps." Then I'd offer him a cup of indifferent tea, "That's very nice of you but I'm afraid I haven't time, how long will it be?" He always stayed for a cup.

Before Diadem started he invited himself to supper on one occasion, and stated when he'd be along. Sure enough he arrived on time but we were still washing. Unperturbed, he sat down and said it was kind of us to invite him, which we hadn't, and not to hurry on his account. It wasn't what the Padre did, though he did a lot, but his method and manner of the doing. He was a character, we were amused, charmed and fond of him, his sincerity shone through and I wish I had told him so.

* * * * * * * *

With the crossing of the Melfa the Hitler line was gone, and the 8th Army Divisions began thrusting forward with increasing momentum. Arce and Ceprano were swallowed up and we realized that at last we were not fettered by well-prepared defences. Our division spent a day or two re-grouping. 112 Bty was taken from the Derbyshire Yeomanry and put under command of the new 61st Infantry Brigade, they were motorised infantry consisting of the 2nd, 7th and 10th battalions of the Rifle Brigade.

After months of stagnant warfare at Cassino, it was now a perpetual 'prepare to move'. There were delaying incidents inevitably, but they were more in the nature of hiccups in the pursuit. There were local battles for local features but none that could halt the armies for any length of time. We passed by to the east of Rome and were well to the north of the Capital by the time it fell on 5th June. This was a time for Ted Newman and his quarter-master stores personnel to go without sleep for a few days. We were using less ammunition perhaps, but hundreds of gallons of fuel for the M10's.

The pattern of events that began to be established was: an advance along one or more roads; a blown bridge across a river; a cautious investigation; some shell and/or mortar fire plus small arms fire; our infantry sent round either side to encircle the obstacle; a night-time bridge building exercise and enemy retreat; a continued advance next day. This sequence was sometimes modified by stronger resistance which would demand a larger preparation and attack on our part. On such occasions it was common practice for our M10's to be called forward to engage enemy posts, or to provide cover if tanks were thought to be in the vicinity.

So the advance north of Rome rolled onward, with little known skirmishes and lesser known engagements, which nevertheless took a constant toll of lives. On the 10th June we were subjected to heavy artillery fire and we lost a number of killed and wounded from 'D' and 'E' Troops. On this occasion I was in yet another small field which our Bty HQ shared with one of our troops and some D.Y. Sherman tanks. Our HQ Sherman was parked about 35 yards from a tank when one of the shells had a direct hit on its turret. Naturally it exploded with a loud crash, it chipped a piece out of the steel and inflicted a series of scores across the turret. I was sheltering underneath our Sherman but looked towards the nearby tank to see what had happened. The tank Commander popped out of the top of his turret and inquired, "Did somebody call?"

We were now making greater use of the M10's as artillery rather than as anti-tank guns. The battery tended to be split in terms of role; one troop in a forward support role with the infantry, one or two troops deployed for indirect fire onto specified objects or areas. Certainly the M10's were earning their keep, indeed they were only rested for maintenance and repairs by the Light Aid Detachment.

Because of this increased artillery action I found myself busier than I might otherwise have been, in the capacity of Forward Observation Officer (FOO). Sometimes we had difficulties with communications. Our wireless sets were not powerful enough, or in some ways not capable of coping with the steep hills and valleys. One moment I could speak clearly to the gun position, the next there was no response whatever. I would then have to drive about to various vantage points to try to re-establish contact, and then I might not be able to see what I wanted.

By the 14th June we had captured Narni and Terni and in doing so had by-passed the beautiful, walled town of Rieti. Seeing this delightful town many years later was like travelling back in time several hundred years; except that it boasted an intimate and exceptionally friendly Bistro where they cater for you so beautifully and where the food and wine was, or is, second to none. The young couple who ran this place were as a host and hostess should be, they were as attentive and hospitable as their food was delicious.

The 17th June saw 'F' Tp back with the Derbyshire Yeomanry and myself acting as FOO as we explored towards Marciano. We engaged a few of the enemy and I was asked to put down some harassing fire on several roads and other places. During this time I watched a German vehicle come down the road towards Marciano, along a part that I had been shelling only 20 minutes before. The vehicle stopped and it would have been very simple to have put a couple of shells on top of it and whoever was in it. I had no real wish to do this, and thought of our journey in Howard's jeep that afternoon at Cassino; so I just watched. He was lucky.

A couple of days later and we were south of Perugia in a field next to our other field artillery regiment, the Ayrshire Yeomanry. There was a large hill, Malbe, west of Perugia, which overlooked Route 75, the road north to Florence and the axis of our advance. Malbe was some 2000ft high and had to be taken. The AY and ourselves put down a lot of fire onto that hill; on the 20th we fired 300 rounds from our M10's and the next day another 154 rounds. The Ayrshires fired their fair share in addition, in 24 hrs we were knee deep in empty shell cases.

Later the same day a Tp of M10's was called for to support the Rifle Brigade who were attacking Malbe. 'F' Troop dashed off along Route 75 and up a very difficult track to reach the RB. Lt Clifford Betts was asked to silence enemy mortars and sniper posts in houses up there. His troop fired high explosive shells, armour piercing shot and their heavy machine-guns, and succeeded in neutralising the mortars and snipers.

That evening, when Capt Newman came with the rations for the troop, he left his truck and was handing round the mail when an enemy shell whined over and banged quite close to his truck. When he returned to the vehicle he found his driver dead and two of his gunners wounded. In such casual ways are the divisions between life and death decided.

Before 'F' Tp left us to join the Rifle Brigade on Malbe, I had been talking one lovely sunny evening with Clifford Betts and another officer. We had been admiring the countryside and comparing it with Africa. Clifford had been with the 8th Army in the Western Desert and had been promoted before joining us some time later. He was now due for special leave in the UK. There was a scheme laid down whereby anyone who had done 4 years overseas was entitled to so many weeks leave in the UK. Clifford had been notified that in one weeks time he would be relieved and would be transported back en route to England. We were chaffing him and telling him it was just an excuse to leave us to finish the Italian war while he had a good time. Clifford said, quite quietly and seriously, "I won't be going back, I have a strong feeling that my number is up".

On Malbe the RB had taken their objectives and began to push on to Corciano. On the 24th the riflemen had sent out a patrol which returned without their officer; he had been wounded and they'd had to leave him. Clifford said he would go and look for him, and Gunner Barber, whom I knew well from the 6 Tp days, went with him. They set off and attempted to reach the RB officer, but in so doing they walked into a minefield. Clifford stepped on one and was blown upside-down against a tree, he was killed instantly. Barber tried to recover him but saw that the place was thickly sown and realized that he couldn't carry Clifford back through the mines on his own, even if he managed to reach him. He rightly, though regretfully, had to leave him.

Not long after the fall of Perugia I tried to pay a fleeting visit to this glorious-looking hill town. Accordingly, I stole off in a jeep and made my way towards the hill on which, in those days, Perugia nestled. (Nowadays it cannot nestle, it is a sprawling town, spilling out on all sides). The road up to the town climbed steeply, twisting and coiling its way round and upwards. There was a high wall on the left of the road as we neared the top, along this wall there was at least a squadron of tanks parked. On reaching the top I continued into a large square surrounded by lovely buildings. Perugia seemed to have escaped destruction and there was a large gathering of soldiers at one section of the square. Switching off the engine I heard music coming from the crowd. On closer scrutiny I learnt that the remarkably good trumpeter, who was belting out some of the forces favourites, was none other than the renowned and popular Nat Gonella. He had come out to entertain the troops, but I'd never heard of an entertainer being so near to the front line before.

We listened with delight and acclaim and gave him additional applause because of his effort to visit the men at the front, rather than the base troops. How he had managed to reach this far forward was a mystery, and I supposed he was going to give a concert somewhere. Then the thought occurred to me that he was not visiting but was actually in the army and was playing his trumpet as Bdr Brown had done in Tunisia. This conjecture was interrupted by a whoosh and bang of a shell hitting a building across the square. The music stopped and the square emptied quicker than a children's classroom at playtime. That was the last I saw of Perugia.

Now our eyes and our guns turned towards Magione, an attractive town of modest size settled on the side of a hill near Lake Trasimeno. This time the force allocated to take and advance beyond this town consisted mainly of artillery. There were armoured cars of the King's Dragoon Guards supported by a Bty of 12th RHA, a medium Bty and our own 112 Bty. I found myself an OP in a very nice house on top of a larger hill facing Magione. The wisdom of this choice was illustrated by the fact that I was joined there from time to time by fellow OP officers from the other regiments.

There were numbers of targets to which the King's Dragoon Guards drew our attention. Often in the past, because our M10's could outrange other artillery guns, we were given more distant targets to neutralize. However, in this situation we were required to take on various emergency targets in front and at the sides of the town. This meant that my guns, which were only 1000 yards behind me, could barely clear my hill in the effort to fulfil our tasks. I had to remind the guns constantly to check the crest clearance before carrying out the orders I'd just passed to them; even so, when the M10's fired, the shriek of shells flying close over my head tended to make me duck. An OP officer from the RHA, who was with me during one period and was unprepared for this, not only ducked when my M10's fired but exclaimed, "I can get this from the bloody enemy without you starting."

46 years later I was staying at San Feliciano on the lakeside 2 or 3 miles from Magione. I looked more closely at this pleasant town and was pleased to record that there were no signs of our earlier destructive behaviour, necessary though it may have been. The capacity for recovery from devastation is almost beyond belief and, I suppose, applies to the whole of Europe and Russia. Visiting many of these war zones in Italy, I am truly amazed at the lack of evidence of previous catastrophe. The only apparent damage still to be seen, that I have found, is showing on the exterior of the castle on Castle Hill, Cassino.

CHAPTER XVI

327 BATTERY AND VILLA GATTAIA

There were aspects of our advance from Cassino, through May, June and July, that I have not talked about. Hopefully anyone reading this story will have realized that the armies were moving virtually all the time. Our battery, as part of this advancing tide, was participating in the battle in one way or another the whole time. There had been no periods of rest, no sight-seeing tours, no opportunities even to have a bath in clean warm water. The divisions were obliged to move along any roads that were available within the confines of their prescribed boundaries. This situation was aggravated by the geography of Italy which denied passage to traffic other than in the valleys between the mountains. Consequently, the labyrinth of roads and tracks were soon churned into dust bowls. We, the participants in all this, were figures of white dust, and hand in hand with dust and dirt and sweat, went sleep, or lack of it.

I used to receive letters from people outside the family in England, saying how wonderful it must be to see the beauty of Italy in all seasons; and had I visited Rome and what did I think of St. Peters? They had been to such and such place for two weeks holiday, had I seen it? They expected I was enjoying all the Italian wine and must be very brown - lucky me.

It was difficult to answer such letters when one had been without sleep for days, without the opportunity to take one's clothes off for long periods of time, without bread or fresh food or milk, or fresh anything. It was pointless to reply that Rome, and all those in Rome, could go to hell for all we cared. It was equally pointless in saying that we had four men killed yesterday trying to scrounge from an empty house, the place was booby trapped and had blown them apart, wasn't that a pity? However, we were able to keep ourselves awake and alert because there was always a reliable supply of shells and bombs falling round us to ensure our attention.

Our hesitant progress pushed slowly northwards in much the same way as it had since Melfa. There was always another river, another hill, another town, another set of circumstances that meant trouble for somebody. Lt Pat Farrell had arrived to take over 'F' Tp, for whom I always had a personal concern. He was keen to play his part, but the battery he had come to join was tired and what would be termed 'battle weary' today. Nerves were stretched and had become frayed. Our people were good soldiers who knew their job, they would survive when less experienced men would have succumbed. There was a limit to their resilience, and senior officers were beginning to see the need for rest and resuscitation. Slowly, bit by bit, small numbers of troops were being withdrawn for short periods of rest. Besides, we were getting short of ammunition.

On 10th July I was given a week's leave and, together with Harry Penman, the Adjutant, went to Rome. It was another world and I felt bewildered and out of place in such contrasting lifestyle. We stayed in a splendid hotel where we had a bath every day and several for the first couple of days. We saw the play 'Blythe Spirit' with an English cast that included Emlyn Williams, whom I first saw in a small theatre in Bromley, Kent, when he was a very young man. The play then, I remember, was 'Night Must Fall', and I hope I'm right when I say that he played the part of Danny. We visited the Coliseum and St. Peters, which was overwhelming, and the opera to see and hear Adriana Guerrini in 'Madam Butterfly'.

It was a week without a dull moment and I was impressed. We naturally spoiled ourselves with food and wine in luscious restaurants. In fact we did all the things the authors of those letters had assumed I had done before. Yet in spite of its history and former glory, there was a touch of 'Twelfth Night' about it, "That surfeiting, the appetite may sicken........" Perhaps it was also to do with a guilty conscience about the fortunes of 112 Battery.

On my return to the regiment I found that Arezzo had been liberated after our M10's had fired a programme of 3 hours duration into the surrounding hills. This, not surprisingly, had used up most of the available ammunition. At this stage King George VI visited the division and Pat Farrell, with a party of gunners and NCO's, had to line part of the road as he passed. Another unexpected incident of a personal nature occurred. I had a message to report to the Colonel on the 23rd July. Wondering what was afloat, I presented myself at RHQ and found that Stanley Edwards was also there. Stanley was the troop commander who had been in the midst of the engagement with the Tiger Tanks at Robaa, Tunisia. He had been promoted Major and was posted to another regiment but had now returned to the 72nd once again.

We stood a short distance from the CO's tent and tried to think what could be behind all this. We questioned each other about our recent movements and activities, but this revealed nothing. Soon the Colonel came and greeted us and took us into his tent. He offered us a drink, which was reassuring up to a point, and then began to chat about the war in general and the role of the army when it was all over. The punch line came when he asked if we'd thought about the army as a career. He went on to say that, if we would like a commission in the regular army, he could arrange for us to be transferred to the Royal Horse Artillery straight away. This, it seemed, would stand us in good stead in the peace-time army.

We both turned down this well-meant and generous offer. Stanley said tactfully that he might have thought seriously about it, but was due to return to his civilian job. I said thank you, but that I had been offered a good job in my father's firm when I returned. This was true enough though I had given little thought to it as yet. We both left feeling rather flattered and chatted together before going our separate ways; we wondered why us?

* * * * * * * * *

On August 1st I was appointed Battery Captain of 327 Battery. This was, in a sense, a promotion, in as much as I automatically became 2nd in command of the battery. However, it meant that I had to leave my old battery which I had joined in 1941 and had served with ever since. Equally, it felt that I was abandoning all those NCOs and gunners whom I had grown to know so well. 327 Battery was armed with two troops of 17 pounders, the third troop was assisting the sappers with road building. This, because the need for conventional anti-tank guns was now strangely small. It seemed a long step from acting as Forward

Observation Officer for the M10's to pushing up rations from behind, and my feelings were confused.

Thus, for the first time in action, in either Tunisia or Italy, I found myself some distance behind the front. It took some time for me to accustom myself to this situation, but it had its compensations. My job was to bring up the daily rations and supplies to the guns. That was relatively easy since, at this time, they weren't near the fighting either. I seemed to spend more time at battery HQ than with 'A' echelon, the term given for the stores and supplies, because I like to keep myself up to date with any news.

327 Battery had an excellent Quartermaster Sergeant who knew more about how to prepare for the battery's needs, and when and from where to replenish his stocks, than I should ever know. It had been his full time job since Heaven knew when and, patient though he was, I could see that my ignorance of such matters was not helping his task, nor were my questions. We got along very well by dint of my doing what I was told, and escorting the couple of vehicles and water truck to the Battery each 24 hours as required. He told me what questions I needed to ask in order to maintain the continuity of this well-tried system, and on these terms it seemed to me that the life-lines of the battery were preserved very well.

By this time the war had ground slowly on past Montevarchi, San Giovanni and Figline, including, to the west, the lovely little town of Greve in the heart of Chianti country. Instead of turning left for Florence, the division was ordered north from Pontassieve to Rufino and Dicomano, its ultimate objective was the breaching of the Gothic Line in the Apennine mountains. The sobering thought was that there were a lot of mountains up there.

The weather began to intrude into the war more and more. We had experienced rain and mud on and off for some time, and these conditions were made so much worse by the continuous weight of traffic and the blown bridges with their individual detours to be maintained. There was an epidemic of trucks rescuing other trucks and tanks heaving at guns. Along many of the mountain tracks it was even a case of men pulling each other out of one quagmire after another. This sounds a fanciful exaggeration, but it is precisely what was happening along the whole front.

Inevitably these conditions, apart from making life thoroughly miserable, slowed the prosecution of the war to a crawl. The likelihood of pushing the Germans out of the mountains into the plains of the Po valley in the north was receding fast. True, Florence fell on August 20th but it had been declared an open city. The Germans had blown every bridge across the Arno except the Ponte Vecchio, here they blew up the buildings at either end in order to block the entrance and exit - a futile exercise without any realistic military purpose. In no time we had built two impressive Bailey bridges to replace two of those destroyed, and the rubble at the ends of the Ponte Vecchio was quickly pushed away.

It was soon obvious that the coming months in the mountains, with their severity of weather, would put additional strain upon the troops at the front. So it was decided that we, and other regiments, should open rest-centres. A place where the men could come to be rested out of danger; where there was warmth, a bath and such entertainment as they could find. To this end, a large and beautiful villa was found in Florence and I was sent to occupy it and make it ready to receive the first party from the regiment within a week. I was given a cook plus assistant cook, and about four men plus an NCO to run the place.

Running the place meant preparing to receive successive parties, each staying about 10 days, and providing conditions as welcoming as circumstances would permit. The preparation included the buying of food to augment the army rations; the cleaning of rooms; provision of fuel for heating and cooking; ensuring enough hot water for endless baths and washing of clothes, providing laundry facilities with clean blankets and towels; medical supplies, maintaining a drying room; providing breakfasts, dinners and suppers for those who wanted them, and literature plus maps of Florence and information generally; maintaining standards of behaviour at reasonable levels and transporting people to and from the city. Lastly I was responsible for the exquisite furniture.

* * * * * * * *

At the risk of stirring the reader's impatience, I believe it might help if I were to explain a little of my personal circumstances before being sent to Villa Gattaia.

It will be remembered that, in order that our M10's could function as field artillery, it was necessary for the battery personnel to undertake conversion courses. There was much vital procedure that all ranks had to understand and needed to become completely reliable in its execution. If we had a weakness, it was in the fact that there were very few officers who could actually shoot the guns from an observation post. In order for the guns to perform, it was necessary for someone to be up front to ascertain the needs of the infantry, or whoever, and to respond quickly to those needs.

For the most part, I had been acting as the Observation Officer for 112 Battery throughout the months from Cassino to Florence. It was rare indeed for me to be back with the guns themselves. Inevitably this meant that my presence was often required in areas which were likely to attract hostile enemy action.

After a time, and depending upon those circumstances, one's nervous system begins to fray round the edges. The feeling is that one is able to sustain the tension less and less. I have said elsewhere that luck is exhaustible; similarly, it may be said that the ability to submit oneself to recurring danger, with little respite, becomes more unbearable with familiarity, not less so. To witness the death or mutilation of others has a constant undermining and debilitating effect. In short, a normal human being is not designed to suffer those experiences indefinitely.

My diversion, to set up the rest camp at Villa Gattaia, came unexpectedly but as a life-line. Although I had been given a different job with 327 Bty, I had felt a kind of delayed reaction to all that had gone before. The war appeared to have no end, the Winter was before us, there seemed nothing to hope for and no comfort to look forward to. The few weeks at Gattaia, and particulary the friendship of those families, who seemed to understand, brought me through a trough and gave me a renewed hope for the future. It was something very special to me and, consequently, is a vital part of my story.

139

As I travelled from the hills to make my first acquaintance with Florence, the sun was shining and the weather warmed as we came from Pontassieve and motored to the outskirts of the city. It was natural to feel pleasure at this time, since the world before us promised to be different from anything that we had known and our anticipation was brimming over. It was the feeling of childhood when we arrived at our holiday destination, everything was wonderful and exciting. With me was my driver and batman Jones, who I always called Sinbad. Both were smiling broadly at this unexpected turn of events and expressed the view that I must have had some influence in high places.

It transpired that the Villa Gattaia was just outside the city itself, south of the River Arno. It was situated in Viale Michelangelo, halfway up the hill towards Piazzale Michelangelo which provides the finest view of Florence to be seen, and one of the finest of any city in the world. The villa's own drive was very steep and twisting from the road, but there, at the top, Villa Gattaia stood in splendour amid the pine trees; it was grand in appearance and large enough for a medium sized hotel. The villa was shaped like an inverted 'L' and incorporated in the smaller side was a stone tower. The tower was open sided at the top like a campanile, this gave a slight ostentation to the whole. The gardens were charming rather than beautiful, with laid out paths and lawns but with unexpected arbours and secluded walks.

On arrival we left my 15 cwt truck in the wide, capacious courtyard, and began to look around the place. In addition to the villa, there were two other houses nearby within the grounds, one at the top of the drive on the right set back from the courtyard, the other also on the right but some 40 yards beyond the villa. Presently, from the first of these houses, there came a lady who was perhaps in her late 50's. She smiled tentatively and, speaking in good English, introduced herself as Signora Pasqui and asked if she could help in any way. I extended my hand telling her not to be alarmed but I should be pleased to explain our presence. This I did as reassuringly as possible and the fact that I had been told to occupy the villa for the reasons I'd just given. I hoped that we should not intrude upon her privacy more than was absolutely necessary.

The lady confirmed that she and her husband, Colonel Pasqui, had been asked by the owner to act as custodians of the villa. The owner was an American lady, a Mrs Loeser (I cannot remember how to spell the name but it was something like that), who was widowed and, upon Italy entering the war, had returned to America. Her husband had been a notable philanthropist in the art world and they had come to Florence to be in the centre, or cradle, of art. They had built Villa Gattaia around their collection of rare and beautiful furniture, pictures and so forth.

It was arranged that I should take an inventory of the villa's contents with Colonel Pasqui the following day. Meantime we accepted the keys to the front and side doors in order to prepare some food and make ready for the night. I took possession of two rooms at the back of the villa at the far end by the tower, mainly because the view was so lovely. The next two or three days were busy ones. Col Pasqui was a veteran of the First World War, he was a kind and gentle man who spoke almost no English but was meticulous in everything he undertook. I grew to like and admire him, and the relationship that was to follow, between

140

the families who lived in the two houses and me, was surprising and comforting.

I learnt that before the war the house at the top of the drive, now occupied by the Pasquis, was the chauffeur's house. The other house beyond the villa was allocated to the gardener. In anticipation of the bombing of Florence, which never happened, except for some of the railway marshalling yards, Mrs Loeser had invited her friends to stay in these houses which were considered out of harm's way. In the first house there were Col. & Mrs Pasqui, their relatives Col & Mrs Conti with Graziella, their daughter and niece of the Pasquis. In the second house were Signor and Signora Salocchi with their daughter Giovanna.

Throughout that September my small party worked hard to provide a relaxing and enjoyable time for the visiting troops. It is true to say that, as we established a workable routine, there was less need for me to oversee the details of this well-run hotel. Consequently there was more time to spend with my new-found Italian friends, for such they had become. So much so, that I returned to spend leaves or fleeting visits with them, until the division moved over to Pesaro and Rimini on the Adriatic coast the following March. This quite special relationship was assisted in its development by my undertaking to teach English to the two girls, Graziella aged 21 and Giovanna aged 20 years, in return for their instruction in Italian. I should perhaps acknowledge that, to spend numbers of hours in pursuit of those aims with those two young ladies, was no real hardship.

In subsequent visits I stayed always with the Pasqui and the Conti families. The former I addressed always as Zia, Aunt, and Zio, Uncle; all of them called me Donald or Donaldo. This meant that I saw and spent more time with Graziella than most of the others. Our friendship grew, perhaps inevitably, into rather more than just friendship. By which I mean simply that we were attracted without breaking any rules of convention in those days.

My visits continued over 6 months and were for me a period of the war that has lasting memories still. At that time, Villa Gattaia provided a haven of sanity, of pleasure and of peace, midst a tempest of physical and emotional torment. The coming winter in the Apenine mountains imposed unreasonable tests of endurance; those occasional visits were a reminder that the world, as exemplified by Firenze and its surrounds and those good people, was waiting to be found again.

* * * * * * * *

There was a fourth family who contributed to this story, they were the nearest neighbours, just down the hill a short distance. The family consisted of Signor Gaio and his three daughters: Lina aged 19, Cilla (Cheela) 17 years and Lia aged 15 years, born on Christmas Day and named Natalia, from Natale. The girls' mother had died about 12 months previously. They were a wealthy family with a beautiful home and all the material benefits, but there was an overriding sadness associated with the loss of the mother. Lina had attempted to fill the gap in her sisters' lives and was quite serene in her acceptance of her position. She was beautiful, loved her music, and was able to restrain her younger sisters without obvious discontent.

Cilla was a cheerful girl with strikingly dark hair which she kept short, she

141

was very attractive but disarmingly unaware of being so. The youngest, Lia, never failed to melt you. She was by nature vivacious and a tomboy, yet combined that with sweetness and being essentially lovable. When she talked, which was as natural to her as breathing and almost as compelling, she did so with all her body and soul. Her eyes, expressions and gestures explained all she wanted to convey even if you couldn't understand the words. She was as full of life and vitality as was possible to be, honest and outspoken and often funny.

My most vivid memory of Lia took place at a family party sometime in early 1945, she was then just 16 years old. Lia had been a little over boisterous and thought she'd better make amends. She left the room for a while and, on returning, was transformed by lipstick and make-up etc, and a long dress made from mosquito netting. Swan Lake was introduced on the record-player and she started to dance her own interpretation of the ballet; it was beautiful in every way. Her unselfconsciousness, her grace, and the way in which she surrendered herself to the music, was spell-binding and brought a lump to my throat. She had no need to learn how to express feelings of tenderness, she just couldn't help it. She was enchanting.

I wrote of this episode at the time, together with an account of what followed. Shortly after she had completed her dying swan, Lia came over to me and, taking my arm, she ushered me away from all the others to a small bench seat. Sitting beside me, and still holding my arm, she told me that she liked me very much but couldn't understand why. She said that, for a husband, she wanted a tall, strong man who was dark and had a moustache. Yet I was none of these, except for a moustache, so why should she like me in this way? And did I like her? Because she was a little afraid that I didn't. As I said, Lia never failed to melt you. I expect she eventually found her tall, dark, strong man. At about that time she gave me the tiniest copy of Dante's "Divina Commedia" in Italian and in its own little box 2" x 1½".

* * * * * * * *

On one ill-chosen day I took Signor Salocchi and Giovanna to see their home at Pistoia, about 15 miles from Florence. The villa had been occupied by the Germans and he wondered about its fate. Signor Salocchi was a rich man with several villas and a happy disposition. Before the war he was the Italian Ambassador in Peru, with his residence in Lima, and now he was living in what was the gardener's cottage. Neither he nor his family were perturbed at this, their only concern was for their son and their son-in-law, both of whom were prisoners of war. The elder daughter Rosanna had a baby boy, Geri, she naturally lived for the day when her husband would return to see his son.

The Arno was high after some days of rain and, before we could return, had burst its banks. The road was under water for considerable stretches and it was impossible to identify exactly where it was. As we met approaching traffic, both lanes had to move from what was thought to be the centre of the road in order to pass. I pulled a little to one side and promptly went nose down into a deep ditch. Within seconds an American truck stopped and threw me a line which I attached to the towing hook; within a few seconds we were pulled back onto the road. My passengers were astonished and I was more than a little surprised. Signor Salocchi expressed the utmost admiration for the efficiency of the Allies - several times. I didn't disillusion him, instead we were grateful to get back to Villa Gattaia. I was given a huge glass flask, or cask, brought from Pistoia. It was filled with gallons of wine for my battery and me, a prize indeed.

That September of 1944 passed so quickly that there seemed scarcely time enough for all the things that happened. Signora Pasqui took me on many tours of Florence, to places that were not necessarily well known as well as those that were. I spent happy hours listening to records with Graziella, mostly opera. Zia actually knew Puccini in her earlier days, so it was to be expected that his music was well represented in the house. She told me that Puccini thought his best work was 'Tosca'.

Graziella and I used to walk and talk together about life in Florence before the war, and the fact that she found it difficult to settle into the life at the university in these troubled times. I tried to tell her about England and my life there. The trouble was that it now seemed that, prior to the war, I had done nothing worth recounting. Perhaps the first 20 years of a person's life are not always filled with accomplishments; but looking back through the mists of the few wartime years, I had really only lived during those years. Whatever I had been before was only a preparation for what was to come, and what had come was a realization of the futility of man, but also his nobility in the degree of his preparedness to face situations that no other animal would dare. We talked of religion but in no revealing depth, only to scorn the divisions and some of the pettiness that separated them. There was little room for any philosophical thought in those war dominated days, it was enough to be alive.

On or about the 20th September, Major Hamilton came to see me. He was on his way to England having been posted to attend some teaching course, and had come to say goodbye. He stayed the night and we talked of the times we had known together, mostly about Tunisia, in the way that people reminisce. It struck me as funny that, in the middle of fighting a war, we could sit together in comfort discussing past adventures and that he, a regular officer, could be returned to England to go on a course. It was then that he said to me quite unexpectedly, "I always knew that you'd come through this lot, and so you will".

My time at Villa Gattaia had to end, at least for a while, and at the beginning of October I was on my way back to the battery.

The goodbyes were difficult, and in some cases tearful. Graziella and Giovanna gave me a lovely book of Florentine sketches and Signor Salocchi found for me a book entitled 'The Medici' by G F Young, Zia gave me a lucky piece of coral.

The parting from Villa Gattaia was truly a wrench for me, particularly since I didn't realize then that I should be returning. As we set off in my 15 cwt Bedford I thought that Florence had seemed never more beautiful. It is nice to record that, although it has changed hands more than once since those days, Villa Gattaia looked exactly the same when I visited it in 1990, except that Salocchi's house had been sold off and a section of the garden bricked off with it. To find Gattaia there, and 'my' house beside it completely unchanged, was a resurrection of the past, almost unbelievable.

CHAPTER XVII

THE MOUNTAINS AND CHRISTMAS 1944

During my absence the war had moved farther and higher into the Apennines. By the end of October there was more activity directed towards keeping warm than engaging the enemy. I heard that the M10's of my old battery had fired hundreds of rounds and I was thankful that it had not been my job to replenish the ammunition, because by now the roads and tracks were either water-logged or frozen. The weather was fast overtaking the plans of mice and men. We had reached the Futa pass with the little town of Firenzuola at its end. The pass was about 3,000ft up, with the mountains all around at heights of 4,000ft and more.

Our supply road was east of Florence from Pontassieve north to Dicomano, west to Borgo San Lorenzo, then north again to Scaperia on the road to Firenzuola. It was a severely twisting road full of hairpins and plenty of places where any driver, who was less than experienced and alert, could so easily go off the road over precipitous drops of hundreds of feet. As the weather grew progressively colder the drivers grew progressively more nervous and every journey took more than twice as long as it would otherwise have done. There was ample evidence in the valleys of the penalties for the unheedy.

Two things worthy of note happened at this time. Firstly, our colonel, Col Slessor, left the regiment to go to Greece and was replaced by Lt Col K A P Fergusson. I didn't know of this change until some time later and it was a further month before I actually met the new Colonel. Secondly, we in 327 Battery received news that we were to take possession of new equipment, namely 3.7 inch howitzers. In consequence, as with 112 Battery before Cassino, our battery had to be trained to become field artillery gunners and with some urgency. In pursuit of this conversion we had to dispatch numbers of officers, NCOs and gunners to a nearby field regiment to learn the new trade. This was exciting stuff for the battery who had been spending much of their time road and bridge making in appalling weather.

Then, after much endeavour by our men and our artillery hosts, the scheme was abandoned in favour of road maintenance again. Apparently the priority was given to the roads because, with the arrival of heavy snow, the delivery of supplies was threatened. 327 Battery were thoroughly disheartened with this change of mind not least because the howitzers would have promoted the battery from labourers to the owners of the most important weapons in the mountains.

By December the word 'living' had become a dubious term for what we were doing. The winter in Africa had been bitterly cold, but this was ridiculous. Those who are avowed travellers in cold climates are careful to clothe themselves appropriately for such journeys. Sleeping in snow may be all right for Polar Bears, but for us, dressed in battle dress and overcoats and a couple of blankets for the night, it was an experience to dwarf most other experiences. Particularly when the wind blew strongly as it was mostly inclined to do.

The snow was growing deeper by the week, but to some it was proving a blessing. Up on the Futa pass it was 4ft deep, enabling the troops to dig trenches and small rooms in the snow thereby escaping from the bitter wind. A hole cut deep and measuring 6ft x 5ft provided enough room for three men who could then share their blankets at night, in this way they could keep themselves relatively warm. Even so, there was an occasion earlier when I heard that, due to the cold, some of our infantry died during one night. Cooking was a problem and any farm buildings or barns were at a premium, but every one had to be cleared of mines and booby traps.

The war drifted to a standstill, even the opposing infantry patrols were unable to probe each other's territory. The only challenge of any kind came from the guns and mortars, and that was spasmodic. There was a limit of firing imposed on our guns and I suspect the same applied to the Germans. The roads were covered by a thick layer of ice and supply trucks had to be kept to a minimum. Much of the supply work was carried out by mules - they were far more reliable than any army transport. Personally I found that the tiny Daimler scout car was the only vehicle capable of coping with the conditions. Its armoured front and sides not only provided a degree of protection against shells and bullets, but the added weight caused the tyres to bite into the ice and so it succeeded in gripping where nothing else could.

Christmas was nearly upon us but there was little anticipation of any revelry. The last two Christmases had been spent in pouring rain in Africa, this one promised to be in penetrating cold, but at least some of the battery had been pulled back out of the hills in order to give Christmas a chance. Surprisingly, I was told to report to RHQ on 23rd December together with Lt Morton, one of the troop commanders.

Dicky Morton was another good-looking, tall, dark and carefree young officer who believed in living every moment that the war made available to him. He had taken advantage of all such moments in Africa and, more particularly, of certain nurses who had shown willingness to share those moments.

We had been told that our presence was required for dinner that evening at RHQ, and, accordingly, should bring our service dress with us. Service Dress was the expression used by the army for our normal uniform as opposed to battle dress; such items, together with other personal baggage, were kept in the sanctuary of 'A' echelon.

* * * * * * * * *

So it was that Dicky and I met our new Colonel and were able to enjoy a most creditable meal, plus wine, which the Colonel had somehow managed to provide. There were a few officers from other batteries who had been invited, and we all had an excellent evening made more pleasurable by the comfort of the house in which RHQ was then established.

At the end of the meal I was somewhat startled when Colonel Fergusson suddenly looked straight at me and said in clear resonant voice, "Mr Vice, the King". My instant response was intuitive and, in the circumstances of several glasses of wine, commendable. Clutching my wineglass, I leapt to my feet and called with some authority "Gentlemen, the King". The loyal toast having been concluded, I felt that the new Colonel could be reassured by the performance of his new regiment; especially so, since the rest of the assembly confided to me afterwards that they would not have known how to respond and congratulated me on my showing.

Had that been the end of the evening, all might have been well, but we were in no hurry to leave and return to our batteries. This was about as near to Christmas as we were likely to get. Our minds, our bodies and our feelings had by this time thawed out to our collective satisfaction, and there was more wine on the table. I was never an active drinker, on the grounds that after a certain intake I tend to feel sick. So that, even in those circumstances, I felt no pressing need to go beyond three or four glasses of wine. Dicky, on the other hand, could do justice to most fortified beverages, nor was he alone in that respect.

Stanley Edwards was by this time 2nd in command of the regiment; he and the doctor were both prepared to recognize the festive season in time-honoured custom. It soon became more a celebration of "Hark the Herald Gunners Sing", and each succeeding rendering of song was offered with relish and fervour. As the evening progressed the 2nd in command and the doctor, among others, became more ambitious in their plans for the future. Many of these were fantasies nurtured in prolonged hardship, but among them was the intention to celebrate Christmas Eve with a meal in Florence. They insisted that Dicky and I should meet them the following evening at the British Officers' Club. By the time this appointment was made, at least three of the four participants were the worse for wear.

On arrival at the Officers' Club in Florence on Christmas Eve 1944 I told our driver and a couple of his mates to buzz off and enjoy themselves. We should not need transport because Stanley had said he would take Dicky and me back to the regiment afterwards. We settled ourselves at a table in the large hotel dining room and ordered a couple of drinks whilst we waited for Stanley and the doctor. In a while we also ordered our meal, and watched and listened to the Italian 'orchestra' which offered us entertainment. This was a kind of two violins, double bass, piano and drums ensemble. with a young girl vocalist. They played a repetition of light and one-time popular items, liberally sprinkled with arias from La Traviata and punctuated with a tune with the title that sounded like 'Amapola'. For some of her operatic presentations the girl was joined by one of the male violinists, as a chorister. It bore a strong resemblance to the days of the Palm Court orchestra.

This was all very fine but it somehow lacked the atmosphere of Christmas Eve joyousness, especially as the assembled diners conveyed a preference for music, or noise, more in sympathy with girl friends and wives. Dicky and I started on our meal, and a bottle of wine, without waiting for our two expected companions. Something had obviously delayed them but we were not unduly perturbed. We had eaten our way well into the third course before the absence of our friends registered any alarm, and doubts entered our conversation about whether Stanley and the doctor were going to show up. It was Dicky who put his finger on the situation without actually recognizing it, "Tell you the truth, I was a bit hazy about the arrangements myself", he volunteered.

We concluded that our dinner was destined to be a two-some and that it was still Christmas Eve so maybe we should make the best of it. However, there was a snag, in fact there were two. One, we had been given to understand that the meal would be the pleasure of the 2nd i/c and neither Dicky or I had any money. Money is the last thing an army needs in action. Two, we'd sent our transport away and so had no means of getting back to the regiment.

Our meal had been at least three quarters consumed by this time, plus the bottle of wine, and we felt a definite unease about our position. Mercifully at this juncture the band packed their instruments and departed, presumably to join their own families, friends and festivities. Dicky thrust me forward to the piano saying, "For Gods sake play while I think of something." Soon there was a group of Americans around the piano suggesting various tunes. They were not supposed to be in our club and Dicky lost no time in explaining our predicament to them. How it happened I don't actually know, but our bill was paid and before long we were being conveyed to the American Officers' Club.

The visit to the American hotel was short-lived. This was partly due to our not knowing the place and feeling slightly out of touch, partly to the fact that our American friends were busy greeting and drinking with their own friends, and partly to the fact that numbers of local prostitutes were beginning to invade the place. Dicky and I slipped out and wondered what we should do, having no money on Christmas Eve was an absurd situation to be in. Had I been alone I should undoubtedly have gone to my friends at Villa Gattaia, but I didn't like the idea of gate-crashing, especially with another.

We walked along the banks of the Arno from the Ponte Vecchio. Presently we heard the sound of music again from another splendid hotel. We entered and ventured towards the sound of the music; as we did so it became obvious that we had trespassed into the South African Officers' hotel. I may be wrong, but I believe this to be the Hotel Lucchese today. Expecting to be challenged and asked to leave, we walked casually into the ballroom and wondered what the hell we were going to do next. The 'Mailed Fists' stitched to our upper arms proclaimed that we were from the 6th Armoured Division and therefore nothing to do with the South Africans. We decided to say that we'd met a couple of SA chaps earlier who had invited us to look in on them here this evening. In fact nobody asked us nor bothered who we were.

Then it happened again, at midnight the band packed up and all the SA officers and their guests were left high if not dry. Dicky thought it was worth another try and persuaded me to pluck at the piano again. So for the next couple of hours, or thereabouts, I was strumming in a determined attempt to recall as many of the favourite dance tunes of the pre-war and early wartime days. Certainly there were plenty of people dancing into the early hours.

Meantime Dicky Morton was circulating among the dancers, who weren't actually dancing at the time, with the oft repeated request of "What about one for the pianist?" This overture, proffered in his most dulcet tones and calculated blandishments, brought an irresistible response of drink, and pockets full of cigarettes, that was positively embarrassing. The drinks were lined up on top of the piano and although Dicky drank two or three to my one, we were unable to keep pace with the supply.

Neither of us was able to say how this ended nor when. The only thing certain is that we both passed out in the ballroom; whether simultaneously or at an interval between is not known, nor does it matter. The next significant detail was that I woke up the next morning in a soft and gorgeous double bed. As I came to, I could hardly help being astonished at rose coloured velvet curtains, beautiful carpet, and an en suite bathroom. Then I felt a body beside me. There can be few more disturbing experienced than that of waking in a daze to find someone sharing your bed who, you feel instinctively, should not be there. Caught in that compromising situation, my mind embraced all kinds of unhappy interpretations. I realized that I was undressed and, with apprehension, I turned to wake up my bedfellow.

Even in my confusion I could recognize the back of Dicky's head and was much relieved to see it. Poking him awake I demanded to know where we were and what we were doing there. Dicky was, if anything, more bemused than I, and took a few aggrieved minutes to address himself to my questions. Having done so he contributed very little. He remembered nothing about the previous night other than the piano and keeping us supplied with drinks. He thought I had fallen off the piano seat but couldn't be sure, and he'd no idea how we'd got where we were nor who had undressed us.

We rejected the idea that the place was in any way disorderly, on the contrary, it exuded splendour and taste. Yet panic was revived when I stealthily opened the bedroom door to see what was beyond. Just at that moment a vision of a very attractive young female in a pink dressing gown swished passed along the corridor. "Christ", said Dicky, "Are you sure?" Not knowing what to do, we washed, dressed and sat down to consider our position. We decided this must be the S.A. Officers' hotel and obviously somebody had put us to bed; our difficulty was that we couldn't pay for this night's lodging. We decided to try to escape without being seen, failing that, we'd have to explain what had happened and offer to send payment as soon as we had access to money.

Creeping to the top of the splendid staircase, we looked below and saw a large entrance hall with the front entrance halfway across the hall. It was not a great distance from the bottom of the staircase to the front porch and we had hopes of success as we crept down the stairs. The staff of the hotel were mostly Italian and nearly all, it transpired, spoke reasonable English. We approached the hall with calm and dignity, and prepared to make a dash for the entrance. Most of the activity was coming from the dining room on our right, and we tended to concentrate on that area. In the event we were accosted by an Italian who emerged from somewhere behind on our left.

The Italian waiter, for so he proved to be, hailed us with a broad smile and bade us "Buon giorno" and were we the 'Inglese officers?' We admitted that we were and didn't quite know what we were doing here. No matter, the waiter gave an understanding laugh and said there was a table for breakfast reserved for us. He escorted us to the table in that very large, elegant dining room and gave us every attention during an excellent breakfast. He explained that everything was already paid for and there was no hurry for us to leave. Needless to say, we were dumbfounded and delighted. Lighting cigarettes while we sipped our coffee, we reflected upon our incredible luck, "Merry Christmas," said Dicky.

After various efforts were made, we eventually managed to contact the regiment and transport was sent to collect us. We returned to RHQ and sought the 2nd in command and the doctor. Dicky and I outlined the series of embarrassments that had befallen us during the past 24 hours. We gave our assurances that, if we were to fall into danger or difficulties associated with the present fighting, we should not look towards RHQ for a lifeline, on that they could rely. We expected regrets and perhaps apologies but, to their eternal shame, none were forthcoming, only chiding, derision and not a little laughter. As we departed for 327 Bty, I warned that, in the circumstances, it would be difficult to accept any further invitations to dinner from the Colonel or 2nd in command.

Back in the hills it was a resumption of survival and trying to keep warm. The next two months were memorable for the distress imposed on thousands of frozen men who sat in frozen holes peering at one another through frozen eyes. Neither British, American, French, South African, Poles nor Germans, Austrians, Hungarians, or whoever, could have given a convincing reason for being where they were. Back in Rome, Naples or London and Washington I imagine the reasons would have been abundantly clear and readily expounded.

Throughout January and February of 1945 the whole of the army was preoccupied with the weather, plus the added ordeal of enemy artillery for those within range. I found that, so long as I could keep my boots dry, I could be miserably cold in comparative comfort; but once my boots became wet, the rest of me suffered immeasurable torment. In order to reduce the intervals of time spent in these conditions, the specialisms of regiments and battalions were ignored, there were just soldiers. We, as gunners, were used as maintenance engineers on the roads but mainly the essential tracks. Others, such as the tank crews, were helping out as infantry holding sections of the line. In this way the various permutations of troops were able to share the debilitating effects of the mountains, and thus enable more frequent withdrawal of troops to more hospitable areas around Florence.

In spite of those efforts, there were many instances of the cruel consequences of the bitter winter. On one occasion I went to a dressing station to visit one of our wounded who had been blown up. I found him bandaged and plastered from head to toe. He had sustained broken arms and legs and his body had been punctured all over by metal splinters. Indeed, according to the doctor, he was being held together by pins and brackets. Nevertheless, he was cheerful and declared that, encased in his bandages, he was warmer now than he'd been for weeks. Opposite him was a wounded German who had been brought in by one of our Infantry patrols. He was unconscious when I saw him, having been operated on at some length in order to repair his badly smashed legs. However, his overall trouble was frost bite. How long he had been lying out in the snow was not known, but he had had one foot amputated, some toes lost off the other foot, and a few fingers had also been taken off. It was still doubtful whether he would survive.

In the early New Year I had a sheep-skin jacket made in Florence which served me well during those times. There were several sheep skins in its construction, a small tent provided the material for the exterior and a felt lining was placed between the skins and the outside. The result was the warmest jacket ever, with a very high collar to care for my ears. It was unfortunate that the wool became discoloured by the smoky fires over which I had squatted whenever possible. To me that coat was worth more than any other that money could buy, it was in fact a life-jacket.

CHAPTER XVIII

FINALE

By the beginning of March there were stirrings within the armies, Spring would be upon the scene in a month or so. I had recently returned from a brief visit to my friends at Villa Gattaia and, as usual, Florence was a different world and the Pasquis were as concerned for me as if I were their son. Graziella had wept when I left and I knew that these infrequent visits were hurtful to her. Such partings saddened me for a long time afterwards and I cursed the war yet again.

The coming Spring offensive had the obvious intention of driving the Germans out of Italy into Austria and, in conjunction with the Russians and the forces in Germany, the destruction of the Nazi armies. All so easy to say and doubtless it would be achieved, but at what cost? Our intentions and options must have been easily identified by the Germans and they had had many weeks, even months, to make ready for them. Until then the opposing armies tried to gain information about each other by taking prisoners and generally caused unpleasantness by discharging shells at one another.

At this time I returned to what I had always considered my rightful Battery, 112. I had not been happy during the months that I'd been away from the old battery, and I'd never felt in tune with my duties as Bty Captain. Maj Mclennan, 112 Bty Commander, was apparently pleased to have me back, and I returned on the understanding that I lost no seniority. I'd only been back with them a few days when Pat Farrell was killed by a shell burst. Pat, whose real name was Terence, was troop commander of Fox Tp, my old 6 Tp of Tunisia. He had been on his way to visit one of the posts guarding a bridge up on the Futa pass and his body was found in a ditch a few hundred yards short of the bridge.

We were naturally saddened by any death in our midst but, like it or not, one simply could not dwell upon such things. Nobody could survive if they brooded about colleagues who were killed. On the contrary, the common practice was not to talk about them and to try not to think about them. However, every now and then the effect was not easily shaken off. I was distressed about Steve Lindsay in Tunisia on a personal basis, and I was incensed by the news of Pat. Partly, I think because it was at a time when we didn't expect casualties, and partly because he was the third troop commander of Fox Tp to be lost in Italy. I cannot explain why, but I was glad when I found Pat's grave in 1990. It is a beautifully sited cemetery on a hillside about 10km from Firenzuola on the road to Imola. The surroundings are extremely lovely and the cemetery is small but tenderly placed among trees and mountains.

Following immediately upon the news of Pat, I was ordered to join an advanced party of representatives from all batteries and RHQ to find billets for everybody at Pesaro, south of Rimini, on the Adriatic coast. There were parties from other regiments, so it was obvious that the division was about to pull out of the line and move over to the eastern coastal plain. We found the necessary quarters without much difficulty and made ready to receive the regiment as and when the individual batteries were relieved.

Altogether we spent a month in Pesaro during which time the regiment was reorganised yet again. This time the batteries became a hotch-potch of all sorts.

We had 'D' Tp with the relatively new 17 pounder anti-tank guns, 'E' Tp retained their M10's and 'F' Tp were given 6 pounders as in Tunisia. For the past 10 months we had been used constantly as mobile field artillery, now with only 4 M10's, that role was no longer a reality. This was a stupid decision and all the members of 112 Battery were angry and felt that their excellent performance in Italy had gone unappreciated.

Two things of note happened during that month. On March 16th a few of us went to Rome to attend and celebrate the wedding of Johnny Gaster to one of the nurses. I remember that her name was Mary and she was Irish. I have often wondered since what happened to them and where they settled after the war. Johnny was lucky considering he was wounded two or three times in Tunisia, including a snipers's bullet right through him around the waist line. His wound looked much more severe than that of Sgt Mortimer who was hit in similar fashion at Cassino and died afterwards. Upon such slender threads of chance did survival depend for so many.

The second occurrence took place at the end of March. Four of us were dining at the officers' club in Pesaro one evening. A small party of Italians had also arrived and eaten there. At the end of the meal one of them rose and called for attention; he then introduced another of their party, I wish I could remember his name, and said his guest was willing to sing an aria for us.

This was so surprising to those present that nobody said anything. In a moment the small orchestral group began to play and the Tenor began singing. His voice was superb, it was electrifying and, in that environment, unforgettable.

As we left, I went to the Italians' table and expressed my thanks to the tenor for his touching and generous performance. To my surprise he asked if I would like to hear more? My eagerness must have been obvious and so I was invited to his house the following Thursday afternoon. Accordingly, at the appointed time, I found the house that afternoon and was admitted through a long hallway and into the sitting room at its end. The sitting room was not large, but spacious enough for comfortable furniture and a grand piano. Assembled were the tenor, I believe he was Giorgio and he was in fact a Czech, his wife, who was a concert pianist, and a friend who, I believe, was a violinist.

Showing me to a chair the lady offered me a glass of wine before sitting down at the piano. She played a sonata and some other shorter pieces, and played beautifully. I remember wondering just what I was doing there in that company. Then Giorgio, as I shall refer to him, asked for my choices of song. Being young and lacking consideration of acoustics for such an artist, I had the nerve to mention various operatic arias like "Che Gelida Manina" from Boheme, and "E Lucevan le Stelle" from Tosca, plus others which I cannot recall. Giorgio then retired to the far end of the hall in order that he should not destroy all the glassware, and the special, private recital began. To the accompaniment of the piano he sang a range of arias including my requests and, needless to say, I was lost for words of appreciation and delight. I was stunned by the quality of this indulgence towards me. That such people with such talents should concern themselves to please me, a mere soldier, was beyond belief. If only we could go back in time to thank people over again. Perhaps it was just an excuse to make music.

In a way, anticipating the launching of an offensive which was expected to deliver the coup de grâce to the German forces, was more nerve-wracking than usual. We expected the enemy would be prepared to fight ferociously in a bid to force the Allies into a peace treaty, and to prevent the collapse of their army as had happened in Tunisia. It could well become a bloody contest, and those of us who had survived the slings and arrows, the shot and shell, or, as Eager Brundell might have put it, 'the grape', were in no mood to take risks at this stage. We were, in a word, not looking forward to the coming weeks. "Oh to be in England now that April's there".

It transpired that our anxieties were unfounded. When the offensive was sprung on 7th April, we found ourselves in divisional reserve, and the 6th Armoured Division itself was in 8th Army reserve. For the first time since landing in North Africa in November 1942 we were not taking part in the early fighting, excluding the landings in Sicily and Italy where our division took no part.

The final battle for Italy centred on the River Po. That river drains the collective waters from the mountains bordering Austria and Switzerland in the north and the Italian Apennines in the south. It stretched across the whole of the north of Italy flowing from west to east and, not surprisingly, it was a huge river making a formidable obstacle.

The essence of destroying the German armies was to cross the Po in several places, some distance apart, so that the breaches could then form pincer movements to entrap the enemy who were still holding the river line. To this end the chosen places were allocated the bulk of the boats and bridging facilities. In the event the river was also crossed in unexpected spots which had to be exploited without delay. We in our regiment divided our batteries into two groups. One group, with Stanley Edwards, was devoted to traffic control for the division, this was an essential role at the time. All the fighting vehicles, tanks, infantry, engineers, signals and supplies had to be directed along obscure tracks, to the river and beyond, as speedily as possible and without chaos.

The other group, which included us, was given the task of building rafts and ferrying the associated traffic across at several points. Everything was rushing to keep up with the leading troops and keeping them supplied with ammunition and all necessities to enable the ground plan to be accomplished. Not- withstanding the fact that those leading troops had advanced many miles beyond the Po, there were many groups and formations of enemy left behind. We were shelled by self propelled guns quite unexpectedly and suffered casualties just when we thought we were far behind the trouble. The Germans had been carved up and had lost cohesion, but they were willing to fight so long as they had orders from someone.

As soon as our sappers arrived to build bridges, we went in pursuit of our division and cantered past Padova, Venice, Pordenone, to Udine. Soon the division was at the Yugoslav and Austrian borders. By the official "Victory in Europe" day, 9th May, we moved towards Austria, but it seemed that our war hadn't ended even if everybody else's had. The trouble, apparently, was that there were hundreds of Yugoslav Communist partisans and a similar number of Italian Communist partisans, all intent upon occupying enemy territory and all intent upon employing the self-help principle. The German commander in those parts, Von Vietinghoff, refused to surrender to anyone but the British, and continued fighting until this assurance was given and able to take effect. The last push in Italy had lasted one month, much of which had been pursuit. It had been very different from our expectation and we were grateful for that.

There it was, without fuss or celebration, no throwing of hats in the air - the war in Europe was over. Since, except for the absence of gunfire, there was no outward sign, many of us were not aware of this historical moment for a little while. As the news spread there was relief and a few handshakes here and there. Most of us simply paused to scribble a few lines home to say that we were safe and there was no further cause for worry. In fact a number of men were killed or badly wounded subsequently, due to the thousands of mines left all over Italy.

I remember going to sleep that night lying under a hedge somewhere. I was awakened by loud screams and I jumped up expecting the worst, so did others who were nearby. Then the frightful sound was repeated, and the adjectives that were aimed at the Peacock which caused the panic were well founded. That bird was very lucky to survive. The fact was that all too many of us had nerves which were in urgent need of repair, and tempers that were short-fused.

Strangely, or perhaps not, it was many, many months after the cessation of hostilities before our reflexes stopped reacting to certain noises and particularly bangs. Much later in England I went flat on the ground when a car backfired loudly just behind me, and years later, when fishing on the River Frome in Dorset, I absolutely froze on the unmistakable bang of an exploding shell some distance away, it was a tank on the Lulworth ranges.

* * * * * * * *

The next day we moved slowly through the hills into Austria. As we crossed the border we came upon groups of terribly ill-looking men stumbling along the roadside in what looked like striped pyjamas. They were incredibly gaunt and weak, hollow eyed and said nothing - they just looked at us not understanding what was going on. Everybody was throwing food to them, such as we had, even cigarettes and matches. A prison or concentration camp had been overrun by troops in front of us, and these pathetic creatures had walked out not knowing where they were going. Some of us were close to tears and when we reached Villach, the first town in enemy territory, tempers were still far from normal.

The people of Villach received short shift from us that night. They wouldn't speak to us and that was fine; we turned numbers of them out of their houses and requisitioned them for the troops and we didn't stand on ceremony. This mood didn't last long but it was very near the surface during the short stay in Villach. Very soon we moved to the north of the Worther See with Klagenfurt at its eastern end. The batteries were spread along this area and we quickly found ourselves some splendid billets in the beautiful surroundings. We were there to keep the peace and to dissuade the Yugoslavs from marauding the villages near to their border. The local people were much relieved by our presence once we explained that the Mailed Fist on our arms had no sinister connotations.

Our sojourn in Austria was regrettably only a three month spell. It was lovely, comfortable, friendly, peaceful and altogether just what we needed. I went home to England from Austria, for one month's leave. It was sometime towards the end of August and I had been overseas for 2 years and 9 months, it felt like half a lifetime. I think my family may have found me rather different from my former self, certainly I felt strange to be there. It was so unreal to be walking round familiar but often deserted places, and even stranger to meet long-established friends. If I'd been honest, it felt rather that I had left all my friends back in the regiment; they all knew and didn't need to ask questions.

During the time I'd been away I had written and received 130 to 150 letters. In so many of those letters I had insisted that there would be so much to say to one another when I returned. Now it seemed there was little to say. I listened to many happenings in my absence, and saw evidence in plenty of bombing all round the area of my home, which itself had been the recipient of a huge mine dropped by parachute. It fell, crushing the garden roller, and knocked a corner off the garage but failed to explode. Coincidentally, the naval officer who came to disarm this mine was the uncle of one of the subalterns in my regiment. He used a pot of my mother's home-made jam as a lubricant.

On rejoining my regiment I was promoted major and assumed command of my 112 Bty. This status was short-lived but I was so proud while it lasted. Then came the unhappy news that the regiment was to be disbanded. This might sound a mundane event, but in reality it was devastating, especially to those of us who had joined it in 1941. We'd been so far together and we'd seen so much. We had shared the extremes of emotion in extremes of circumstance. I felt, rightly, that I could never settle in any other organisation in the army. Ted Newman and I were posted together to join the 15th Royal Horse Artillery, but to me that regiment could never replace the 72nd Anti-Tank Regiment, RA.

A Share of Time

Such life as we enjoy - a share of time,
We strive to preserve to longevity.
What fulfilment of hopes and loves sublime
Could you realise in such brevity?
Stark noise and shouts and shells and awful dread
Were your companions of that time ago.
I see you still, though you were blanket-wrapped
and dead;
Your aspirations and your dreams left fallow.

D.G.A.L.

"COMBAT AND COMPETITION" by David Ince, DFC,Bsc. A fascinating story of a gunnery officer turned Typhoon pilot. Operating with 193 and 257 Squadrons through the summer of 1944 to the bitter end of Hitler's dying Reich. As a trained test pilot, the author marketed advanced flight control systems. He is a dedicated glider pilot, chief instructor, active in sailplane development testing and a past member of the British team squad. Foreword is by Air Chief Marshal Sir Christopher Foxley-Norris, GCB,DSO,OBE,MA,CBIM,FRAeS. ISBN 1 872308 23 6. HB price £15.95, SB £14.95.

"DEATH OR DECORATION" Ron Waite's fascinating story of a pilot from day one of his training, through to operational missions and beyond. His six years of war with No. 76 Squadron, 1658 and 1663 HCUs makes enthralling reading. Foreword by Wg Cdr P. Dobson, DSO, DFC, AFC, (CO No 158 Squadron). A jolt to the memory for those who were there...A seat in the cockpit for those who were not! ISBN 1 872308 08 2.
HB price £14.95, SB price £13.95.

"ESCAPE FROM ASCOLI" by Ken de Souza of 148 Squadron. This book is a fore runners of **"Una Bell Passaggiata"**. Ken's vivid and fascinating tale of survival in the desert, against the odds. His escape from PG70 Italian POW camp, operating with the SAS and final get-away from Occupied Italy. Foreword by Air Chief Marshal Sir Lewis Hodges, KCB,CBE,DSO,DFC. President of the RAF Escaping Society.
ISBN 1 872308 02 3. HB. Price £12.95

"FAITH, HOPE AND MALTA GC" The author is Tony Spooner, DSO, DFC. The foreword by Air Marshal Sir Ivor Broom, KCB,CBE,DFC**,AFC, himself an ace Malta pilot. It is the gripping story of the Ground and Air Heroes of Army, Air Force and Navy defenders of the George Cross Island.
ISBN 1 872308 50 3. Price £16.95.

"FEAR NOTHING" David Watkins accurate history of 501 (F) County of Gloucester Squadron, Auxiliary Air Force. The 'part-timers' were in action from May 1940 over France followed by the Battle of Britain. Later re-equipped with Spitfires, Tempests and the Vampires. Foreword by Wg Cdr K.MacKenzie, DFC,AFC,AE.ISBN 1 872308 07 4. HB. Price £14.95

"FROM PILLAR TO POST" by Norman Harris. An interesting and well written narrative of the author's journey through life. Commencing with an RAF Admin. career in 1939, posted to East Africa. On demob from the RAF, involved in local politics, Elected Mayor of Nairobi, then Minister for Information and Broadcasting in the Kenya Government. Move to Australia, the author writes with insight & clarity. There are excellent descriptive passages. A Serviceman's journey through life, full of humour in the reporting of everyday incidents that beset the wanderer. Foreword by Air Marshal Sir Maurice Heath KBE,CB. ISBN 1 872308 65 1 SB Price £14.95.

"GREEN MARKERS AHEAD SKIPPER" by Gilbert Grey. Aged 15 at the outbreak of WWII the author had completed a tour of 34 operations serving as a Flight Engineer with 106 Squadron before his 20th birthday. Foreword by Wg Cdr M J Stevens, DFC, RAF,(Ret'd) who comments: "What a wonderful book for passing on to posterity because it describes what it was really like being a member of the aircrew in a Lancaster bomber in 1944." ISBN 1 872308 11 2, SB. Price £15.95.

All available ex-stock: J & KH Publisher
P O Box 13, Hailsham, E. Sussex BN27 3XQ